New Directions
in Sociology

D1479288

New Directions in Sociology

Essays on Theory and Methodology in the 21st Century

Edited by Ieva Zake *and* Michael DeCesare

McFarland & Company, Inc., Publishers
Jefferson, North Carolina, and London

LIBRARY OF CONGRESS CATALOGUING-IN-PUBLICATION DATA

New directions in sociology : essays on theory and
  methodology in the 21st century / edited by Ieva Zake
  and Michael DeCesare.
      p.   cm.
    Includes bibliographical references and index.

    ISBN 978-0-7864-6342-8
    softcover : 50# alkaline paper ∞

    1. Sociology.   2. Sociology — Methodology.
  I. Zake, Ieva.   II. DeCesare, Michael, 1975–
  HM585.N4587   2011
  301.01 — dc22   2011014383

BRITISH LIBRARY CATALOGUING DATA ARE AVAILABLE

Cover image © 2011 Shutterstock
Front cover design by Bernadette Skok (bskok@ptd.net)

Manufactured in the United States of America

McFarland & Company, Inc., Publishers
  Box 611, Jefferson, North Carolina 28640
    www.mcfarlandpub.com

TABLE OF CONTENTS

PART I: THEORY

Section One—Inspirations from the Past

Section Two—New Paths Forward

v

PART II: METHODOLOGY

Section Three—Tactical Innovations

Section Four—Strategic Approaches

INTRODUCTION

Ieva Zake *and* Michael DeCesare

This volume is an invitation to consider the current state and future prospects of sociology from the point of view of the next generation of sociologists. What do we want sociology to become in the future? In which directions, particularly in terms of sociological theory and methodology, are we heading? And what can younger sociologists suggest? These are the primary questions we are concerned with.

From the point of view of sociological theory, this volume's mission is to build connections to the classical authors as well as contemporary social theorists who have already come to be treated as "classic," such as Mills, Foucault, Bourdieu, and others. In this respect, the present volume points out the canonical status of what is presented as contemporary theory in many undergraduate and graduate courses and explores the issue of what comes after these perspectives.

In terms of methodology, this volume has two purposes. The first is to critique the currently dominant approach — namely, statistical analysis that is almost willfully ignorant of conceptualization, operationalization, and measurement problems— by discussing topics that are decidedly non-numerical. The second is to introduce new thinking about old methods, as well as innovative thinking about future methods.

It is rare that an author or editor treats both theory and methodology between the same two covers. Although this volume is separated into sections on theory and methodology, we fully intend for it to encourage readers to discuss sociological theory and methodology *together*. We believe that it is quite unfortunate that, for the most part, the two have lived in isolated worlds where one of them pursues novel, often outlandish conceptions of society, while the other persistently emphasizes positivist and quantitative methods of research. We also believe that the former has done little to inform the research process, while the latter has often disregarded theorists' criticisms and suggested revisions. What is the impact of new theoretical ideas on sociology's methods? And how do cutting-edge methods inform sociological theory? By asking these questions, this volume introduces an array of new theoretical perspectives along with innovative approaches to methodology in order to help students begin thinking of the two as intimately connected parts of the sociological enterprise.

As much as we believe that theory and methodology are connected, and should be thought of and treated as two sides of the same sociological coin, we have deep misgivings about the current state of each. Stepping away from discussing the goals of this volume, we now turn to a consideration of what it is that dissatisfies us about current sociological theory and methodology.

The End of Sociological Theory? Applied Sociology and Posthumanism

Since the decline of postmodernism during the first decade of the 21st century, a certain sense of emptiness, even vacuum has set in among many sociological theorists. What is next? Where to turn? What ideas are important for the future of sociology? These kinds of questions are being currently asked with an increasing sense of urgency.

At least two new directions seem to be emerging in sociological theory, though neither appears particularly promising. One of the recently forming directions is the growing tendency to see sociology as an applied discipline, which some sociologists advocate with fervor. An increasing number of sociology departments will be expected to turn their research and teaching in this direction simply to justify their existence. The proponents of sociological practice suggest exchanging inquiries about the nature of society with evaluation of successes of social programs, detecting discrimination, improving living conditions and preventing social problems and preparing professional sociologists-practitioners to do all this (see, for example, the self-definition of applied sociology at http://www.aacsnet.org). This practical sociology applies sociological insights for the purposes of clinical action, that is, sociology is used to diagnose some sort of social ill and create and also carry out a plan for its cure. This means that public policy, planned community change and social work become the central goal of sociological research and teaching. In this turn toward applied sociology, as one my colleagues often loves to exclaim, "Theory is dead!" because the only measure of the value of sociological knowledge is its application for practical purposes such as social planning and policy. There are a number of reasons why such practical or policy oriented sociology can appeal to sociologists and their students. One of them is a desire to turn sociology into an instrument for "helping people." Participating in policy evaluation and creation can be also exciting because the sociological theories of the 20th century have often been wrong and can no longer be trusted. The only sure path to relevance for sociology then appears to be its application to fixing social ills. This direction in sociology has been encouraged also by those who advocate so-called "public sociology," which sees as its aim to fight the numerous levels and forms of social inequality (Burawoy 2005; Beck 2005).

There are, unfortunately, certain costs associated with this turn toward application. By becoming practical, sociology immerses itself into the therapeutic culture and its industries that have evolved in and around the modern state. Sociology becomes another entrance point for those interested in the healing and rescuing of reality from itself through administrative means. Contrary to the claim that by becoming more applied, sociology is trying to get more in touch with the world around it and become more relevant, it is doing exactly the opposite — enclosing itself in the ideal of perfectable reality through the application of supposedly scientific knowledge. Instead of teaching students what we (can) know about social reality, and the limitations of our knowledge and questions that need further exploration, applied sociology offers itself as an indispensable instrument for transforming the society according to advice generated by sociology itself. It presents itself as the justification for introducing social reforms based on its supposedly "scientific" findings. In this way sociology can rule the facts and present itself as a reformative force at the same time.

In sum, when sociology turns itself from a method of inquiry into a tool for planned social change, it becomes encapsulated within itself and at the same time undistinguishable from such value-based professional fields as social work and public policy. If, however, sociology would remain a theoretically based research perspective and not a public policy instrument, it would be a resource for public debate and thus accountable to those taking advantage of its research results. It would have obligations toward the public, which it can quickly lose by becoming applied. Therefore this turn toward "less theory and more practice" appears threatening to the future of sociology as a form of knowledge.

Another emerging trend aims to create a sociological theory that would eliminate humans and their societies as subjects of sociological research. This direction is a further evolution of sociological postmodernism, which introduced skepticism about reason, rationality, truth and intersubjective communication. The new (post)postmodernism distinguishes itself from its earlier forms by its particular interest in animals and the physical and physiological aspects of human existence (such as cells). Its influence in sociology is increasing, although some of the most well-known texts in the animal-oriented postmodernism come from sources other than sociology (literary criticism, philosophy, etc.). Sociology is ready to accept the turn toward animal studies as exhibited in the works of symbolic interactionists such as Arnold Arluke (2002; 2006), Clinton Sanders (1999) and Janet Alger and Steven Alger (2002). Michigan State University's sociologists have created an interdisciplinary specialization in animal studies, and the American Sociological Association has an Animals and Society Section.

One of the most notable social thinkers of the late 20th century, Donna Haraway, recently published books with titles such as *The Companion Species*

Manifesto: Dogs, People and Significance of Otherness (2003) and *When Species Meet* (2007). In fact, her work has initiated what could be called the Age of the Animal in the social sciences. She brings topics such as animal consciousness and animal morality from the realm of zoology and animal psychology into social science, and argues that animals are just as much members of society as humans and therefore humans have no right to declare themselves to be the rulers over other creatures. Haraway and those who advocate the Age of Animal in social sciences see all humans, animals and machines as intertwined and they are interested in humans only because people are organisms that share the world with other "critters" and technologies. The goal of the new theory is to go against human exceptionalism with full force. Similarly, Nicole Shukin (2009) has developed an analysis of capitalism from animals' point of view. She analyzes the ways in which animals are treated symbolically and practically under capitalism in great detail, and argues that by looking at how a capitalist economy creates and exploits the idea of a species divide tells a lot about the nature of this economic system.

This sort of analysis of the social and economic systems from the perspective of how they define and use the difference between humans and animals has been labeled "posthumanism." One of its main points is that the distinctive lines between animality and humanity, the self and the other, the mind and body, society and nature, the organic and technological have been socially constructed and thus could or should be erased (Wolfe 2010). This theory sees itself as a direct descendent of the ideas of postmodernist Jacques Derrida and his notion of studying all living creatures as being so diverse that their plurality cannot be understood by creating a simple distinction between the human and the animal. Due to this position, posthumanists remove humans as the center of sociological (as well as philosophical and other interdisciplinary) investigations in order to demonstrate that people are animal-like, instead of trying to prove that animals are people-like (see, for example, Acampora 2006; 2010).

By bringing to the forefront the notion of human animalness, posthumanists also reject notions of disembodiment, that is, that humans can transcend their biological nature and that human rationality can exist autonomously and is not determined by the human body. Posthumanists argue that in order to understand the human experience, we have to see them as animal-like bodies that are a part of biological evolution and something that coexists with other non-human forms such as technology (Wolfe 2010). Posthumanists suggest that people are driven by emotional and physiological processes even in their political decisions (Protevi 2009). It is also not surprising that although posthumanism claims to be a new academic perspective, those who use it are closely connected to political activism on behalf of animals (see, for example, Sztybel 2010 on the ideas of sociology having to adopt "the best caring stance" and become an active advocate on behalf of the animals).

Of course, issues such as the perceptions of animals by humans are extremely interesting. However, it is not completely clear how posthumanists can present themselves as social scientists if a large part of their interest lies with the non-human world. How exactly is it possible to study animal "self-hood" and "identity" (Myers 2003; Irvine 2004) sociologically? What are the consequences to sociology as a study of society if we assert that we live in a "mixed species society" (see, for example, Sanders 1999)? These recent directions in research do not just study the treatment of animals by society; they actually build their analyses from the point of view of animals or animality. This would imply taking the sociological perspective away from its focus on people by erasing them as subjects of its intellectual interest. Posthumanism could even produce a sociology that would envision a world without people and still somehow think of itself as a "social science." Our concern is that once sociology takes up this posthumanist turn toward animals and animality as the central elements of human reality, and there are signs of this gradually happening (on these trends see, for example, Sanders 2006), it will end up arguing that humanity is insufficiently authentic, while the animal kingdom represents the only true existence worthy of scholarly attention. We suspect that the turn toward animals in sociology could become a radical attack on human existence as a source of knowledge, which could potentially threaten sociology as the science of human societies.

In sum, the direction of making sociology into an applied discipline will eventually turn it into a political, therapeutic and policy-based, thus losing all of its analytical benefits. Applied sociology does not need theory because it is merely an obstacle on the path of activists set on making the world a better place and resolving all social problems. Meanwhile, the posthumanist animal studies in sociology could blur the line between animals and humans, thus undermining the notion of human society as an object of sociological theory and research. These two emerging tendencies could soon pose grave danger to sociology as a whole and its theory in particular by removing it from true exploration and analysis of social processes.

The New Methodology: Spreading "Statisticism" and Turning out Textbooks

The situation regarding methodology is no less dire. Methodology, the study of our methods of research, fell out of favor among American sociologists several decades ago. Long gone are the days of debating the validity, reliability, and precision of measures, scales, and indices. Since the 1970s, sociologists have gone about their work as if all of the debates over measurement and method have been settled, and as if statistical analysis represents the highest form of sociological analysis. Serious discussions about general methodological concerns have virtually disappeared.

One tangible indication of sociologists' general lack of interest in methodology is the American Sociological Association's (ASA) annual Section membership counts, which represent the most reliable data we have regarding both the relative and absolute popularity of sociology's many subfields. Of the 49 current ASA Sections, Methodology ranked 28th overall in 2010. In terms of *student* members, the Methodology section ranked even lower — 32nd to be exact — which suggests that Methodology is not a particularly important topic among the next generation of sociologists (American Sociological Association 2010).

Two major trends have accompanied sociologists' growing neglect of methodology over the past few decades: an explosion in the number of sociological journal articles that rely on statistical modeling, and a proliferation of research methods textbooks that purport to introduce students to everything that sociologists claim to know about methodology. Amidst the onslaught of statistical journal articles and methods texts, one is left to wonder: Where have all the sociological methodologists gone?

Once upon a time, American sociologists took the study of research methods seriously. Hubert Blalock, Otis Duncan, Walter Wallace — these sociologists of earlier generations combined a knowledge of the philosophy of science with a mastery of the tools of social science, in the hope of refining the purposes for which and the ways in which sociologists collected and analyzed data. What resulted were productive debates over philosophy and epistemology, as well as unique and pragmatic suggestions about the most fruitful ways to carry out sociological research. But most sociologists of subsequent generations, in response to the changing structural and cultural contexts of social scientific inquiry, became preoccupied with other concerns. With personal computers and statistical software widely available for the first time during the latter half of the 1970s, nearly every sociologist suddenly had access to — if not the ability to correctly use — advanced statistical techniques. The trend, quite naturally, led more and more sociologists toward refining those techniques, and away from discussing their epistemological and conceptual foundations.

A textbook industry began to develop at roughly the same time. The appeal of codifying sociological knowledge — a proxy for achieving scientific respectability — coupled with the financial rewards that would come from widespread course adoption, attracted teaching sociologists to the possibility of writing a textbook. Trampled by the rush to write the latest and greatest textbook (and any subsequent editions) was, among other things, most of the interest in continuing to develop a holistic methodological approach to the sociological enterprise. Methodology came to be defined not by methodologists, but by textbook authors.

The trends toward more sophisticated statistical methods on the one hand, and less sophisticated methods textbooks on the other, contributed to the disappearance of sociological methodologists on par with Blalock, Duncan, Wallace, and others. Bombarded by high-level statistical techniques in sociological journals, sociologists who were trained after the mid–1970s easily overlooked the methodological steps that precede data analysis; namely, operationalizing concepts and measuring variables. They were not taught to question — and, to be fair, could not be expected to question for themselves— the measurement of each variable that was included in those elegant statistical models. And when they were asked to teach research methods to undergraduates, their first preparatory step was to order examination copies of methods textbooks. Upon reviewing them, they quickly found that there was an apparent consensus about what research methodology has been, about what it is, and about what it should be. Any lingering questions they might have had about methods were all answered by the textbook. The past 35 years, in other words, have witnessed a growing, yet often blind, confidence in statistical methods, on the one hand, and an unquestioning devotion to methods textbooks, on the other. This has proven to be a lethal combination for the advancement of sociological methodology.

Regarding the former, there is no doubt that as a group, sociologists have become very good at developing and refining statistical techniques of analyzing data. What sociologists have not done nearly as well is continue the vital work, begun during the early 20th century, of improving the measurement of social variables and clarifying their conceptualizations of constructs. Instead, sociologists have assumed that their conceptualizations and measurements are perfect — or at least good enough to proceed unthinkingly to statistical modeling.

Duncan (1984) famously dubbed "statisticism" the naïve faith in statistical analysis as a superior research method. It is not difficult to find examples of the "syndrome" of which Duncan warned sociologists. One need only glance at the contents of just about any issue of any sociological journal to discover the extent to which statistical analysis pervades the field. The prevalence of "statisticism" has grown to a degree that even Duncan probably could not have imagined.

We write this Introduction after the publication of the April 2010 issue of the *American Sociological Review*, the American Sociological Association's flagship journal. In typical fashion, most of the issue's contributions rely on statistical modeling, but one article in particular illustrates the point we make here: Jennie Brand and Yu Xie's (2010) piece on who benefits most from a college education. The authors utilize a range of impressive statistical analyses. But they never entertain — at least not in the published article itself— the possibility that the variables in their models have been measured inadequately. It is precisely that lack of consciousness, that lack of critical thought about methodology on the part of researchers, that we hope to begin to correct with this volume.

But it is not only researchers who are to blame for the current state of affairs; it is textbook authors as well. In a few telling paragraphs, Earl Babbie, the author of the most successful research methods textbook on the market, briefly summarized the book's evolution in the Preface to its most recent edition. Preceded by his book *Survey Research Methods*, Babbie's *The Practice of Social Research* debuted in 1975 and was an immediate success. Thus began the time of the methods textbook in sociology. *The Practice of Social Research* appeared in its 12th edition in 2010; during its unprecedented run, it has been used in about 30 different disciplines, and in 2000, a two-volume Chinese edition was published. Other authors have enthusiastically followed Babbie's lead over the past 35 years, in the hope that they would find the same success.

As a result, dozens of methods texts, specific to sociology, are now available from a variety of publishers; many have gone through multiple editions over the last 10 years or so. Yet regardless of the author or the publisher, each text looks similar to its competitors: roughly 15 chapters, arranged in roughly the same order, which cover roughly the same material. Like other subfields of sociology, methodology has been institutionalized for profit, and codified in the sacred textbook.

These two preoccupations of many methods-inclined sociologists of the past 40 years have left at least some sociologists dissatisfied, disappointed, and disillusioned. High-level statistical techniques and cookie-cutter textbooks, though the orders of the day, will not define American sociology forevermore. Indeed, they *cannot* define American sociology if the field hopes to survive the 21st century. They will be replaced, in time, by other engrossments. Whatever those happen to be, we hope that they represent not simply another analytic technique or a different breed of textbook, but a return to the fundamentally important methodological questions that characterized an earlier time period in American sociology.

*   *   *

Neither of the two theoretical directions we outlined at the beginning of our Introduction seems promising to us. This realization inspired us to work on this book, as we sought ideas that would still be sociological, would not be determined by the perspectives of the previous decades, and would be promising in terms of keeping sociological theory and methodology alive. At the same time, we also wanted to point out that, fortunately, there exist younger scholars who are not content to write formulaic methods textbooks and who do not believe that fanciful statistical analyses represent the highest form of sociological methodology. Will the methodological approaches and theoretical directions that these young authors espouse prove fruitful, or will they fail? We do not claim to know the answer. What we do know is that the contributors to this volume present new ideas, they offer fresh insights into old and forgotten ideas, and they point to some exciting paths forward.

New voices, whether they speak of sociological theory or methodology, have sometimes been heard above American sociology's intellectual din. But they have more often been drowned out by the chorus of tradition and habit. We hope this volume can soften the din and quiet the chorus, if only long enough to allow these new, youthful, energetic voices to be heard.

References

Acampora, Ralph. 2006. *Corporal Compassion: Animal Ethics and Philosophy of Body*. Pittsburgh: University of Pittsburgh Press.
_____. 2010. *Metamorphoses of the Zoo: Animal Encounter after Noah*. Lanham, MD: Lexington.
Alger, Janet, and Steven Alger. 2002. *Cat Culture: The Social World of a Cat Shelter*. Philadelphia: Temple University Press.
American Sociological Association. 2010. Final 2010 Section Membership Counts. http://www.asa.org.
Arluke, Arnold. 2002. A Sociology of Sociological Animal Studies. *Society and Animals* 10(4): 369–74.
_____. 2006. *Just a Dog: Understanding Animal Cruelty and Ourselves*. Philadelphia: Temple University Press.
Beck, Ulrich. 2005. How Not to Become a Museum Piece. *The British Journal of Sociology* 56(3): 335–43.
Brand, Jennie E., and Yu Xie. 2010. Who Benefits Most from College? Evidence for Negative Selection in Heterogeneous Economic Returns to Higher Education. *American Sociological Review* 75: 273–302.
Burawoy, Michael. 2005. For Public Sociology. *American Sociological Review* 70(4): 4–28.
Duncan, Otis D. 1984. *Notes on Social Measurement: Historical and Critical*. New York: Russell Sage.
Haraway, Donna. 2003. *The Companion Species Manifesto: Dogs, People and Significance of Otherness*. Chicago: Prickly Paradigm.
_____. 2007. *When Species Meet (Posthumanities)*. Minneapolis: University of Minnesota.
Irvine, Leslie. 2004. *If You Tame Me: Animal Identity and the Intrinsic Value of Their Lives*. Philadelphia: Temple University Press.
Myers, Eugene. 2003. No Longer the Lonely Species: A Post-Mead Perspective on Animals and Self. *International Journal of Sociology and Social Policy* 23(3): 46–68.
Protevi, John. 2009. *Political Affect: Connecting the Social and the Somatic*. Minneapolis: University of Minnesota Press.
Sanders, Clinton. 1999. *Understanding Dogs: Living and Working with Canine Companions*. Philadelphia: Temple University Press.
_____. 2006. The Sociology of Human-Animal Interaction and Relationships. http://www.h-net.org/~animal/ruminations_sanders.html
Shukin, Nicole. 2009. *Animal Capital: Rendering Life in Biopolitical Times*. Minneapolis: University of Minnesota Press.
Sztybel, David. 2010. Animal Absolutes: Liberation Sociology's Missing Links. Part II of II Essays on Animals and Normative Sociology. *Journal of Critical Animal Studies* 8(1/2): 126–75.
Wolfe, Cary. 2010. *What Is Posthumanism?* Minneapolis: University of Minnesota Press.
Xie, Yu, and Xiaogang Wu. 2005. Reply to Jann: Market Premium, Social Process, and Statisticism. *American Sociological Review* 70: 865–70.

PART I: THEORY

1. HERMENEUTICS AND SOCIOLOGY
Deepening the Interpretive Perspective
Isaac Reed *and* Benjamin Lamb-Books

Human beings live in a world of meanings: signifying to each other their wants and needs; misunderstanding intentions and correcting these misunderstandings; telling stories of good and evil, loss and salvation; using compelling rhetoric to achieve political victories and retain social power; deploying categories that call forth actions and mold collective intentions; the list goes on. The point is that social action is embedded in and molded by the meanings people use to get on with their lives. For this reason, sociology, and the human sciences as a whole, are hermeneutic in that they require the social researcher to interpret meaning if she is to make sense of social life in a new and useful way. In hermeneutic sociology, the investigator uses theory to develop interpretations of social action; by mobilizing theory in this way, she is able to intensively study social processes so that the human subjects under study can be understood, explained, and criticized.

The arguments for a hermeneutic sociology are partially available through the sociological canon, but remain, in their fully articulated form, outside that canon. In classical theory courses, Max Weber's concern with interpretation is contrasted to the more naturalistic sociological theories of Karl Marx and Emile Durkheim. Likewise, the symbolic interactionists' interest in concrete processes of meaning–construction is often contrasted to the analytical realism of structural functionalism. And finally, "postmodern" skepticism about the production of sociological knowledge often addresses itself to discourse, and indeed concerns itself with meaning albeit in a different way than the symbolic interactionists did. However, though the project of interpretive sociology is often outlined and debated, the specifically hermeneutic tradition of thought in social theory in the West is less well-known. In this chapter we construct a reading of this line of thinking and, by doing so, outline a specifically hermeneutic understanding of social theory and social research. We conclude with three questions for contemporary hermeneutics, which we view as signposts for what may develop in twenty-first century social theory.

The term "hermeneutics" refers, in a general sense, to the science, art, and philosophy of interpreting meaning, and in particular, the meaning of texts. Perhaps this is part of why hermeneutics' influence on sociology has always been tendentious: in its origins in the modern West, it is less concerned with people themselves and more concerned with the restoration and interpretation of one of their most celebrated productions, texts. Hermeneutics, as such, can be traced back to Antiquity, but its modern form emerges from disputations during the renaissance about interpreting Homer. Influenced by an emergent modern humanism, scholars began to object to the allegorical readings of Homer that interpreted *The Iliad* and *The Odyssey* in Christian terms, and thus hermeneutics was born via disputes over the validity of interpretation. In its modern form, then, hermeneutics developed via the fields of Classical philology and Biblical interpretation; methods of interpretation were tested in the fires of translating Plato and restoring sacred Christian texts. For this reason, hermeneutics has, since the early modern era, retained an association with high culture, religion, and thus also with politically conservative intellectual work. However, as with so many things, so with social theory: the 1960s saw a radical shift in the possibilities and implications of hermeneutics. In some ways, however, the "cultural turn" of the 1960s found a like-minded predecessor in debates about history and knowledge that animated German intellectual life in the latter half of the 19th century. In particular, the work of Wilhelm Dilthey can now be seen as a necessary reference point for any social theory that concerns itself with interpretation.

Historical Hermeneutics

Hermeneutic social theory as we now know it has its origins in German romanticism and the *Geisteswissenschaften*. The latter term was originally a German translation of J. S. Mill's "moral sciences." More literally it refers to the "sciences of the spirit" but it has come to mean "human sciences" or "human studies" in general, conceived in opposition to the methods and objectives of the natural sciences. This now-classic opposition, which influenced Wilhelm Dilthey's work, separates the method of explanation in the natural sciences from the method of understanding in the human sciences. The *Geisteswissenschaften* was a mixed German response to a British empiricism that was ambitiously applying the scientific rationality of physics and astronomy to the study of human society. On the one hand, Wilhelm Dilthey, Heinrich Rickert, and Max Weber admired the rigor of scientific methods, especially inductive logic, and accepted the goal of producing valid and general knowledge of human history. On the other hand, they rejected the idea of a *mechanistic* explanation of human action and events. In their work, attempts to "explain away" history without taking into account the mental dimension of human life were carefully and vigorously attacked.

In engaging in this *methodenstreit* (the "fight over methods"), various German thinkers drew on the work of Friedrich Schleiermacher and his conceptualization of the "hermeneutic circle" (1998). A hermeneutic circle is evident when part of a text can only be understood through a preliminary grasp of the whole text, and when the inverse is also affirmed: understanding a part will increase the understanding of the whole. Schleiermacher thought there were a multitude of hermeneutic circles constituting interpretation, one of them being the relation between the author (part) and his historical context (whole), another between a text (part) and the author's life and work (whole). In each case there is a reciprocal relation between parts and whole that is characteristic of the process of understanding in general. The interpretation of a text itself is the fundamental model however.

Hence in Schleiermacher we find the archetypical image of hermeneutics: the investigator puzzling over the meaning of a text he does not yet understand. Schleiermacher also emphasizes importance of historical contextualization and the need for the investigator to reconstruct the author's cultural and linguistic context when considering a text. However, for all of these contributions, Schleiermacher was ultimately committed to the 19th-century romantic ideal of the "genius" artist — except that for Schleiermacher, the genius of the artist must be matched by the genius of the interpreter. In fact, the interpreter should know the text better than the author — it is from Schleiermacher that we inherit the idea that the goal of hermeneutics is to understand the author better than the author understood or understands herself.

This theory of artistic genius (and of interpretation) betrays a certain individualist bias in Schleiermacher's work. When Schleiermacher focuses on the genius of artistic creation and when he argues that hermeneutics is the inversion of rhetoric (i.e. hermeneutics as the movement from speech to thought), he seems to reduce hermeneutics to the study of authorial intention. Hans-Georg Gadamer and Paul Ricoeur would, in the twentieth century, criticize this displacement of meaning as too psychological and argue that the author's biography is not necessarily relevant for understanding the meaningful subject-matter and truth-claims made by the text itself. The early work of Wilhelm Dilthey is also susceptible to the same criticisms.

For example, in his *Introduction to the Human Sciences* (1988 [1883]), Dilthey tried to ground the epistemology of the human sciences on a universal psychology. His early social theory of understanding does not articulate the necessary mediation of understanding through historical texts, language, and so on. Instead, he sometimes claims that meaning is immediately intelligible (a very non-hermeneutical position!). But over the course of his life, Dilthey fully reconstructed his views on this matter and thus developed the first major statement of historical hermeneutics, starting with his 1900 essay, *The Rise of Hermeneutics* (1996), and then in his paradigm-setting work, *The Construction of the Historical World in the Human Sciences* (1910).

In the latter, Dilthey states that the human mind can only understand itself through its objectifications or historical expressions (1976, 172–3, 191). Humans are constantly and meaningfully articulating their inner experiences through externalized expressions such as speech, texts, laws, actions, etc. Dilthey has a rather dualistic vocabulary here for what is actually inseparable: each expression has an "inner" and an "outer" dimension.[1] The inner dimension is the meaningful mental structure emerging from lived experience; the outer is the physical sensuous embodiment of the meaning-system, e.g. written words on a page. Self-understanding or the understanding of others must be based not on introspective reason or un-mediated empathy, but rather on the inter-connections between mind, experience, meaning, and external expressions:

> The totality of understanding reveals—in contrast with the subjectivity of experience—the objectifications of life. A realization of the objectivity of life, i.e. of its externalizations in many kinds of structural systems, becomes an additional basis for the human studies.... The great outer reality of the mind always surrounds us. It is a manifestation of the mind in the world of the senses—from a fleeting expression to the century-long rule of a constitution or code of law. Every single expression represents a common feature in the realm of this objective mind.... We live in this atmosphere, it surrounds us constantly. We are immersed in it. We are at home everywhere in this historical and understood world; we understand the sense of meaning of it all; we ourselves are woven into this common sphere [1976, 191; emphasis dropped].

The argument that contextualizes this passage is Dilthey's claim that the *Geisteswissenschaften* have a distinctive object of study: mental structures of meaning. To understand human social life and historical events, an account of this subjective order is an absolute necessity. Methodologically, getting at this inner reality requires an interpretive approach dealing with the medium of "objectifications." Dilthey thus defines understanding as the process of recovering the mental content that was experienced and expressed through any given diversity of objectifications. Like Schleiermacher, understanding is achieved through hermeneutical circles requiring contextualizing historical and linguistic study.

What are these objectifications of mind that Dilthey references? Here the departure of Dilthey from the neo–Kantian philosophies that so influenced Weber becomes apparent.[2] By developing and secularizing one of Hegel's terms, Dilthey firmly commits to understanding meaning as a supra-individual structure that is relatively stable and indeed exerts considerable power over any given group or individual. Dilthey writes that the "outer reality of mind" consists of "language, custom, and every form or style of life as well as the family, society, the state and the law," not to mention all art, religion and philosophy as well (1976, 194). Thus Dilthey affirms the Hegelian idea that social-historical practices and institutions are objectifications of a shared inner reality, that a set of meanings implicitly structure customs, conventions, and behaviors. However, Dilthey does not accept Hegel's metaphysics of absolute knowledge in which Reason can deduce the teleological progress of meaning-structures throughout history.[3] Instead, in his later writings, Dilthey proposes a research program for studying meaning-systems through historical hermeneutics. His point is precisely that we cannot know the inner world of this or that set of human beings via metaphysical speculation or *a priori* introspection. Instead, we must do the hard hermeneutic work of finding our way in the lives of others by familiarizing ourselves with the external manifestations of the meanings that drive their action.

By thus proposing that meaningful webs of relationships exceed the individual and "possess an independent existence and development of their own through the content, value and purpose which they realize," (1976, 181)[4] Dilthey asserts that meaning in social life takes on a structure. This has tremendous implications for social science: on the one hand, it implies that social science must of necessity engage in the task interpreting meanings. On the other hand, it suggests that this task can indeed succeed, since meaning is not as evanescent, individualized, or radically subjective as it is sometimes thought to be. Rather, meaning has a *structure,* and it is this structure to meaning that the social researcher must grasp if she is to explain the social actions she is interested in.

Finally, Dilthey maintained that to interpret the meanings that gave a certain historical era its structure, the investigator had to use general concepts, even if the object of his investigations remained what Weber called a "historical individual," which is to say, a particular complex of meanings that is not repeated anywhere else in history. Thus, in Dilthey's work, we find the outline of a dialectic between lived experience and highly generalized theory as the key to producing valid knowledge of history (1976, 187–8). He thus holds steadfastly to the possibility that the investigator can, and should, attain a certain degree of epistemic privilege,[5] by making a distinction between an everyday understanding and the "higher" understanding that produces knowledge in the human sciences.[6]

Philosophical Hermeneutics

Dilthey wanted to demonstrate how scientific knowledge of history was possible. For him, hermeneutics was primarily a textual methodology that, when transferred to the discipline of history, could deploy general or universal concepts to make historical times and places far removed comprehensible. In the 20th century, however, Martin Heidegger recast hermeneutics as a philosophical approach for interrogating the meaning of Being. Heidegger's student, Hans-Georg Gadamer, would join his teacher in working through this new, overtly philosophical, turn in hermeneutics.

In the Introduction to *Being and Time*, Heidegger presents his philosophy as a "hermeneutic phenomenology" of "fundamental ontology" (1996, 33). Thus Heidegger distances himself from the particular epistemological concerns of any one academic discipline and especially from the social sciences.[7] His broader question is: what is the meaning of Being? Since meaning entails interpretation, he describes his philosophy as hermeneutical. However, there is a key difference between Heidegger and Dilthey's theories of interpretation. For Dilthey, hermeneutics is a systematic rule-based art for obtaining knowledge of something. For Heidegger, hermeneutics involves a much more passive process of letting Being speak for itself — Heidegger's technical definition of phenomenology is letting the concealed disclose itself through appearance, which Heidegger hopes Being will do for philosophers with the right hermeneutic orientation.

Hermeneutics, then, serves the philosophical function of determining the right posture that would enable Being's unconcealment. Thus for Heidegger, understanding is a matter of finding the right presuppositions that adequately fit with the "thing-in-itself."[8] In Heidegger's view, an existential analysis of the human being will function as the pre-understanding necessary to interrogate the meaning of Being. A sort of ontological hermeneutic circle is at work throughout *Being and Time*: to understand Being we must develop the pre-understanding humans *already have* of beings (Division I) and then develop the temporality of the human-being as the horizon for Being's self-disclosure (Division II). This ontologization of the hermeneutic circle leads Heidegger to analyze the practice of pre-understanding in humans, that is, the prepositional structure of all practical understanding, what is also translated as the "fore-structure of understanding."

Heidegger relates understanding to the situatedness of human beings in the world and their practical projects within the world. This theoretical move — to the practical, perhaps never-quite-articulated way in which human beings know how to hammer a nail or how to throw a baseball — has had a deep effect on twentieth century philosophy and social theory. Thinkers as different as Richard Rorty, Stanley Fish, and Pierre Bourdieu could be said to have Heideggerian strands to their thinking insofar as they find human *practices* irreducible to the rules they supposedly follow, or the logics that supposedly support them.

But what Heidegger does for the hermeneutic tradition in particular is add the level of situational meaning to an interpretive theoretical framework — an idea anticipated in some of Georg Simmel's work,[9] but never fully connected, in 19th century hermeneutics, to the kinds of structural "objectifications" of human life that so interested Dilthey. Heidegger leaves Schleiermacher behind: in philosophical hermeneutics the problematic of understanding has shifted from the author's experience behind a text to the practical tacit intelligence exercised by human beings in situations. He thus shifts from a historical hermeneutics of objectifications to an ontological hermeneutics of practical understanding.[10] Heidegger seeks to show how humans use everyday tools pre-reflectively, i.e. before a conceptual subject-object division ever emerges. Practical understanding, then, is an ability possessed by human beings and exercised in all situated action.

For the social sciences at least, what Heidegger suggests is a hermeneutics of everyday life, and many contemporary theorists have been influenced by his assertion that humans in the world are always already exercising understanding. This has two implications. Methodologically, it confirms a fundamental differ-ence between social and natural science — by studying humans, social researchers are interpreting interpreters. Analytically, it suggests a helpful dis-tinction in sociological hermeneutics between situational meaning and cultural or systemic meaning.[11] This type of situationally dependent meaning could also be called performative meaning because elements of a situation only acquire meaning through their relation to the social performance of which they are a part (though, as cultural sociology is quick to point out, performances tend to be iterative and call upon wider codes and systemic meanings). Thus we suggest that any hermeneutic sociology needs to take into account at least two types of meaning: not only codes and narratives that make up culture, but also the situational meaning that emerges from practical involvement in the world and social interactions.

Hans-Georg Gadamer (2004 [1960]) takes Heidegger's meditations on the situatedness of human action, and reapplies them to Schleiermacher's original problem — the investigator confronted with a text she does not yet fully under-stand. He thus develops a broad meta-theoretical framework for knowledge and an enduring protest against basing the human sciences on the natural sci-ences. According to Gadamer, Dilthey was still too seduced by the natural sci-ences in his concerns with empirical epistemology and inductive methodology.[12] Instead, Gadamer connects the interpretation of texts to a different model of truth: experiencing a work of art. Truth, as experienced in the work of art, is not an object that becomes known through method. Instead, truth is an event that absorbs the subject in its own world-disclosure.

Gadamer defines understanding as the experience of a "fusion of horizons" between the present horizon of the interpreter and the world encountered in the text. To say that both the interpreter and the text have a distinct horizon is another way of saying that they both are situated in a specific context and their meaning — and claim to understanding and truth — is shaped by that con-text. Gadamer's notion of horizons leads him to reject the "Enlightenment's prejudice against prejudice," which he finds not only in naturalism and posi-tivism, but also in the German historical school and its methodologists (2004, 273). The traditional prejudices that situate the interpreter make up the specific horizon of the present, and Gadamer states, "to try to escape from one's own concepts in interpretation is not only impossible but manifestly absurd. To interpret means precisely to bring one's own preconceptions into play so that the text's meaning can really be made to speak for us" (2004, 398). "Prejudice" could be better translated as "pre-judgments" in the sense of a preliminary conception of the whole needed to understand the parts in a hermeneutic circle. This has radical implications for the interpretation of meaning for Gadamer. If it is not possible to neutrally excavate the original meaning of the text within its own historical horizon — due to the historicality of all understanding — then any interpretation will always be a blending of two different horizons. Thus, for Gadamer, meaning is co-determined by elements of the world of the text and by the historically-conditioned consciousness of the present reader.[13]

As Susan Hekman (1984) has argued, Gadamer articulates some very broad meta-theoretical ideas that fit well with a hermeneutic approach to social science. His fundamental idea — that understanding involves a "fusion of horizons" — correctly identifies the deep symmetry of knowledge in the human sciences, in which human subjects create knowledge about other, already knowledgeable, hermeneutic subjects. Hermeneutic sociology thus depends on the development of knowledge in a symmetric relationship between the investigator's meaningful context and the meaningful context of the humans whose actions she is interpreting (Reed 2010). However, the way Gadamer describes this relationship is ultimately insufficient for social science because he tends to conflate many different kinds of fore-understanding under his category of prejudice.[14] Gadamer packs into "historical prejudices" or "prejudgments" *all* aspects of the investigator's meaning-bound life experience. But perhaps the social theories developed in dialogue with colleagues are a different sort of meaning than the reinvented traditions that give religious experience coherence, or the authority of a technical expert who we rely on when using an elevator.[15] Is it not possible that we judge theories based upon their resourcefulness for constructing valid interpretive explanations and how such explanations do or do not render action intelligible by providing adequate interpretation at the level of meaning and the level of cause (Weber 1978, 10–1)?

Gadamer, then, poses the problem of the context of the interpreter, but does not solve it. We think this is because, in the end, Gadamer's theory of understanding is actually rather one-way: despite a co-determination of meaning, the crux of understanding focuses on how the reader is addressed by the text and how the reader applies the aesthetic truth-events made by the text to her present horizon. Gadamer's theory of application as essential to understanding is never reversed, say, for the application of carefully crafted theories to the world of the text, a reversal that would open the door to the possibility of social explanation.

The Metaphor of the Text or Cultural Hermeneutics

To summarize, Dilthey took the textual methodologies of hermeneutics and applied them to history and proposed that the human studies are possible precisely because the inner, lived experiences of human subjects are mediated by structures of meaning that span time and space. Heidegger pointed to the way in which meaning was not just encoded into culture, but ontologically present in situations and in the practical, temporal understandings of the human beings who act in them. Gadamer pointed to just how sharp the break must be between natural and social science, because of how the symmetry problem affects the nature of truth in the latter. But, for hermeneutics to really become an epistemic frame for social research, the following problem must be directly addressed: why should these textual methodologies be useful for studying — and explaining — social action? It is to this question that some of the most innovative theoretical work associated with the "cultural turn" is addressed.

Paul Ricoeur's work on hermeneutics and the human sciences transitions away from existential concerns, and towards a concern with history, society, and action.[16] In his work, the break between speech and writing is used as leverage to push the study of action into a new phase. Any written text, Ricoeur explains, is defined by its distance or distanciation from spoken dialogue.[17] For instance, in a conversation between speakers, meaning has an immediate character because "the subjective intention of the speaking subject and the meaning of the discourse overlap each other in such a way that it is the same thing to understand what the speaker means and what his discourse means" (1981, 200). If a misunderstanding occurs in a conversation, a round or two of question and answer is usually enough to restore understanding (of course, not always). In the case of written discourse however, the addressor and the addressee can no longer regulate the transmission of meaning in this way through more interlocution. Not only is the potential audience widely opened through writing's fixation of discourse, but the inherent polysemy in language — how words and sentences can have multiple meanings—cannot be immediately restricted and the intended meaning can no longer as easily be determined through contextualization (1981, 44). As the context of the reader departs from the context of the author, the intended univocal meaning becomes more equivocal. *Pace* Gadamer, for textual understanding, the conversational metaphor of dialogue loses its coherence because "with writing, the conditions of direct interpretation through the interplay of question and answer, hence through dialogue, are no longer fulfilled" (1981, 45).

In his well-known essay *The Model of the Text*, Ricoeur (1981) argues that valid knowledge about social action can be obtained by treating action as a text-analogue and using hermeneutic methods of understanding. Ricoeur accepts Weber's definition of social action as subjectively meaningful and as the proper object of social scientific knowledge and explanation. The essay is dedicated, then, to strengthening the argument that action can indeed be understood and interpreted like a text. The success of this argument depends, for Ricoeur, on demonstrating the similar constitutive features of both texts and action.[18] Let us take a closer look at this argument.

First, Ricoeur argues that both actions and texts are inherently meaningful objects of analysis— they come to the analysis with meanings that are already there. The references for this argument are many, but in addition to Max Weber, Ricoeur points to the speech-act theory of J. L. Austin and John Searle to argue that actions are only actions insofar as they communicate some sort of meaning. In addition, action can have unintended effects much like the texts can have meanings not consciously intended by their author. Texts are semantically autonomous, as are actions historically autonomous, from their authors.[19] The meaning of texts and actions can multiply, shift, and change — as well as sediment and become tremendously powerful in ways not intended — as history proceeds. Both texts and actions are plurivocal, but this plurivocity is limited by their reception in specific historical contexts.

Methodologically then, the interpretation of action is not altogether unlike literary criticism or structural linguistics, fields which offer advantageous methods to social science in Ricoeur's assessment. Ricouer's ground for comparison here is how methods for understanding both texts and actions depend upon some detachment of meaning from the event of its instantiation. The written text fixes meaningful discourse (Dilthey's objectification), that later readers can then encounter. The study of action also relies upon a form of objectification mediating meaning, not between the writer and the reader but between the actor and the social scientist. Within Ricoeur's argument by analogy, there is an implicit recognition that social scientists are always operating within a context of investigation different from the context of the social action to be explained. The meaningful nature of social action enables theorists to reflect on that meaning in a different context through an interpretive process much like translation.

Ricoeur has high hopes for the metaphor of the text. He writes that "the paradigm of reading, which is the counterpart of the paradigm of writing, provides a solution for the methodological paradox of the human sciences" (1981, 209). The paradox he is referring to is the traditional dichotomy between naturalistic explanation and interpretive understanding in the *Geisteswissenschaften*. Ricoeur thinks Dilthey conceded too much ground by letting the natural sciences monopolize the definition of causality and explanation (216). Though he is attempting to reconcile understanding and explanation within one sociological hermeneutic, Ricoeur does not wish to retain a classical conception of mechanical causality.[20] Instead, "a new kind of explanatory attitude" emerges from the structuralist movement in literary criticism that can be extended to the task of social explanation. Ricoeur envisions structural analysis as a necessary stage of explanation within a larger hermeneutic project (218). Structuralism abstracts from experiences and processes to classify elements and types within a larger system thanks to general theoretical categories and concepts. But these abstractions are then re-integrated into a concrete interpretive explanation — a return to the specific meanings of a set of social actions that were efficacious at a specific time. Thus Ricoeur's newly rendered hermeneutic achieves a dialectical synthesis between explanation and understanding in order to produce "depth interpretations" or "critical interpretations" (ibid). In the terms we are developing here, we could say that interpretive explanation is what results when the situational and systemic meanings of social action are analyzed together.

We can note that one of the most well-known social scientists of the 20th century, Clifford Geertz, put this metaphor of action-as-text directly into practice. In his essay on the Balinese cockfight, Geertz wrote (1973, 448, our emphasis):

> If one takes the cockfight, or any other collectively sustained symbolic structure, as a means of "saying something of something" (to invoke a famous Aristotelian tag), then one is faced with a problem not in social mechanics but social semantics. For the anthropologist, whose concern is with formulating sociological principles, not with promoting or appreciating cockfights, the question is, what does one learn about such principles from examining *culture as an assemblage of texts?*

Geertz's meditations on the means by which an anthropologist can, and cannot, understand other cultures than his own are deeply connected to his own "readings" of different cultures in Indonesia and Morocco. In so far as Geertz's research practice exemplifies the philosophical standpoint that Dilthey developed, one can think of Geertz as an anthropological application of Dilthey's vision for the study of history (for an extended reflection on Geertz's work and his interpretive perspective, see Reed 2008).

Thus in following Ricoeur we can say that the metaphor of the text is useful for social research because of the way in which it captures the structured, meaningful wholes in which persons, and their various social actions, are immersed. It is also useful because it suggests a link between the idea of a hermeneutic sociology and the practice of translation. Translations produce interpretations that can more or less preserve the spirit of a text; roughly the same meaning-system can be comprehended within a different language. The structure of translation as the go-between that connects two linguistic contexts not only offers suggestive parallels for interpretive social research, but also provides a definitive premise of hermeneutics: key elements of meaning can be transferred from one context to another even though translated meaning is never completely identical to original meaning.[21]

Three Questions for Contemporary Hermeneutics

Hermeneutics, thus, articulates a set of precepts for social research and the use of theory in that research. The hermeneutic social investigator should, via the interpretation of meaning, become highly sensitive to historical and cultural difference, but in so doing she increases, rather than decreases, her epistemic privilege and explanatory power. Her ability to do this is premised upon the way in which social meaning relies upon the inner, subjective lives of individuals but is not reducible to them. Rather, meaning has a structure, and creates a landscape upon which individuals must move, if they want to act. Construed so, hermeneutic social theory is poised to re-emerge as an influential frame for the human sciences. What needs to be done for this to be so? We pose three questions for hermeneutics.

1. What kind of meaning system is social theory?

Above, we criticized Gadamer's hermeneutics for failing to differentiate between communally crafted concepts for social-scientific inquiry and the inevitable, particularistic biases affecting an individual's pre-understanding. This raises the question of what exactly social theory is and how it works to further the goals of interpreting, explaining, and criticizing the social world. If theory is its own language game, what differentiates it from other language games? We think that the answer lies in considering how the abstractions and generalities of social theory can, when repeatedly confirmed as epistemologically useful, grant a certain amount of epistemic privilege to the investigator. Theory can help to create a distinctive fore-structure, which, when fused with the structures of meaning in the context of social action, makes knowledge deep, effective and explanatory.

A hermeneutic sociology will develop the idea that while there is no absolute ground from which to evaluate the "objectivity" of a social explanation, there are nonetheless better and worse explanations, much as there are better and worse translations of a text (but no perfect translation). A literal translation misses the point in a way a thin, anti-theoretical description does. Thus, hermeneutic sociology needs to develop an account of the vast pluralism of social theory wherein seemingly incommensurable pictures of social life are built up and used in different ways at different times by different investigators to deepen their understanding of this or that set of social actions. Perhaps this pluralistic promotion of multiple social theories is, in fact, a necessary prerequisite to good social research rather than a sad indication that sociology has not yet entered a time of "normal science" (Kuhn 1996).

2. What is the relationship between hermeneutics and critical theory?

As suggested earlier, recent developments in social and political theory indicate that hermeneutics can and has shed its conservative label. In one line of thought, Habermas has developed Gadamer's notion of horizonal fusions into his own theory of rational dialogue. Within the inter-subjective practice of dialogue, several ethical assumptions are constantly being made that ensure the felicitous transfer of meaning (unless the situation is affected by systematic distortions). Habermas wants to build a more robust normative-critical theory from these foundations in the universal nature of communication. This has been taken further by some of Habermas's best interpreters, especially by the philosopher and feminist theorist Maeve Cooke (1994). However, contemporary hermeneutics has also developed an alternative framework to both Habermas's universal discourse ethics and his well-known post-structuralist critics.[22]

In another line of thought, Georgia Warnke (1993a) finds an ally in hermeneutics for overcoming the false universalism of Habermas and others who also aspire to such foundationalist thought. Warnke develops a hermeneutic feminism (1993a, 92–7) that makes a hermeneutic justification for pluralism of valid interpretations. She defends a loose conception of tradition that is not static but itself constituted by pluralistic, moral arguments (that is, as opposed to tradition being defined by agreement and deference to authority). Hermeneutic feminism more than tolerates legitimate interpretive differences; it sees them as mutually productive and morally edifying. Warnke describes how a hermeneutic political philosophy promotes inclusive, multidimensional understanding and democratic deliberation.[23] Michael Walzer (1987), another hermeneutic political theorist, likewise finds a democratic ethics in the pluralistic dimension of hermeneutics. He appropriates hermeneutics for the interpretive element in social criticism. Like Geertz, Walzer expands a "thick" and "thin" distinction to describe possible attitudes toward culture including moral judgments. Thin criticism, including all types of philosophical ethics, is unnecessarily detached and minimalist towards morality. In contrast, thick social criticism requires a hermeneutics that can extract ideas and principles already embedded in the local thicket of moral culture. Hence Walzer calls this local meaning-centered criticism immanent — it starts from and stays within a culture's moral frameworks of belief.

3. Can a validity-seeking, historicist hermeneutics develop an analytics of social power?

This, in the end, will be the crucial question for hermeneutics, for so much of the most innovative theoretical development in the human sciences of the last fifty years has developed, to quote Susan Sontag, "against interpretation" (1961). Another way of saying this is that many contemporary readings of social theory would draw a bright line between the focus on "deep meaning" and the focus on "social power" (e.g. Asad 1993). There may be a variety of reasons for this, but one of them surely is the way Clifford Geertz and Michel Foucault are read as thinkers whose intellectual projects were radically different, even perhaps directly opposed, to each other. Though the differences in focus and concern of Foucault and Geertz are palpable, we dissent from the way in which these two thinkers have become iconic figures in post-positivist theory, the one standing for critical theory, and the other for the ethnographic imagination.

In his descriptions of his archaeological and genealogical method, Foucault claimed to leave interpretation behind and insisted in a variety of ways that he was merely describing or setting out the workings of discourse and the intersections of truth and power (Foucault 1972, 135–211).[24] Foucault has also criticized several tendencies of modern hermeneutics found especially in Freud and Heidegger. Foucault exposed Freud's hermeneutics of unconscious desire as a ruse of bio-power and an artifact of confessional technology (Foucault 1978). Foucault has also sought to historicize the primordial universalist ontology in Heidegger's philosophical hermeneutics (as well as Claude Levi-Strauss's universalist anthropology).

We understand these critiques to be sharp indictments of philosophical hermeneutics, but not as destructive of historical hermeneutics. We believe that close examination of Foucault's own empirical work reveals a deep hermeneutic sensitivity and an ability to ferret out the meanings of various actions, institutions, and practices. Thus we think that hermeneutics, as a program for social theory in the twenty-first century, is quite commensurate with the study of discourse, power and practice, properly understood. Another way of saying this is to suggest that the next step for social theories of power, will involve a re-engagement with and re-invention of the questions surrounding interpretation, explanation and the use of abstract theory. We can see the dawning of a new era of theory, which will leave the problematic of postmodernism behind. We hope that pluralistic hermeneutic sociology will lead the way in this renaissance.

Notes

1. Daniel Suber (2010) explains why this distinction does not make Dilthey a dualist contra Rickert and others.

2. The neo–Kantian movement in 19th century German philosophy re-invigorated the subjective turn in epistemology by transposing Kant's focus on the universal-rational structures internal to the human *mind* into a method for examining value, historical particularity, and other concerns of the emerging human sciences. As a result of the influence of the philosophical language of the neo–Kantians, many early non–Marxist sociologists in Germany displayed a tendency towards what we would now call methodological individualism. Though it is by no means clear that Weber was himself a methodological individualist, Dilthey's defense of the more Hegelian notion of subjectivity or spirit anticipates the structuralist and post-structuralist theoretical influences on cultural sociology — in particular, the idea that the realm of value has a structural order of its own, being collective or cultural. See, for example, Charles Taylor's (1985) critique of modern positivism and behavioralism for a similar argument about the inter-subjective nature of meanings.

3. Arguing explicitly against Hegel, Dilthey writes, "But, today, the task is the reverse [of Hegel's] — to recognize the actual historical expressions as the true foundation of historical knowledge and to find a method of answering the question how universally valid knowledge of the historical world can be based on what is thus given" (1976, 195).

4. Exhibiting several intellectual tendencies shared with other more well-known classical sociologists, this quote fruitfully compares with later Durkheim on the autonomy of collective representations—a motif celebrated as the "autonomy of culture" by contemporary cultural sociology—and Weber's notion of the "spirit" of capitalism as a complex historical set of intelligible elements.

5. In the course of this chapter, we use the term "epistemic privilege" to describe the way in which, in our view, the hermeneutic investigator seeks to secure a sort of knowledge that is superior in its insight and rigor to everyday opinion. In particular, we expect hermeneutic investigation to produce knowledge that is empirically responsible and that can also access "deeper" explanatory truths about the social actions under study. In doing so, we do believe we are hewing to Dilthey's original vision, but articulating it through concepts that were unavailable to him. More generally, the debates over epistemic privilege can be seen as having three poles: *empiricist*—where epistemic privilege is granted by the investigator following specific rules of inference from data; *standpoint*—where epistemic privilege is made possible, if not guaranteed, by the social position of the knower (e.g. the "standpoint of the proletariat" or "feminist standpoint"); and *postmodernist*—in which the very possibility of epistemic privilege is effaced in favor of a more contingent, intersectional, and playful understanding of the identities of knowing human beings and their claims (for this distinction between the three epistemologies, see Harding 1986). Hermeneutics, in our view, shares with empiricism and standpoint theory the demand for empirical responsibility and, with recent renditions of standpoint theory (e.g. Wylie 2003), a non-reductive vision of the way in which the inclusion of various located perspectives on social life can enhance the range of proposed interpretations of a given phenomenon that an investigator considers. Ultimately, our view is that theory can indeed do a lot for epistemic privilege, but only if used in a way *not* consistent with naturalist or realist models that assimilate social knowledge into natural science.

6. Due to Dilthey's philosophy of life, the latter higher understanding always emerges from everyday understanding according to Dilthey. While a distinction between different types of understanding may be useful when analyzing the nature of social theory itself as a meaning-system (see our conclusion), Dilthey's positing of a universal second-order kind of relationship is in many cases doubtful, as when inheriting concepts from the social-scientific tradition.

7. While epistemology refers to how valid knowledge is obtained, ontology is the philosophical practice of making truth-claims about the generic being of things, humans, human nature, social facts, etc.

8. Thus, Heidegger is also distancing himself from Kant who thought that the "thing-in-itself," i.e. mind-independent reality, is inaccessible to human scientific reason. Heidegger is trying to move beyond all such subject-object dualisms in the history of metaphysics. By considering his hermeneutics to be a project in "fundamental ontology," Heidegger signals his desire to think through Being itself in a more original way than has ever been done. For Heidegger, this involves examining the temporal, practical and yet poetic nature of Being.

9. In addition to Simmel's well-known work on dyads and triads, see Simmel (1977).

10. Ricoeur summarizes this as a "shift in philosophical locus" in the history of hermeneutics, and that Heidegger "de-psychologizes" hermeneutics by recognizing the primacy of being before knowledge (1981, 56). While most social theorists no longer doubt this "primacy," the epistemological implications Heidegger draws are more debatable.

11. See also Eliasoph and Lichterman (2003) for another rendering of this distinction.

12. Gadamer associates an overly objectivistic "historical consciousness" with Dilthey. Gadamer reads Dilthey as denying the historicality of all understanding, and in particular the historically-located investigator himself. However, recent commentators have defended Dilthey by demonstrating that he was indeed aware of a sort of value-relevance of the historian. See especially Harrington (2001) for a critique of Gadamer's dialogism and the resultant misreading of Dilthey.

13. "The real meaning of a text, as it speaks to the interpreter, does not depend on the contingencies of the author and his original audience. It certainly is not identical with them, for it is always co-determined also by the historical situation of the interpreter" (Gadamer 2004, 296).

14. Habermas criticizes Gadamer for not considering the distinctive "fusion of horizons" between a natural language and a theoretical language in *The Hermeneutic Claim to Universality* (1990). This leads us to question the nature of social theory as a distinctive sort of meaning-system (see concluding section to this chapter).

15. The notion of authority and Gadamer's normative safeguarding of it inevitably provoke concern about the relation between philosophical hermeneutics and politics. The debate, in so far as it does not revolve around specific biographical details of Gadamer's academic trajectory, concerns whether the meaning of the terms authority and tradition in Gadamer's work were close to their common usage, or in fact quite different. For us, even if Gadamer's terms are interpreted liberally and granted their own Gadamerian usage, there is still the problem of differentiating theory as a different and perhaps unique element of the investigator's meaningful context, a theoretical criticism somewhat autonomous from the political debate. See Warnke (2002) for a generous consideration of the implications of Gadamer's ideas for ethics and politics.

16. On the other hand, a more recent attempt to bring philosophical hermeneutics back to social sciences is Anthony King's *The Structure of Social Theory* (2004). King uses the ontologies of meaningful experience and shared understanding present in Gadamer and Heidegger as an antidote to the dualistic, structure v. action dichotomy that governs so much contemporary social theory.

17. Both speech and written texts though are forms of discourse for Ricoeur. Discourse here is simply meaningful language.

18. Ricoeur sets up the analogy between texts and actions as follows: "My claim is that action itself, action as meaningful, may become an object of science, without losing its character of meaningfulness, through a kind of objectification similar to fixation which occurs in writing.... This objectification is made *possible* by some inner traits of the action which are similar to the structure of the speech-act and which make doing a kind of utterance. In the same way as the fixation by writing is made possible by a dialectic of intentional exteriorisation immanent to the speech-act itself, a similar dialectic within the process of transaction prepares the detachment of *meaning* of the action from the *event* of the action" (1981, 203–4).

19. Semantics is term from linguistics that designates the meaning dimension of language and not its form (the latter is studied as syntax).

20. On the reconciliation between understanding and explanation in the social sciences, also see Apel (1987).

21. In *On the Logic of the Social Sciences*, Jürgen Habermas (1988, 143–51) also connects hermeneutics to the experience of translation. Habermas uses this analogy in a polemic against the grammatical closure logically entailed by Wittgenstein's philosophy of "forms of life."

22. For a more developed account of how hermeneutic sociology can connect with and reorient critical theory, see Reed (2007).

23. See Warnke (1993b) on how this hermeneutic political philosophy engages other political theorists including Habermas, Rawls, and Taylor.

24. This was a point taken up in much detail and to great effect in that keystone of Foucault commentary, *Michel Foucault: Beyond Structuralism and Hermeneutics* by Dreyfus and Rabinow (1983).

References

Apel, Karl-Otto. 1987. Dilthey's Distinction Between "Explanation" and "Understanding" and the Possibility of Its Mediation. *Journal of the History of Philosophy* 25:131–149.

Asad, Talal. 1993. *Genealogies of Religion: Discipline and Reasons of Power in Christianity and Islam*. Baltimore: Johns Hopkins University Press.

Cooke, Maeve. 1994. *Language and Reason: A Study of Habermas's Pragmatics*. Cambridge: MIT Press.

Dilthey, Wilhelm. 1976. *Selected Writings*. New York: Cambridge University Press.

_____. 1988. *Introduction to the Human Sciences: An Attempt to Lay a Foundation for the Study of Society and History.* Detroit: Wayne State University Press.

_____. 1996. The Rise of Hermeneutics. In *Hermeneutics and the Study of History.* Vol. 4, *Wilhelm Dilthey: Selected Works,* ed. Rudolf Makkreel and Frithjof Rodi, 235–58. Princeton: Princeton University Press.

Dreyfus, Hubert L., and Paul Rabinow. 1983. *Michel Foucault: Beyond Structuralism and Hermeneutics.* Chicago: University of Chicago Press.

Eliasoph, Nina, and Paul Lichterman. 2003. Culture in Interaction. *The American Journal of Sociology* 108(4): 735–94.

Foucault, Michel. 1972. *The Archaeology of Knowledge and the Discourse on Language.* New York: Pantheon Books.

_____. 1978. *The History of Sexuality, Volume 1: An Introduction.* New York: Pantheon Books.

Gadamer, Hans-Georg. 2004. *Truth and Method.* New York: Continuum.

Geertz, Clifford. 1973. *The Interpretation of Cultures: Selected Essays.* New York: Basic Books.

Habermas, Jürgen. 1988. *On the Logic of the Social Sciences.* Cambridge: MIT Press.

_____. 1990. The Hermeneutic Claim to Universality. In *The Hermeneutic Tradition: From Ast to Ricoeur,* ed. Gayle L. Ormiston and Alan D. Schrift, 245–72. Albany: State University of New York Press.

Harding, Sandra. 1986. *The Science Question in Feminism.* Ithaca: Cornell University Press.

Harrington, Austin. 2001. *Hermeneutic Dialogue and Social Science: A Critique of Gadamer and Habermas.* New York: Routledge.

Heidegger, Martin. 1996. *Being and Time.* Albany: State University of New York Press.

Hekman, Susan. 1984. Action as a Text: Gadamer's Hermeneutics and the Social Scientific Analysis of Action. *Journal for the Theory of Social Behavior* 14(3): 333–54.

King, Anthony. 2004. *The Structure of Social Theory.* New York: Routledge.

Kuhn, Thomas. 1996. *The Structure of Scientific Revolutions.* Chicago: University of Chicago Press.

Reed, Isaac. 2007. Cultural Sociology and the Democratic Imperative. In *Culture, Society, and Democracy: The Interpretive Approach,* ed. Isaac Reed and Jeffrey C. Alexander, 1–18. Boulder: Paradigm.

_____. 2008. Maximal Interpretation in Clifford Geertz and the Strong Program in Cultural Sociology: Towards a New Epistemology. *Cultural Sociology* 2(2):187–200.

_____. 2010. Epistemology Contextualized: Social-Scientific Knowledge in a Postpositivist Era. *Sociological Theory* 28(1): 20–39.

Ricoeur, Paul. 1981. *Hermeneutics & the Human Sciences.* New York: Cambridge University Press.

Schleiermacher, Friedrich. 1998. *Hermeneutics and Criticism: And Other Writings.* Cambridge, UK: Cambridge University Press.

Simmel, Georg. 1977. *The Problems of the Philosophy of History: An Epistemological Essay.* New York: Free Press.

Sontag, Susan. 1961. *Against Interpretation and Other Essays.* New York: Picador.

Suber, Daniel. 2010. Social Science between Neo-Kantianism and Philosophy of Life: The Cases of Weber, Simmel, and Mannheim. In *Historical Perspectives on Erklären and Verstehen,* ed. Uljana Feest, 267–90. New York: Springer.

Taylor, Charles. 1985 [1971]. Interpretation and the Sciences of Man. In Philosophy and the Human Sciences: Philosophical Papers, 15–57. Cambridge: Cambridge University Press.

Walzer, Michael. 1987. *Interpretation and Social Criticism.* Cambridge: Harvard University Press.

Warnke, Georgia. 1993a. Feminism and Hermeneutics. *Hypatia* 8(1): 81–98.

_____. 1993b. *Justice and Interpretation.* Cambridge: MIT Press.

_____. 2002. Hermeneutics, Ethics, and Politics. In *The Cambridge Companion to Gadamer,* ed. Robert J. Dostal, 79–101. New York: Cambridge University Press.

Weber, Max. 1978. *Economy and Society.* Berkeley: University of California Press.

Wylie, Alison. 2003. Why Standpoint Matters. In *Science and Other Cultures: Issues in Philosophies of Science and Technology,* ed. Robert Figueroa and Sandra Harding, 26–48. New York: Routledge.

2. The Austrian School
Old Ideas in Economics and New Research Opportunities in Sociology

Joshua McCabe *and* Brian Pitt

The German speaking world has historically been the birthplace of some of sociology's most influential theorists. These theorists include Karl Marx, Max Weber, and Joseph Schumpeter. The same period that produced the latter two theorists also saw the birth of a school of economics known as the Austrian School. The school began with Carl Menger, one of the fathers of the so-called "marginalist revolution," and Friedrich von Weiser, an economist who called for a new *socio*economics. While economics as a discipline eventually became synonymous with the neoclassical paradigm, the students of Menger and Weiser continued the tradition as it was practiced in early 20th century Austria. Ludwig von Mises, who was part of the second generation of Austrian thinkers, was both a member of the German Sociological Society and a friend of Max Weber. Although the school has lain outside the mainstream of economics, Menger and his students have been rediscovered by several prominent sociologists (see Swedberg 1998, 173–204; Granovetter 2002, 44–5). To date, the vast majority of adherents to the Austrian School are still found in economics, but a new generation is emerging in sociology.

This makes a good occasion for reexamining some of the connections between the Austrian School and sociology. The Austrian School is very much in the tradition of Weberian sociology with an emphasis on the causes and consequences of human action. Mises (1998, 10) defined economics as studying the following:

> Human action is purposeful action.... Action is put into operation and transformed into an agency, aiming at ends and goals, is the ego's meaningful response to stimuli and to the conditions of its environment, is a person's conscious adjustment to the state of the universe that determines his life.

The emphasis on action implies a causal analysis. The only difference between Mises and Weber is that the latter stipulated that action be social in nature. Mises did not make this distinction. For him, analyses of Robinson Crusoe's actions do not have to undergo any fundamental change when Friday comes into the picture. Regardless, it is unclear that this distinction had any effect as Weber never undertook a study of non-social action while Mises only used the fabled autarkic individual as a heuristic device to explain economic principles. Mises (1957, 159) emphasized the inherent social nature of man elsewhere.

Another supposed disagreement between Weber and Mises centered on the idea of rationality. Weber broke down action into a typology based on orientation. While instrumental and value actions were both rational; affectual and traditional action might be considered nonrational. Affectual actions "consist in an uncontrolled reaction to some exceptional stimuli" and traditional action is an "almost automatic reaction to habitual stimuli" (Weber 1978, 25). For Mises, all action was rational by definition. He was aware of Weber's typology but rejected it. Acting man "indulges in these habits only because he welcomes their effects" (Mises 1998, 47). For example, while a man might cry after learning that his wife has died (affectual action), he may also make the choice to hold back his tears if his children are present. Therefore, he has implicitly made a rational choice to cry. Similarly, individuals who make a habit of drinking tap water in the United States learn quickly that this is not a rational choice in certain developing countries. This does not necessarily mean that Weber and Mises had contradictory definitions of rationality. Callahan (2007), channeling Alfred Schutz, argued that they were talking about two different features of social action with Weber's typology being a complement to Mises' definition.

Of course, unlike mainstream economics, contemporary sociological theory has moved beyond positivism and even Weber's simple version of interpretation. Students of sociology have plenty of alternatives to choose from: the rational choice theory of James Coleman; the critical theory of Jürgen Habermas; the post-structuralism of Michel Foucault; the postmodernism of Zygmunt Bauman; or the critical realism of Roy Bhaskar. What is the value-added by the Austrian approach relative to some of these other schools of thought?

In this chapter, we hope to explore several areas where we believe the Austrian School can bring unique insights to sociology. First part discusses the methodology of the Austrian school. Second part explores two key components of the Austrian perspective on knowledge and subjectivity. Third part delves into spontaneous order analysis — the Austrian research program that closely parallels Max Weber's interpretive sociology. Fourth part looks at several of the more interesting applications of Austrian School theory to both economic and seemingly non-economic phenomena. We conclude by arguing that the Austrian School is uniquely positioned to tackle some of the important questions in sociological theory in our post-positivist era and discuss these advantages relative to other schools.

Methodology

The methodology employed by the Austrian School is one of the more controversial aspects of the research program. It has its origins in Germany at the turn of the 20th century. A *methodenstreit* or "battle of methods" had been raging over what should be considered an objectively valid truth in the social sciences. On one side were Gustav von Schmoller and the Historical School. On the polar opposite side were Carl Menger and the Austrian School.[1] These two approaches could not be further apart. In terms of methodology, Mises (1957, 199) described the Historical School as follows:

> The fundamental thesis of historicism is the proposition that, apart from the natural sciences, mathematics, and logic, there is no knowledge but that provided by history. There is no regularity in the concatenation and sequence of phenomena and events in the sphere of human action. Consequently the attempts to develop a science of economics and to discover economic laws are vain. The only sensible method of dealing with human action, exploits, and institutions is the historical method.

According to Historicists, the study of history came first and economic "laws" were to be formulated from the data collected by social scientists. The Austrian School, on the other hand, believed that theory came before history. Mises, we will add, took a position of extreme apriorism. According to him, social sciences, such as economics or sociology, started with the self-evident postulate that man acts. Theorems were then logically deduced a priori from this postulate and built upon axiomatically. These fundamental axioms were universally valid and absolutely true. For this reason, most Austrians went to the extreme of rejecting positivism as well. Empirical tests can neither prove nor disprove logically deduced axioms. This did not mean that Austrians rejected the use of econometric, statistical, or ethnographic techniques. Rather, they saw them as tools for writing historical accounts of events informed by theory. History was still important insofar as it was the application of social theory to actual people and events. The Austrian School's unique methodology could contribute to the debate on theory and historical sociology (see Ragin and Zaret 1983; Kiser and Hechter 1991; Quadagno and Knapp 1992; Mahoney 2004). Their position might be characterized as what Mahoney (2004, 468) called "outcome explanation" where the researcher "does not test the outcome that comprises the final proposition, since this is simply a descriptive referent for one or more historical cases."

Other aspects of Austrian methodology have much in common with that of Max Weber. A common theme in both Weber's and Mises' work was the necessity of employing methodological individualism. Mises (1998, 41–2) argued:

> Praxeology [the science of human action] deals with the actions of individual men. It is only in the further course of its inquiries that cognition of human cooperation is attained and social action is treated as a special case of the more

universal category of human action as such.... [W]e must realize that all actions are performed by individuals.

Neither Weber nor Mises denied that individuals were part of a collective. Both, in fact, dedicated countless pages to the study of collective entities such as bureaucracy, the state, and capitalism (see Mises 1944; 1951; 1998; Weber 1978; 2003). Methodological individualism simply asserts that action only had meaning or purpose to individuals. We may speak about what "society" values or where the "market" is going in colloquial terms, but society and the market have no purpose of their own apart from the subjective intentions of individual actors. Ultimately, the social scientist must go down to the level of the individual in order to explain cause and effect. Additionally, Mises, like Weber, took a value-neutral approach to the social sciences. According to Weber (1957, 54), "an empirical science cannot tell anyone what he *should* do—but rather what he *can* do—and under certain circumstance—what he wishes to do." Mises agreed unconditionally with Weber on this topic more than any other. Echoing Weber almost verbatim, Mises (1998, 10) argued, "Science never tells a man how he should act; it merely shows a man how he must act if he wants to attain definite ends." The Table I below gives a sense of where the Austrian School stands in contrast to other prominent schools of thought.

Table I

	Value-Oriented	Value-Free
Positivist	Analytical Marxism	Rational Choice Theory
Non-Positivist	Critical Theory	Austrian School

According to Austrian School, there is nothing inherently problematic with the application of positivism to the natural sciences. Positivism only becomes problematic when individuals try to apply it to the social sciences. Hayek attributed such a movement to early French sociologists such as Saint-Simon and his student, Auguste Comte. According to Comte (1911, 131), "each branch of knowledge is necessarily obliged to pass through three different theoretical states: the theological or fictitious state; the metaphysical or abstract state; last the scientific or positive state." In each stage, one kind of science can only come after another and build on it. For example, math came first, then astronomy, physics, chemistry, and biology. This had already occurred within the natural sciences and Comte saw it as his goal to apply it to the social sciences, which he simply saw as "social physics."

While the goal of Comte was the unification of all the sciences, Hayek believed in a strict methodological dualism between the natural and social sciences. The rejection of positivism and historicism stems from what Austrians saw as the fundamental difference between the natural and social sciences. In the natural sciences, we study objects which possess no purpose of their own. When we combine two atoms of hydrogen with an atom of oxygen, we always get a certain chemical reaction which results in water. The facts involved are objective in that the molecules cannot purposefully act otherwise. While researchers investigating natural phenomena are able to set up controlled experiments that yield objective results, the "facts" of the social sciences are of a completely different nature. Sociologists, for example, study the purposeful actions of individuals who each have their own subjective value and perception of the world around them. "So far as human actions are concerned," according to Hayek, "the things are what acting people think they are" (Hayek 1952, 47). A causal explanation of social phenomena requires the interpretation of each actor's motives by the researcher. One cannot explain the reasons for someone's action if they do not understand how that person perceives their situation. Similar to the idea of Alfred Schutz's woodchopper,[2] even something as physically objective as a hammer is something specific to each person viewing it according to Hayek. In this way, we must engage in *verstehen* or the hermeneutical approach. Compared to natural scientists, who try to study the world without regard to the opinions of man, the social scientist actually takes the opinions of man as his object of study. For these reasons, the facts of the social sciences are always subjective. In contrast to the positivist approach dominating neo-classical economics (Friedman 1953) and some strands of sociology (Durkheim 1982), the Austrian approach is much more interpretive. It is at this point that disagreements within the Austrian School begin to arise over what this means for research in the social sciences.

Believing that a focus on a priori theorizing limited the application and relevance of Austrian ideas in economics and sociology, a small group of Austrians turned to the philosophical hermeneutics of Hans-Georg Gadamer and other continental thinkers (Lavoie 1990; Vaughn 1994, 127–33). They believed that this would put the work of the Austrian School on a more solid philosophical footing and enable them to use qualitative techniques such as ethnography. Scholars are still debating the success of integrating hermeneutics into Austrian theorizing. Recently though, there has been a renewed interest in the works of Alfred Schutz as an acceptable alternative to hermeneutics (Storr 2009). As Prendergast (1986) has pointed out, Schutz was actually an early member of the Austrian School and a good friend of Mises. *The Phenomenology of the Social World* (Schutz 1967) is an attempt to reconstruct Weber's methodology to meet Austrian objections. Schutz did this by reformulating Weber's concept of ideal type to move it from the realm of comparative history to the realm of a priori theory. This allowed him to keep Mises' separation of theory and history while opening up new directions for further research.

Knowledge and Subjectivism

The unique contributions of the Austrian School on this subject fall under four broad observations: (1) the limited and fragmented nature of knowledge;

(2) the role of the price mechanism as a coordination signal; (3) the subjective nature of knowledge and human action; and, (4) the problem of intersubjective understanding.

Knowledge has played a very special role for the Austrian School starting with Friedrich Hayek (1948). The original impetus for Hayek's work was the so called "socialist calculation debate" of the 1920s. Mises (1935) argued that rational economic planning was impossible under socialism since there would be no prices to coordinate economic actors. In a market economy, prices serve to move land, labor, and capital to where they are most urgently needed and used most efficiently. Market socialists, such as Oskar Lange and Abba Lerner, responded that a socialist planner could still utilize prices as accounting devices in a manner similar (or at least similar enough) to the market. Therefore socialism could be, at minimum, as efficient as market allocation of resources.

Hayek's response to the critique of the market socialists was to take the debate beyond the idea of simple resource allocation. Such discussions assumed omniscient actors, but in reality, the knowledge necessary for the rational allocation of resources was fragmented among countless individuals. Austrians after Hayek called this the "knowledge problem." In fact, he characterized it as *the* central problem of economics as a social science. In contrast to the neoclassical assumption of perfect knowledge, Austrians put an emphasis on the division of knowledge in society. Hayek was concerned with the kind of knowledge which "by its nature cannot enter into statistics and therefore cannot be conveyed to any central authority in statistical form" (Hayek 1948, 83). Prices are a way to convey the knowledge of the "particular circumstances of time and place" available to individual actors in a signaling mechanism accessible to other actors without firsthand knowledge. In contrast to the equilibrium analysis of neoclassical economics, Hayek saw competition as a discovery procedure. Market competition, much like in sports, is necessary to discover the most efficient arrangement of resources. The analogy is apt. Modern sports are replete with statistics on just about anything and everything. Despite this, we would find it absurd to pick the best team based on their statistics. The same is true in the economic sphere. Competition serves to reveal the most efficient outcome given our limited knowledge of something as complex as society.

Eliminating the assumption of perfect information opened up new possibilities for economic analysis. The neoclassical homo economicus (economizing man) was envisioned simply as an economizer. Both his means and ends were given. All that was left was to take the path of least resistance. This left no room for entrepreneurship (however defined) in neoclassical models. "The theoretical firm is entrepreneurless," remarked Baumol (1968, 66), "the Prince of Denmark has been expunged from the discussion of Hamlet." Additionally, this left no room for knowledge creation.[3] The Austrian conceptualization of the entrepreneur was much more helpful. Specifically, the entrepreneurial function as envisioned by Mises and Kirzner was especially relevant to the topic here.[4] Mises

(1998, 336) described the entrepreneur as the individual who was the "first to understand that there is a discrepancy between what is done and what could be done." In contrast to homo economicus, Mises's homo agens or acting man actually manipulated his given means as well as "the very perception of the means-ends framework within which allocation and economizing is to take place." Homo agens possessed "alertness toward fresh goals and the discovery of hitherto unknown resources" (Kirzner 1973, 33–4). In a world of constantly changing tastes, resource scarcity, and technological changes, the entrepreneur acted as an arbitrageur moving heterogeneous land, labor, and capital to its highest valued use. We never actually reached equilibrium, but in most cases, we were moving toward it (Kirzner 1997).[5]

Concordantly, Austrians put much emphasis on the subjective nature of all knowledge and human action. According to Hayek (1952a, 53), "Neither a 'commodity' or an 'economic good,' nor 'food' or 'money,' can be defined in physical terms but only in terms of views people hold about things." Even something as objective as the price of iron or wool is simply conveying an inter-subjective understanding "about things which people have certain beliefs and which they want to use in a certain manner" (Hayek 1952a, 56. On this see also Ebeling 1986). Hayek later added a base in cognitive psychology to augment his argument. In *The Sensory Order*, Hayek (1952b) argued that the mind is a kind of system of classification. People make mental maps based on their experiences and these maps evolve as we gain new knowledge. In many ways, the work of Hayek builds off of Weber (1978) and Schutz (1967) while preceding the important work on "social construction" done by other Schutz-influenced sociologists such as Berger and Luckmann (1967).

Ludwig Lachmann developing the ideas of Weber and Schutz, took a radically subjective approach to human action. "The future is unknowable," according to Lachmann (1976, 55), "but not unimaginable." This problem exists because the data of the social world always necessitates interpretation by each individual (1971, 39).

> It is only too clear that different men with the same knowledge, acquired perhaps in schools to which all men had equal access, in a society dedicated to the ideal of "equal opportunity for all," will nevertheless apply different parts of their common knowledge to a given situation, because their judgment on what is relevant to it will differ. Different men's action is in reality oriented to different knowledge drawn from different sources of experience, but different knowledge may flow even from the same experience.

Yet, planning is not unimaginable as people have the ability to rationally cope with radical uncertainty. As mentioned above, Hayek pointed to the price mechanism as a process that makes inter-subjective understanding and coordination possible. Lachmann extended this idea to institutions as well. "An institution," according to Lachmann (1971, 49–50), "provides means of orientation to a large number of actors. It enables them to coordinate their actions by means of orientation to a common signpost." In this way, institutions were a form of embedded knowledge which creates order.[6] As will be discussed in the next section, these institutions are the result of both purposeful planning and spontaneous ordering of individual action. More recently, Young Back Choi (1993) has put forth a theory of institutional change. Echoing Weber's discussion of usage, custom, convention, and law, Choi shows how social institutions provide stability and how entrepreneurs bring about social change when these same institutions fall behind the times and start producing suboptimal outcomes.

Spontaneous Order Analysis

Spontaneous orders have the following properties: (i) they are (social) regularities (or institutions) that are best defined as "orders" (as opposed to "organizations"); (ii) they are the emergent result of purposive human action, but not the result of human design; (iii) the components of a spontaneous order follow particular rules of conduct; and (iv) spontaneous orders have a self-reinforcing feedback mechanism. These call for elaboration.

Friedrich Hayek averred that a spontaneous order was a social institution that was best defined as an "order." It is important that we make clear what Hayek meant by "order" because not all social institutions were spontaneous orders. Hayek (1973, 35–40) clarified this point by distinguishing "orders" (or spontaneous orders) from "organizations" (or made orders). Throughout the three volume work, *Law, Legislation, and Liberty*, Hayek (1973; 1976) used different language in order to highlight the distinction. For example, he used the Greek terms "taxis" and "kosmos" to refer to made orders and spontaneous orders, respectively. Specifically, Hayek stressed the distinction between an order and an organization by discussing the difference between an economy and "catallaxy" or the market order. An economy, Hayek (1976, 107) said, consists of "activities by which a given set of means is allocated in accordance with a unitary plan among the competing ends according to their [agreed upon] relative importance." Hayek named households, farms, and enterprises as representative of institutions that were the result of human design because their resources were allocated according to a single order of ends that was *deliberately* arranged.

Spontaneous orders, however, do not fall within this category. Rather, spontaneous orders comprise those organizations, such as households, farms, and enterprises, whose actions and interactions produce the emergent and *undesigned* order such as "the market order." It is important to recognize, however, that orders and organizations are inextricably linked. For example, the purposeful actions and interactions of enterprises with the goal of obtaining profit contribute to the undesigned social order, such as the "market order," or what Hayek called "catallaxy." However, enterprises receive feedback, in the form of prices, from the unplanned "market order," that assists them in their purposeful actions and interactions to obtain profits. As Hayek (1983, 35) stated, "A system of market-determined prices is essentially a system which is indispensable in order to make us adapt our activities to events and circumstances of which we cannot know." In short, spontaneous orders provide the necessary feedback that aids organizations and actors in their purposeful activities.

Given the proximate interaction between orders and organizations, it is best to conceive of a spontaneous order as a continuum rather than as a pure dichotomy (Horwitz 2007). Nevertheless, there are important distinctions. Organizations are structures that are simple enough to be directly perceived by inspection and are able to serve specific purposes. Spontaneous orders, on the other hand, may be too abstract to be directly perceived and serve no specific purpose. That is to say, due to their level of complexity, and the multiplicity of actors and organizations that compose them, spontaneous orders do not, and cannot, serve specific purposes. For example, a Fortune 500 company (an organization) has a specific purpose, to maximize profits, whereas the English language (a spontaneous order) has no specific purpose. Rather, the English language exists to serve numerous and varied purposes determined by the multitude of people who use it.

Also, spontaneous orders are social regularities, which emerge due to individuals and organizations following particular rules of conduct, which are independent of any particular end. Ends-independent rules or canons that enable individuals to pursue manifold ends, rather than being directed toward a specific, agreed upon end, also characterize spontaneous orders. These rules may be framed negatively or positively. For example, "Thou shalt not kill," and "Do not steal," are framed in the negative. But, "Respect private property" and "Meet contractual obligations" are framed in the positive. As noted, the positive rules are suitably abstract so as to ensure that whatever the end, these are the rules that one must follow in order to pursue it. These rules may be tacit, however. As Hayek (1973, 43) stated, "That rules in this sense operate without being explicitly known [i.e., articulated] to those who obey them applies also to numerous rules which govern the actions of men and thereby determine a spontaneous order." It seems to us that while the rules consistent with spontaneous orders serve to circumscribe our ends, they reduce the inescapable uncertainty of life and assist in the plan co-ordination of a number of individuals and organizations. To recap, understanding spontaneous orders calls for not only recognizing many institutions as the result of human action, but not human design, but also detecting how rules serve to co-ordinate the activities of multitudinous individuals, households, firms, and corporations that are all pursuing numerous and varied ends.

It seems to us that spontaneous order research is focused on investigating how purposive social action engenders unintended complex rules that redound in institutional mechanisms which facilitate purposive social action. In short, spontaneous order research investigates how micro motives translate into macro behavior. As Boettke and Coyne (2005, 155) have written, spontaneous order analysis

> proceeds from context to the action arena to incentives to patterns of interactions, to outcomes, which are evaluated and, in turn, influence the interactions. The context is defined by the physical and material conditions existing in a society, the attributes of the community in question, and the rules that are in use in that society. The different action arenas generate incentives that, in turn, engender a pattern of social interactions. The pattern of interactions results in outcomes that either reinforce the context of choice or conflict with it.

This is precisely the intellectual task that Max Weber set out for his interpretive sociology. In fact, the components of Weberian interpretive sociology nearly mirror the steps of spontaneous order research. Step one in spontaneous order analysis, according to Boettke and Coyne (2005), proceeds from context to the action arena. This, we contend, parallels direct observational understanding in Weberian interpretive sociology. Step two in spontaneous order analysis, claim Boettke and Coyne (2005), explores incentives. This, in our view, parallels using motives to penetrate empirical reality in Weberian interpretive sociology. Step three, in the research program of spontaneous orders, according to Boettke and Coyne (2005), examines patterns of interaction. To us, this connotes how actors orient their behavior to others and the meaning that actors invest in their action according to Weberian interpretive sociology. Step four, of the spontaneous order analysis, as per Boettke and Coyne (2005), explores outcomes, which are evaluated and, in turn, influence the interactions. For us, this constitutes the causal explanation of the intended, secondary, and truly unintended consequences of social action in Weberian interpretive sociology.

In referring to Weber's interpretive sociology, we are drawing attention to what Weber writes in the first paragraph and its elaboration in Chapter 1 of *Economy and Society*. According to Weber (1978, 4),

> Sociology is a science concerning itself with the interpretive understanding of social action and thereby with a causal explanation of its course and consequences. We shall speak of "action" insofar as the acting individual attaches a subjective meaning to his behavior — be it overt or covert, omission or acquiescence. Action is "social" insofar as its subjective meaning takes account of the behavior of others and is thereby oriented in its course.

How does this relate to the spontaneous order approach? Foremost, it is clear that this component of Weberian interpretive sociology and the spontaneous order approach differ a great deal from mainstream economics and sociology due to its focus on meaning *and* intentionality. Rarely do mainstream economists emphasize meaning and seldom do mainstream sociologists stress intentionality. This is true of economic sociology as well (see Boettke and Storr 2002). Mainstream economics focuses, almost exclusively, on revealed preference, and disregards meaning, in order to understand human action. Mainstream sociology, in contrast, highlights meaning, but gives short shrift to intentionality. Without combining meaning and intentionality, as Weber and spontaneous order theorists do, it is difficult to comprehend the manifold reasons, for example, as to why the woodchopper is chopping wood. Thus, neither mainstream economists nor mainstream sociologists adequately bring Weberian explanatory understanding into their frameworks.

In this section, we have argued that there is a close relationship between Weber's interpretive sociology and the Austrian economists' spontaneous order approach. We have, hopefully, articulated that both approaches to the study of social life are profoundly concerned with "orders" or the regularities of socio-economic life. And it should now be clear that Weberian interpretive sociology and the spontaneous order approach posit that an individual's behavior may be affected, influenced, or even directed by social structures and relations but not determined by them. Most importantly, we anticipate that mainstream sociologists whether micro, meso, or macro, will incorporate the spontaneous order approach into their research programs.

Moving Beyond Economics

While the contributions of the Austrian School to economic sociology have been documented elsewhere (Mikl-Horke 2008), our focus will be on its application to several subfields beyond the traditional realms of economics. This section will outline of few examples of Austrian insights applied to areas such as cultural studies, organizational theory, and the study of anarchy.

Max Weber famously defined the state as an entity which "claims the monopoly of the legitimate use of physical force within a given territory" (Weber 1998, 77–8). He assumed that a state was necessary for the market and civil society to thrive, but what happens when no single entity can claim monopoly status in the use of force? The study of anarchy (which is simply another way of saying the establishment of order in the absence of a state) within the Austrian School can be traced to the writings of Murray Rothbard (1973). While Rothbard took a natural rights approach, others since him have focused on applied theory and historical case studies.

Anderson and Hill (2004) examined the so called Wild West of the American frontier in the 19th century. These territories, not yet subject to state or federal jurisdiction, have often been portrayed as lawless regions subject to widespread violence and banditry. Contrary to popular myth, Anderson and Hill found that the Wild West was not as wild as popularly believed. A variety of private law enforcement mechanisms arose to adjudicate disputes. Land clubs settled disputes over property boundaries, cattlemen's associations helped ranchers avoid the tragedy of the commons on the open range, and mining camps helped establish mineral rights in a way that evolved to the special cir-

cumstances of the time and place. These arrangements emerged through negotiation among individuals which gave rise to norms of trust and reciprocity.
The functions normally associated with the state — law and order, protection
of property, and social welfare — were provided by social institutions and but-
tressed by economic forces.

Leeson (2009) examined history's most notorious outlaws, the pirates who
roamed the open seas in the late 17th and early 18th centuries, and found a
plethora of social mechanisms that ensured order on pirate ships. He discovered
that pirate ships established elaborate constitutions, checks and balances, and
democratic procedures to prevent captain predation and guarantee harmony
among crew members. Most constitutions included provisions for social insur-
ance and workmen's compensation in the case of injuries. Most interestingly,
Leeson found that pirate ships were often bastions of racial tolerance. Black
crew members made up a substantial proportion of many ships. A lack of state-
enforced slavery aboard ships forced pirates to come to grips with their racial
prejudices and accept blacks as equal partners in the quest for treasure. Group
cohesion was vital. A captain who did not gather the best crew possible or
ensure group cohesion among his men might soon find himself hanging from
the gallows. Leeson's point is that culture and institutions matter even among
outlaws. Leeson (unpublished) also has two promising projects looking at the
economics of modern day gypsy curses as well as the economics of "trial by
ordeal" in the middle ages. In both cases, he shows how seemingly irrational
superstition can serve as a rational institution in these specific cases to efficiently
maintain order within the community.

Sobel and Osaba (2009) looked at the rise of youth gangs in urban areas
across the United States. Many of these areas, while technically under the jurisdiction of municipal authorities, are neglected in terms of provision of law and
order. Sobel and Osaba found that youth gangs, rather than being a cause of
violence, were usually a reaction to a preexisting rise in urban violence. They
labeled gangs "pseudo-governments" who provided protection to members in
dangerous neighborhoods. While gangs with a monopoly on a particular neighborhood often limited the amount of violence there, they found that competition between gangs often fueled violence. This work complemented that done
by urban sociologists such as Anderson (2000) and Venkatesh (2006).

Others have discovered that spontaneous orders have arisen, not just for
law and order, but to allow trade and create markets as well. Benson (1989)
traced the evolution of the Law Merchant over several centuries and its ability
to facilitate international trade in the absence of a global authority. Stringham
(2002) found that more complicated institutions, such as stock exchanges, may
still arise in the absence of government enforcement mechanisms. The London
stock exchange was developed in the 18th century in the city's coffee houses.
Stockbrokers formed self-policing clubs which relied on social norms and non-
coercive "shunning" of those who broke the rules to prevent fraud and facilitate

trade among stockbrokers. Stringham (2003, 321) also found the same mechanisms at work in 17th century Amsterdam where they "enabled extralegal trading of relatively sophisticated contracts including short sales, forward contracts, and options."

Cultural studies seem like an unlikely match for economic analysis (Chamlee-Wright and Lavoie 2000), but this is exactly where many Austrian economists have been doing their best work. The study of culture received most of its impetus from the work of Hayek (1973; 1988) who envisioned culture as part of an extended or spontaneous order. "The Mind" according to Hayek (1988, 21), "is not a guide but a product of cultural evolution and is based more on imitation than insight or reasoning." By this he meant that culture was not something rationally invented by individuals or groups. Instead, it was a shorthand mechanism that allowed individuals to interact with each other in a world of uncertainty. Chamlee-Wright (1997) combined interpretive anthropology with Austrian analysis in a study of urban female entrepreneurship in Ghana. She utilized both ethnographic and quantitative techniques to uncover the cultural and economic factors that shaped the structure of the market and the behavior of its participants. The study revealed a discrepancy between the de jure laws passed by municipal and national authorities and the complex social norms and rules that actually govern day-to-day life in the market. Elsewhere, Chamlee-Wright (2005) explained the failure of popular programs such as micro-lending to take hold in Zimbabwe because of the inability of international NGOs to take local indigenous culture into account in their lending practices. Chamlee-Wright's ethnographic work also pointed to the market as what Storr (2008, 135) called a "social space" where "meaningful extraeconomic conversations" can occur. Just as neoclassical accounts of atomistic economic actors bear no resemblance to reality, sociological accounts of hyper-rational, almost anti-social market participants make little sense as well. Markets were not only "embedded" in society (Granovetter 1985; Mises 1957), but markets also enlarged and created new social relationships.

Austrians have also documented the resilience of culture over time and under institutional changes. Storr (2006) updated Weber's work on the Protestant ethic in Europe and applied it to the Junkanoo ethic of the Bahamas. Powell, Ford, and Nowrestah (2008) and Leeson (2007) looked at the persistence of customary law in Somalia and its ability to alternatively adapt under circumstances of oppressive government and statelessness. They found that decentralized clan-based law limits violence between members of different clans and allowed Somalis to trade over long distances without resort to government authority. Chamlee-Wright (2010) has done extensive work looking at post–Katrina New Orleans. She found that the Vietnamese community there tapped into various cultural resources, including a common collective narrative and their local Catholic church, in order to rebuild their community faster than others in New Orleans.

Austrian School vis-à-vis Other Contemporary Theories

We have touched upon the main tenets of the Austrian approach and their possible application to several sociological topics, but why should the Austrian School be considered an improvement compared to contemporary alternatives? To answer this question, we must examine several diverse schools of thought popular amongst sociologists today. While the rational choice theory of James Coleman (1990) is open to the same critique of positivism discussed earlier and warrants no further elaboration here, much of sociology today is marked by a variety of post-positivist approaches.

Orthodox Marxism has been on the decline, but several offshoots have flourished in the post-war period. The critical theory of Jürgen Habermas (1967; 1971) has taken the lead among adherents to the Frankfurt School. Unlike previous critical theorists, he did not denigrate traditional theory relative to critical theory. Instead, according to him, the problem lies in the application or scope of each kind of theoretical approach. According to Habermas, there are three types of interests. Each has their own social location, a location in the world of knowledge, and their own consequences in terms of action orientation.

The first is the technical interest. It is socially located in the control of our environment and circumstances. In the world of knowledge, we see this in fields like engineering. It has an action orientation which can be described as instrumental-rational. The second is the practical interest. It is socially located in social integration, that is, subjective and inter-subjective understanding of the world around us. In the world of knowledge, we see this in the historical and cultural sciences—the hermeneutical or *verstehen* approaches. The action orientation is meaningful action or substantive rationality. The last is the emancipatory interest. It is located in the practice of critical reflection. In the world of knowledge, we see this in critical theory and psychoanalysis. Its action orientation is an ideological critique seeking out distorting communication which achieves power. Believing that most decisions are made through distorted information that plays to the interests of the dominant groups in society, the goal is to make it more likely that any norm or political outcome is achieved through undistorted communicative action.

Additionally, Habermas situated the first two interests within two separate parts of society. The system world of the economy and the polity was identified with the technical interests in their quest for control over nature and society. The system world was subject to the kind of rationalization about which Weber worried. In the state, we saw the iron cage of bureaucracy taking hold. In the economy, we saw everything being reduced to a numerical price. The life-world of society, on the other hand, was identified with the practical interests in the desire for mutual understanding and communicative reason. The problem arose as the technical interests of the system world attempted to "colonize" the life-world. How does this apply to positivism?

Positivism is not in and of itself something we need to criticize. Instead, Habermas saw as problematic the attempted application of positivist methods to the social sciences. Like Habermas, Hayek objected to the methods of the natural sciences being applied to the social sciences on both analytic and normative grounds. We have already discussed Hayek's analytical critique which he shared with Habermas. It is on the normative side of the argument that they diverge. Both Habermas and Hayek begin on comparable grounds. Echoing Habermas' discussion of the technical interests, Hayek criticized Comte (1952b, 351): "It cannot be too much emphasized in any discussion of Comte's philosophy that he had no use for any knowledge of which he did not see the practical use. And 'the purpose of the establishment of social philosophy is to reestablish order in society.'" As mentioned above, Habermas saw the colonization of the social sciences by positivism as a result of the rise of the market and its logic. For Hayek, just the *opposite* was true. "Scientism" led to social engineering as people came to believe that a science of society meant that we could manipulate the units much like we do in the natural sciences. Hayek was also quick to point out that both Saint-Simon and Comte were socialists. "Central economic planning," Hayek (1952b, 173) said, "is nothing but an application of engineering principles to the whole of society based on the assumption that such a complete concentration of all relevant knowledge is possible." Unlike Habermas, who was a critic of what he saw as the hegemonic power of market logic, Hayek took a *wertfrei* or value-free approach to social science. Although Hayek and other Austrians are often associated with a *laissez faire* ideology, there is nothing intrinsically ideological in their methodology and theory (Boettke 1995; Prychitko and Storr 2007). In fact, recent work by a Marxist economist has successfully integrated the economic analysis of Hayek with a normative quest for social justice (Burczak 2006). Thus, the Austrian School, unlike critical theory, gave us a value-free critique of positivism.

Postmodernism has been another popular school of thought. "Modernity" is an oft-used concept in sociology which refers to the period starting from roughly around the time of the Enlightenment to recent times. According to contemporary sociologists, modernity is characterized by the rise of industrial capitalism and the movement toward the rationalization of state, market, and society. Schumpeter (1962) believed that the "creative destruction" of capitalism would give way to the rational planning of socialism. Max Weber (1978) spoke of the "iron cage" of bureaucracy. Habermas, as we have just seen, was concerned about the "colonization of the life-world." Sociologists of all stripes predicted a creeping rationalization in all aspects of life.

Just when we think we have reached the pinnacle of modernity though, some sociologists have declared that recent decades have ushered in a new era of postmodernity or what Zygmunt Bauman (2000) called "liquid modernity." In contrast to modernity, postmodernity is characterized by an increasing uncertainty and constant change. If modernity was best represented by Taylor's "one best method" and Ford's emphasis on lifelong employment then post-modernity is best represented by Microsoft's constant innovation and reliance on contingent workers. What made Bauman's conception of modernity and postmodernity so unique was his emphasis on the role that order plays in each period. Capitalism and rationalization were still important, but they were part of a larger desire for order. Bauman (2001a, 78) argued that in modernity, "the desire to manipulate probabilities and to make human affairs regular and amenable to planning and control was high up in the minds of the principle advocates and actors of industrialism, democracy, and incredibly, capitalism." Elsewhere, he argued that modernity "prompted an incessant drive to eliminate the haphazard and annihilate the spontaneous" (Bauman 2001b, 192). From this perspective, contemporary neoclassical economics is thoroughly modern in Bauman's sense of the term. The neoclassical emphasis on closed-system general equilibrium analysis is a perfect example of modern social science. Such models are supposed to account for all possibilities within the system and lead to a single equilibrium. In many ways, the evolution of mainstream economics exemplifies modernity's need for order and rationalization after the Enlightenment. We have seen what a thoroughly modern economics looks like, but how would a postmodern model of economics look? Bauman (2001b, 175) gives us a hint in a description of postmodernity that is worth quoting at length:

> What the theory of postmodernity must discard in the first place is the assumption of a *systematic character* of the social condition it purports to model: the vision of a system (a) with a degree of cohesiveness, (b) equilibrated or marked by an overwhelming tendency to equilibration, (c) defining its elements in terms of the function they perform in that process of equilibration or the reproduction of the equilibrated state. It must assume instead that the social condition it intends to model is essentially and perpetually *unequilibrated*: composed of elements with a degree of autonomy large enough to justify the view of totality as kaleidoscopic — momentary and contingent — outcome of interaction. The orderly, structured nature of totality cannot be taken for granted; nor can its pseudo-representational construction be seen as the purpose of theoretical activity. Randomness of the global outcome of uncoordinated activities cannot be treated as a departure from the pattern which the totality strives to maintain; any pattern that may temporarily emerge out of the random movements of autonomous agents is as haphazard and unmotivated as the one that could emerge in its place or the one bound to replace it, if also for a time only. All order that can be found is a local, emergent and transitory phenomenon; its nature can be best grasped by a metaphor of a whirlpool appearing in the flow of a river, retaining its shape only for a relatively brief period and only as the expense of incessant metabolism and constant renewal of content.

Contrast Bauman's description of postmodern theory with Langlois' (1986, 171) description of the Austrian economist, Ludwig Lachmann:

> Lachmann is the scourge of determinism, the apostle of disequilibrium, the prophet of the kaleidic. Thus, in many, if not most, eyes, his role appeared as that of gadfly — or, at best, of methodological conscience — to his fellow theo-

rists. His is the salutary albeit annoying task of reminding us that the future is unknowable, that expectations must diverge, and that there are forces of disco-ordination as well as of coordination.

The similarities between Bauman's description of postmodern theory and Lan-glois' description of Lachmann are uncanny. Hayek had applied subjectivism to values, preferences, and knowledge of market conditions, but could it be applied even further? According to Lachmann, the answer was yes. This led Lachmann (1976, 59) to argue that "The future is unknowable, though not unimaginable." Others have labeled this as a "radical subjective" approach.

According to Lachmann (ibid), the market "cannot diffuse 'superior expec-tations' in the sense which it diffuses superior knowledge [i.e. prices] because *ex ante* no criterion of success can exist." The kaleidic nature of the market, with its constant stream of new information, causes individuals to regularly change their expectations of the future and thus change their actions. Burczak (2006) also has pointed out the postmodern nature of Hayek's economics. Aus-trian theory eschews general equilibrium analysis in favor of open-ended processes and spontaneous order analysis. In essence, the market is the quin-tessential postmodern institution. Furthermore, postmodern thinkers, among which we might include structuralists and poststructuralists such as Foucault, often fall prey to some form of relativism or nihilism. In their rebellion against any sort of systematic theory, they have thrown out the baby with the bathwater. The Austrian School, on the other hand, successfully meshes a priori, universal laws of action with the subjective perceptions and action-orientation of human actors across time and space.

Of all the contemporary schools of thought, the Austrian School has had the most interaction with critical realism whose proponents have led the charge against neoclassical economics. According to critical realists, the positivist method employed by modern economics, which argues that causal relationships can be established from the observation of correlations in empirical data, is not sufficient or in some cases necessary at all. As much as we have tried to stress the differences between neoclassical and Austrian theory though, the two have much in common. Austrians still employ the language of neoclassical theory — rational choice, utility, marginalism, and methodological individualism — while avoiding the pitfalls of mathematical modeling and closed-system equilibrium analysis. Much like critical realism, the Austrian School embraces open processes, causal-realism, emergence, and a prominent role for social structure. Martin (2009, 518) called this the "Austrian paradox" for the apparent love-hate relationship between the two approaches. Most critical realists have taken special care to distance themselves from Austrian economics (Lawson 1997) or have ignored it altogether.

We argue that the Austrian approach offers significant advantages over critical realism. Austrian subjectivism permits one to keep rational choice the-ory while allowing something beyond strict instrumental-rationality and admitting actors make errors. Austrian spontaneous order analysis avoids reifying social structures through emergence theory (Bhaskar 1979) as they exist *only* in the actions of individuals. Unlike critical realists, Austrians can have their structural cake and eat it too. Lastly, Austrian theory keeps universalism while open to local variation and particulars in historical accounts.

Notes

1. The label "Austrian School" is a result of this conflict. Schmoller used the term "Austrian" in a derogatory manner to characterize Menger and his students at the University of Vienna. It implied that they were not true Germans. Most members of today's Austrian School are actually American.
2. Schutz (1967, 26–7) argued that, as an example, we cannot simply assume that a man we observe wielding an ax is chopping wood. Rather, we must look at the larger context of meaning.
3. For example, in Stigler's (1961) model, the actor does not create knowledge, but again is simply a manager who decides how much to invest in the search for knowledge.
4. For a wider survey of Austrian theories of entrepreneurship, see Klein (2008).
5. Taking a radical subjectivist approach, others such as Lachmann (1976), argued that we cannot even discern whether the market process was an equilibrating or disequilibrating force.
6. For a further elaboration of Lachmann's theory of institutions and a defense against accusations of postmodern nihilism, see Foss and Garzarelli (2007).

References

Anderson, Elijah. 2000. *Code of the Street: Decency, Violence, and the Moral Life of the Inner City*. New York: W.W. Norton.
Anderson, Terry L., and Peter J. Hill. 2004. *The Not So Wild, Wild West: Property Rights on the Frontier*. Stanford: Stanford University Press.
Bauman, Zygmunt. 2000. *Liquid Modernity*. Cambridge: Polity Press.
_____. 2001a. *Conversations with Zygmunt Bauman*. Cambridge: Polity Press.
_____. 2001b. *The Bauman Reader*. Edited by Peter Beilharz. Oxford: Wiley-Blackwell.
Baumol, William J. 1968. Entrepreneurship in Economic Theory. *The American Economic Review* 58(2): 64–71.
Benson, Bruce L. 1989. The Spontaneous Evolution of Commercial Law. *Southern Economic Journal* 55(3): 644–61.
Berger, Peter L., and Thomas Luckmann. 1967. *The Social Construction of Reality: A Treatise in the Sociology of Knowledge*. New York: Random House.
Bhaskar, Roy. 1979. *The Possibility of Naturalism*. Brighton: Harvester Press.
Boettke, Peter J. 1995. Why Are There No Austrian Socialists? Ideology, Science and the Austrian School. *Journal of the History of Economic Thought* 17(1): 35–56.
Boettke, Peter J., and Chris Coyne. 2005. Methodological Individualism, Spontaneous Order and the Research Program of the Workshop in Political Theory and Policy Analysis. *Journal of Economic Behavior and Organization* 57: 145–58.
Boettke, Peter J., and Virgil Storr. 2002. Post-Classical Political Economy in Weber, Mises, and Hayek. *American Journal of Economics and Sociology* 61(1): 161–91.
Burczak, Theodore A. 2006. *Socialism after Hayek*. Ann Arbor: The University of Michigan Press.

Callahan, Gene. 2007. Reconciling Weber and Mises on Understanding Human Action. *American Journal of Economics and Sociology* 66(5): 889–99.

Chamlee-Wright, Emily. 1997. *The Cultural Foundations of Economic Development*. London: Routledge.

_____. 2005. Entrepreneurial Response to "Bottom-up" Development Strategies in Zimbabwe. *Review of Austrian Economics* 18(1): 5–28.

_____. 2010. *The Cultural and Political Economy of Recovery: Social Learning in a Post-Disaster Environment*. London: Routledge.

Choi, Young Back. 1993. *Paradigms and Conventions: Uncertainty, Decision Making, and Entrepreneurship*. Ann Arbor: The University of Michigan Press.

Coleman, James S. 1990. *Foundations of Social Theory*. Cambridge: Harvard University Press.

Comte, Auguste. 1911. *Early Essays on Social Philosophy*. London: Routledge.

Durkheim, Emile 1982. *The Rules of Sociological Method*. New York: Free Press.

Ebeling, Richard M. 1986. Toward a Hermeneutical Economics: Expectations, Prices, and the Role of Interpretation in a Theory of the Market Process. In *Subjectivism, Intelligibility, and Economic Understanding*, ed. Israel Kirzner, 39–52. New York: New York University Press.

Foss, Nicholai J., and Giampaolo Garzarelli. 2007. Institutions as Knowledge Capital: Ludwig M. Lachmann's Interpretative Institutionalism. *Cambridge Journal of Economics* 31(5): 789–804.

Friedman, Milton. 1953. *Essays in Positive Economics*. Chicago: University of Chicago Press.

Granovetter, Mark. 1985. Economic Action and Social Structure: The Problem of Embeddedness. *The American Journal of Sociology* 91(3): 481–510.

Hayek, Friedrich A. 1948. *Individualism and Economic Order*. Chicago: University of Chicago Press.

_____. 1952a. *The Counter-Revolution of Science: Studies in the Abuse of Reason*. Indianapolis: Liberty Fund.

_____. 1952b. *The Sensory Order: An Inquiry into the Foundations of Theoretical Psychology*. Chicago: University of Chicago Press.

_____. 1973. *Law, Legislation, and Liberty: Rules and Order*. Chicago: University of Chicago Press.

_____. 1976. *Law, Legislation, and Liberty: The Mirage of Social Justice*. Chicago: University of Chicago Press.

_____. 1983. *Knowledge, Evolution, and Society*. London: Adam Smith Institute.

Horowitz, Steve. 2007. Is the Family a Spontaneous Order? Paper presented at the Atlas Foundation "Emergent Orders" conference, Portsmouth, New Hampshire, October 27–30.

Kirzner, Israel. 1973. *Competition and Entrepreneurship*. Chicago: University of Chicago Press.

_____. 1997. Entrepreneurial Discovery and the Competitive Market Process: An Austrian Approach. *Journal of Economic Literature* 30: 60–85.

Kiser, Edgar, and Michael Hechter. 1991. The Role of General Theory in Comparative-Historical Sociology. *American Journal of Sociology* 97: 1–30.

Klein, Peter. 2008. Opportunity Discovery, Entrepreneurial Action, and Economic Organization. *Strategic Entrepreneurship Journal* 2(3): 175–90.

Lachmann, Ludwig. 1971. *The Legacy of Max Weber*. Berkeley: The Glendessary Press.

_____. 1976. From Mises to Shackle: An Essay on Austrian Economics and the Kaleidic Society. *Journal of Economic Literature* 14: 54–62.

Langlois, Richard N. 1986. Coherence and Flexibility: Social Institutions in a World of Radical Uncertainty. In *Subjectivism, Intelligibility, and Economic Understanding*, ed. Israel Kirzner, 171–91. New York: New York University Press.

Lawson, Tony. 1997. *Economics and Reality*. London: Routledge.

Lavoie, Don. 1990. *Economics and Hermeneutics*. London: Routledge.

Leeson, Peter T. 2007. Better Off Stateless: Somalia Before and After Government Collapse. *Journal of Comparative Economics* 35(4) 2007: 689–710.

_____. 2009. *The Invisible Hook: The Hidden Economics of Pirates*. Princeton: Princeton University Press.

_____. (unpublished). Gypsies. http://www.peterleeson.com/Gypsies.pdf.

_____. (unpublished). Ordeals. http://www.peterleeson.com/Ordeals.pdf.

Mahoney, James. 2004. Revisiting General Theory in Historical Sociology. *Social Forces* 83(2): 459–89.

Mikl-Horke, Gertraude. 2008. Austrian Economics and Economic Sociology: Past Relations and Future Possibilities for a Socio-economic Perspective. *Socio-Economic Review* 6: 201–26.

Mises, Ludwig Von. 1935. Economic Calculation in the Socialist Commonwealth. In *Collectivist Economic Planning*, ed. Friedrich A. Hayek, 87–130. London: Routledge.

_____. 1944. *Bureaucracy*. New Haven: Yale University Press.

_____. 1951. *Socialism*. New Haven: Yale University Press.

_____. 1957. *Theory and History: An Interpretation of Social and Economic Evolution*. Auburn: The Ludwig Von Mises Institute.

_____. 1998. *Human Action: A Treatise on Economics. Scholar's Edition*. Auburn: The Ludwig von Mises Institute.

Powell, Benjamin, Ryan Ford, and Alex Nowrasteh. 2008. Somalia After State Collapse: Chaos or Improvement? *Journal of Economic Behavior & Organization* 67(3–4): 657–70.

Prendergast, Christopher. 1986. Alfred Schütz and the Austrian School of Economics. *The American Journal of Sociology* 92(1): 1–26.

Prychitko, David L., and Virgil Storr. 2007. Communicative Action and the Radical Constitution: The Habermasian Challenge to Hayek, Mises, and Their Descendents. *Cambridge Journal of Economics* 31(2): 255–75.

Quadagno, Jill, and Stan J. Knapp. 1992. Have Historical Sociologists Forsaken Theory? Thoughts on the History/Theory Relationship. *Sociological Methods & Research* 20(4): 481–507.

Ragin, Charles, and David Zaret. 1983. Theory and Method in Comparative Research: Two Strategies. *Social Forces* 61(3): 731–54.

Rothbard, Murray. 1973. *For a New Liberty*. New York: Macmillan.

Schumpeter, Joseph A. 1962. *Capitalism, Socialism, and Democracy*. New York: Harper Perennial.

Schutz, Alfred. 1967. *The Phenomenology of the Social World*. Evanston, IL: Northwestern University Press.

Sobel, Russell S., and Brian J. Osoba. 2009. Youth Gangs as Pseudo-Governments: Implications for Violent Crime. *Southern Economic Journal* 75(4): 996–1018.

Stigler, George J. 1961. The Economics of Information. *The Journal of Political Economy* 69(3): 213–25.

Storr, Virgil. 2006. Weber's Spirit of Capitalism and the Bahamas' Junkanoo Ethic. *Review of Austrian Economics* 19(4): 289–309.

_____. 2008. The Market as a Social Space: On the Meaningful Extraeconomic Conversations That Can Occur in Markets. *Review of Austrian Economics* 21(2/3): 135–50.

_____. 2009. Schutz on Meaning and Culture. *Review of Austrian Economics* 23 (2): 147–64.

Stringham, Edward. 2002. The Emergence of the London Stock Exchange as a Self-Policing Club. *The Journal of Private Enterprise* 17(2): 1–19.

_____. 2003. The Extralegal Development of Securities Trading in Seventeenth-Century Amsterdam. *The Quarterly Review of Economics and Finance* 43(2): 321–44.

Swedberg, Richard. 1998. *Max Weber and the Idea of Economic Sociology*. Princeton: Princeton University Press.

Vaughn, Karen I. 1994. *Austrian Economics in America: The Migration of a Tradition*. Cambridge, UK: Cambridge University Press.

Venkatesh, Sudhir. 2006. *Off the Books: The Underground Economy of the Urban Poor*. Cambridge: Harvard University Press.

Weber, Max. 1949. *The Methodology of the Social Sciences*. New York: Free Press.

_____. 1978. *Economy and Society*. Berkeley: University of California Press.

_____. 1998. *From Max Weber: Essays in Sociology*. New York: Routledge.

_____. 2003. *The Protestant Ethic and the Spirit of Capitalism*. New York: Dover.

3. KARL POPPER'S CRITICISM OF SOCIOLOGY

Renewing the Call for an Open Sociology

Ieva Zake

Just as classical sociological theory, contemporary theory has also developed a canonical set of theorists and schools of thought. Judging by how contemporary theory is taught in the current textbooks and readers, this canon includes authors such as Max Horkheimer, Herbert Marcuse, C. Wright Mills, Jurgen Habermas, Anthony Giddens, Michel Foucault, Pierre Bourdieu, Dorothy Smith, in some cases Jacques Derrida and Zygmunt Bauman, Ulrich Beck, Stuart Hall and a few others. They are presented as the most important voices that have shaped the sociological theory since the end of World War II and they are usually grouped in set perspectives. A quick look at this list reveals pre-dominance of conflict, critical, post-structuralist, post-modernist, multi-culturalist and feminist theories with some symbolic interactionism. The overall features of this canon indicate that contemporary sociologists think that their primary mission is to advance criticism of capitalism, liberal (representative) democracy, and various forms of oppression, inequalities and social hierarchies. In addition, direct intervention into the social processes, deconstruction of social structure and its beliefs, and exposure of and opposition to ever-increasing layers of dominance are the most important techniques used by the contemporary sociological canon. In other words, it appears that the critical theory's original idea that theory has to be combined with a liberating practice because social facts are not there to be studied, but changed by social sciences, had cast a lasting shadow over the sociology of the late 20th century.

This orientation of the canon of contemporary theory is particularly interesting considering which authors and ideas are missing from it. And there are quite a few of those. For example, Friedrich Hayek and Leo Strauss[1] are never discussed as a part of the sociological theory of the late 20th century. Another telling omission is the work of Karl Popper, including his famous book *The Open Society and Its Enemies* (1963). It came out soon after World War II and was as an elaborate and well-argued critique of social philosophy of the pre-

and post-war period. Popper's main target was the notable influence of Plato, Georg Wilhelm Friedrich Hegel and Karl Marx in contemporary analyses of the society. His concern was that these authors' ideas contained a large dose of totalitarianism and that they had played a major role in shaping the most murderous ideologies of the 20th century, namely, Communism, Nazism and Fascism. He was particularly worried that these dangerous ideologies and popular social theories drew their intellectual inspiration from the same sources. He found this disconcerting because he believed that science and its method had to lead to the creation of an open and democratic political system as opposed to a closed and government-controlled society. Unfortunately, the social sciences of the day with their indebtedness to Plato, Hegel and Marx were failing to bring about more democracy. Moreover, not only did they not warn their societies about the dangers of totalitarianism, but they even helped support oppressive political regimes.

Popper's arguments about the shortcomings of social sciences were in the past and remain today difficult to accept or even discuss for most sociologists. The goal of this chapter is to demonstrate how Popper's perspective is at odds with the direction of the dominant contemporary theories and to argue for continued relevance of Popper's theory for the future of this discipline. The chapter proposes that although Popper's criticism of sociology has been conveniently forgotten in the canon of contemporary theory, his critical insights deserve a discussion because they point out some of the inherent problems in sociological perspective as a whole.

Popper's Criticism of Sociology

In order to explicate the conflict that emerged between Karl Popper and sociological theorists, this chapter focuses primarily on the two "sins" of which Popper accused contemporary social sciences—historicism and holism. These two ways of thinking, according to Popper, led sociology directly toward irrationalism and mysticism, which translated into sociologists' eventual support for a controlling and all-powerful state and blindness to the threats of Communism, Nazism and Fascism.

What was historicism? According to Popper, it consisted of three elements. First, there was the historicist method of "the principle that we can obtain any knowledge of social entities or essences only by applying the historical method, by studying social changes. But the doctrine leads further ... to the worship of History and its exaltation as the Grand Theatre of Reality as well as the World's Court of Justice" (1963, 7). In other words, historicism was an intellectual tendency that focused on social change over time and argued that, by studying it, we could reach the best understanding of the nature of society. In other words, historicism claimed that all societies are essentially products of history. The social is the historical, according to historicism, and therefore it approached transformation or change as the ultimate manifestation of social reality. What worried Popper here was that historicism saw change as good, even morally superior, while tradition and continuity as suspect. Historicists (sociologists who followed ideas of Marx and Hegel such as, for example, critical and conflict theorists) glorified and demanded continuous alterations and they were not interested in understanding how societies could last. Consequently, they were motivated to study society because they admired change for its own sake and many of them even became activists involved in creating social transformations.

The second element was an argument that only change could make apparent the inherent potentialities of any society, and the third element of historicism claimed that there was such a thing as the true essence of a society that, again, could reveal itself only through social change (7–8). A historicist would argue that only in a state of transformation the society could become complete and authentic. Those who followed the historicist perspective were convinced that during revolutions or dramatic social calamities (riots, demonstrations and open conflicts) societies were realizing their full potential because change alone could force societies to rise to the occasion and meet historical expectations.

Overall, in historicism the glorification of history (as a change) led to the glorification of revolution, which, to Popper, was a highly unproductive, even dangerous way to think about any society. He was concerned that such an uncritical admiration of radical transformation could lead sociologists to mistakenly support idealistic extremists forcing their compatriots into murderous social experiments or dictators claiming to be building whole new societies, that is, creating new histories. Popper's warning to sociologists was that by following historicist logic they might lose an ability to notice the threatening tendencies inherent in social movements for radical change.

At the same time Popper pointed out that historicism also assumed that history evolved in stages and had a pattern that could be formulated in a "law of historical change." Due to this, individual agents of history mattered little to historicists. They were convinced that change was generated by history's own logic, that is, history made itself, while people were merely fulfilling the dictates of the historical process. There were some slight differences between various historicists on this issue. Some of them argued that each society had its own unique laws of historical change, while others insisted that there was one generalizable law that governed all social change and that it could be discovered by social scientists and used to predict the future stages of history for any society. Popper opposed both of these positions and suggested instead that history was influenced by too many factors to be summarized in a form of one or many laws. It has to be noted also that although Marx and Hegel as historicists believed in history unquestionably leading toward the perfect state, many of their followers had given up on such utopian concepts. Nevertheless, they continued to believe in history following its path of change that was independent of individuals and their will.

The second sin of sociology, according to Popper, was holism. It was an assumption that society was a unified collective that had a nature of its own and that this nature was not necessarily a sum of individuals' contributions. Moreover, holism argued that the whole could determine the characteristic features of its members and that the whole was legitimately entitled to demanding obedience from its constituting parts. According to holists (again, such as Hegel and Marx and their followers), the social whole was the one that progressed through the stages of historical change, not its individual members. Therefore holists were also historicists and the other way around.

Holists also demanded that sociology had to analyze society as a unified and coherent whole and get at its rules of development instead of trying to understand its parts, that is, individuals. This, according to Popper, was a slippery slope, which led sociology toward dangerous irrationalism and mysticism. Following holism, sociologists attributed powerful characteristics to social collectives and treated them as "real entities, which must be comprehended, intuitively, as wholes, in order that their place in the historical process be explained" (Cohen 1963, 250). Just as historicism deified history, holism deified society as a unified organism that could be understood only if seen as one unit. In Popper's view neither were rational scientific approaches, but rather beliefs based on irrational intuitions that could not be substantiated empirically.

Popper blamed the development of holism on Hegel and Marx who had brought Plato into sociological theory. All three of them considered society to be superior to the individual and tended to believe "that the state and the nation is more 'real' than the individual who owes everything to them" (Popper 1963, 99). Their holism became particularly explicit in contemporary social theories of modern state, according to Popper. They treated the state as embodiment of the whole society. To them, the state was complete, homogeneous and self-sufficient. Popper saw such thinking as an example of collectivism (that is, an idea that a group is more important than individuals who constitute it) according to which the state possessed "a conscious and thinking essence, its 'reason' or 'Spirit'" (37). In Popper's eyes, a statement that society, state or nation possessed some mystic inner essence was completely irrational because the presence of such a "soul" could not be proved empirically, but had to be believed. And this was exactly opposite to how scientific research worked.

What concerned Popper was that historicism and holism as it was used in sociology erased human agency in understanding social processes. This led sociology to overstate the power of the so-called elites or by contrast — marginalized groups, abstract historical processes, macro-level state structures, social institutions and identity-based collectivities. In other words, by employing historicism and holism sociology viewed society as possessing an inner force (soul or spirit), which for the most part could not be detected and measured in an empirically sound way. Since this "spirit" of the social whole could not be located using rational methods, sociologists began identifying it intuitively and found it in a wide array of places. Each school of contemporary sociology believed that the "spirit" of the society resided somewhere else, which inevitably caused the sociologists to introduce personal and political values into sociological research. There was no rational method for proving that the mystic spirit of a society could be found in either economy, culture, history or ethnic, class or gender identity. Consequently, sociologists, especially those who followed ideas of Marx and Hegel, fell into a danger of advocating non-scientific biases.

What did Popper want sociology do to instead? In his mind, if sociology aspired to be anything like a science, it had to rethink its approach to history and society in general. It had to admit that it was individuals, not whole societies and their spirits that were agents of history. Of course, individuals' actions were extremely diverse and often unpredictable, which meant that sociology would have to abandon its project of articulating generalizable abstract rules of social change. History was far too complex, in Popper's view, and any attempts to predict it through theoretical models were exercises in mysticism and manipulation that tried to make the world fit a theory regardless of the facts. Popper rejected such efforts as non-scientific. He was highly concerned that contemporary theory was too involved in forcing the facts to match (politicized) theories, thus leading sociology further away from its scientific mission and turning it into a political ideology.

Instead of looking for generalizable historical patterns, Popper suggested that social sciences use the logic of the situation (97), which meant focusing on how particular individuals in each specific situation find a solution, make a decision and generate a social change. The task of sociology was, to him, to analyze "the unintended social repercussions of intentional human actions" (96–7). Such research could be based on empirical studies of social processes and cases over time. This would be a rational and ultimately scientific approach to social reality, according to Popper, because it would treat humans as rational beings, who could be understood using rational methods. Becoming a science meant adopting "a common language of reason" and establishing "something like a moral obligation towards that language, the obligation to keep up its standards of clarity and to use it in such a way that it can retain its function as the vehicle of argument" (239). Only by studying society in a rational way, sociology could avoid becoming a hostage to political ideologies and unproven beliefs.

Sociology's Treatment of Popper

How were Popper's ideas received among sociologists? His criticism went after some of the most basic assumptions of what sociologists as members of their profession thought they were supposed to be doing such as study history and treat society as larger than a sum of individuals' actions. Sociologists had been trained to analyze society as an abstract construction with its pattern of development and they were supposed to look at collectivities as opposed to focusing on individuals. Moreover, many sociologists were eager to follow calls for political action as opposed to pursuing rational analysis of social complexities. But Popper was telling them that such an understanding of social research was irrational and even politically dangerous. Therefore, as shown below, the reaction of sociologists to Popper was predominately dismissive.

Rejection

Negative responses to Popper's ideas appeared soon after the wider publication of his work. While some criticized his ideas of the logic of scientific discovery (Gluck 1960), others wrote that Popper's analysis of historicism fell short because it was badly defined from the start and could not convince any historicist to give up what they were doing (Sorokin 1958; Coates 1958; Lynd 1951). In the early 1960s, Popper was criticized for overstating the influence of historicism in American sociology of the day (Cohen 1963). The argument was that American sociology already was focused on empirical research and did not contain much theory and notions of societies as wholes. Popper was criticized for building accusations on a "special, limited, partial or outmoded view" of sociology, which he thought was representative of the whole discipline (Gluck 1964, 218).

In the 1970s and 80s, criticism against Popper intensified by going after the foundations of his theory. Some authors painstakingly tried to prove that Popper's arguments against historicism simply were not valid and could not be sustained under a philosophical investigation (Urbach 1978) and that science itself was ideological and politicized (Purkayastha 1989). Others mounted a more aggressive attack arguing that Popper's own beliefs about science, rationality and liberal democracy were utopian (Freeman 1975; Sica 1987). Freeman, for example, declared that Popper did not hold his own theory up to the standards that he demanded of others, which made his approach non-scientific and populist. Freeman accused Popper of being too obedient to the regulations of scientific research, while sociologists who practiced utopianism in their studies were advancing exciting experiments and possessed a truly critical spirit (1975, 32).

Claims about Popper's implicit political bias and ideological agenda strengthened toward the end of the 1970s. Some critics argued that Popper's ideas were utterly political: "Popper's doctrine succeeds not only in masking the true relations of power in capitalist society. It also justifies and helps sustain central command planning" (Friedmann 1978, 82). His critics stated that objective scientific knowledge as such did not exist and therefore it could not claim any moral authority over other forms of knowledge such as, for example, an epistemological model that sought knowledge based on social practice (84). This model introduced new facts into the world and solved social problems as opposed to accumulating formal knowledge. Popper's critics were more likely to support this model as opposed to demands for rigorous scientific truth. Overall, by the late 1970s many sociologists had come to believe that Popper was wrong for thinking that sociology could be an empirical science and demanded instead that sociology follow normative principles and practical goals.

Others did not go as far as to suggest an alternative epistemology, but tried to show that Popper was driven by his essentially irrational belief in liberal democracy (Sica 1987) and that he tied his political position and theory of knowledge together too much (Krige 1978). They also blamed him for being a vehement anti–Marxist (McLachlan 1980). It seemed obvious to these critics that Popper's goal was to create an ideology of pure science according to which power would go to the scientific community. Popper was also accused of having a limited goal such as elimination of badly designed scientific theories, while real social scientists boldly criticized badly functioning social and political systems. In other words, sociologists saw themselves as trying to do something real and meaningful, while Popper was only seeking scientifically tested descriptions of social reality (McLachlan 1980, 305). As argued by sociologist Michael Burawoy (1989), research programs that followed agendas for political change were actually much better suited for social sciences than theories based on principles of scientific objectivity. According to Burawoy, if sociology were to try to be a science it would have to collect facts to refute theories, but there were some sociological theories that Burawoy would have liked to preserve even if facts went against them. So what he proposed was thinking of theories in sociology as "research programs" that did not assume objectivity, followed moral values and were conceptually open (Burawoy 1989, 794). Overall, Popper's demand that sociology be committed to scientific objectivity was a major stumbling block for the sociologists of the later part of the 20th century. Not only were they not sure that Popper's approach could help social scientists eradicate subjectivism and irrationalism, but also they were unconvinced that this was at all necessary (Jacobs 1990).

By the late 1990s, some critics of Popper decided that his Eurocentrism and belief in "truth," "objectivity" and science was hopelessly out of date (McDonald 1997), while others argued that Popper's influence had been profound, even dominant, especially in convincing sociologists that they could share methodology with the natural sciences. According to these authors, Popper had turned social scientists into glorified technicians and made sociology so scientific that even his critics could not help but become scientific (Aronowitz and Ausch 2000, 703). In order to resist this "scientification" of sociology, they pointed out that Popper had put science on a pedestal of rationalism without realizing that all scientific pursuits were culturally determined. Therefore sociology's "goal should be one of social transformation, always sensitive to inequality in material and culture resources and power as it is distributed across race, class, gender, nation and sexuality" (715). As an openly value-based science, sociology would begin with an intuition that would generate reflections about the society, its nature and the need to change it. To the critics of Popper such a critical and political position was superior to the scientific method that he had proposed.

Another way to reject Popper was by arguing that not only science itself was politically grounded, but also "reason and politics are ... interdependent in the production of scientific knowledge and truth" (Brown and Malone 2004, 106). According to this position, the structure of scientific communities and the way that they acquired knowledge was already political and therefore it was pointless to pretend that scientists were capable of generating non-political knowledge (120). In the most recent publications, sociologists have continued the past practice and argued that Popper was wrong about social revolutions (Patnaik 2004), about history having no pattern (Goldstone 2004) and about the usefulness of the scientific principles of falsifiability in social sciences (Gorski 2004).

Acceptance

There have been noticeably fewer sociologists who have found Popper's criticisms of sociology useful, especially in the era after the 1960s and 70s. During the early 1950s, Popper's work received some positive reactions especially as far as his criticism of modern totalitarianism was concerned (Cook 1951; Watkins 1951). Later, some sociologists argued that the issues he has raised about the nature of sociological inquiry were relevant and had to be taken seriously (Phillips 1973). One such worthwhile concern was disconnection between philosophy of science and sociological methodology, which had led to the ignorance on the part of sociologists "especially those engaged in empirical research" about "the possible influence of their implicit theory on their work" (24). It was argued that Popper's methodological suggestions could lead sociologists toward a more rigorous discussion about their theoretical assumptions.

It is notable that Popper's ideas generated positive response chiefly among economists and political scientists, not sociologists. Economists appreciated the benefits of Popper's critical rationalism (Caldwell 1991) while political scientists considered Popper's methods to be useful tools for evaluating various theories, including his own (Pickel 1989). Political scientists also pointed out the uniqueness of Popper's concept of liberal society as based on rationality, reason and a free exchange of ideas (Vernon 1976).

Meanwhile, sociologists who discussed Popper noted his influence in methodology, but not in theory (Lynch and Bogen 1997). Popper's ideas were discussed in relation to methodological individualism, which is a method where "actions had to be explained as attempts by individuals to pursue goals in the light of their beliefs and the logic of their situations" (Wettersten 2006, 31). But again, it was noted that Popper's method of institutional individualism actually had been used more in political science and economics than sociology (Udehn 2002, 498–500).

John Wettersten (2006) was among the rare sociologists who took Popper's theories seriously and examined their potential for resolving some of the pressing issues of sociological inquiry. He pointed out that sociology along with other social sciences had to deal with a serious dilemma. On the one hand, sociologists wanted to see individuals as rational beings, but, on the other, they perceived societies as systems with their own properties and an ability to determine individuals. Popper's theory, according to Wettersten, was an attempt to resolve this problem by saying that we could preserve individualism in science and democracy, while still analyzing how individuals' actions interact with the larger structures of the society in sociology. This would allow sociologists to describe society as a system without making assumptions about individuals as mere products of the system. In addition, this would also suggest that social sciences could advocate policies that help remove social or political limitations to the free pursuit of individuals' interests (54).

Unfortunately, the kind of serious engagement with Popper's ideas as represented by Wettersten's writing was rare in sociology. In most cases sociologists were not interested in using or even carefully examining Popper's observations about the inherent problems of sociology. Instead, the sociologists who turned to Popper's theoretical suggestions pursued somewhat unusual projects that involved major rethinking of Popper's original ideas. For example, one theorist in the 1980s argued that ethnomethodology and Popper's method of falsification possessed striking similarities because they both could help us see that there were no sure "guarantees that we are right in our decision to accept or reject a theory. We can never be certain that our theory is true" (Tilley 1984, 39). In other words, it was argued that both ethnomethodology and Popper assumed that there was no foundational truth and that a quest for certainty was hopeless. Popper's theory was then identified as a convincing reason for most sociologists to become ethnomethodologists.

A similar example of a somewhat strange use (or abuse) of Popper's ideas was an argument that his notion of scientific sociology could justify theories that aimed to solve social problems and followed normative criteria to achieve social justice, even using state action (Caputo 2007). Even though Popper's theory as such gave no indication that he would consider value-driven theories scientific or believe that there was no foundational truth, these sociologists argued that he would still accept them as valid for building knowledge. Such reinterpretation stretched his ideas to serious lengths and eventually lost sight of his criticism of historicism and holism.

In sum, sociology of the second part of the 20th century was not responsive to Popper's critique. In fact, it was overtly hostile to it and either accused Popper of bias or appropriated only the more convenient parts of Popper's theory, while ignoring his criticism of sociology. The aversion toward Popper's critique in contemporary sociological theory could be explained as due to the fact that sociology was in fact committing the two sins of historicism and holism. The following part of this chapter demonstrates this in three dominant theoretical perspectives in contemporary sociological theory, namely, the critical theory of Frankfurt School, the conflict theory of Ralf Dahrendorf and C. Wright Mills, and the feminist theory of Dorothy Smith.

Historicist and Holist Tendencies in 20th Century Sociological Theory

The following discusses relevant aspects of some of the most influential sociological theories of the late 20th century and analyzes them by applying Popper's criticism of holism and historicism. The goal here is to reveal the extent to which Popper's insights uncover embedded problems in contemporary sociological theory. Ultimately, it is shown here that Popper's analytical approach continues to be a valid instrument for evaluating sociological conceptions, particularly as far as their scientific efforts are concerned. The three theories discussed here are consistently included in contemporary theory textbooks where critical theory is defined as a link between classical Marxism and its contemporary versions such as conflict theory, and feminist theory is treated as one of the fastest growing and revolutionizing areas of the last couple of decades.

Critical Theory

Critical theory undoubtedly was and still is a multifaceted set of ideas. Its major contribution was bringing the psychoanalytical ideas of Sigmund Freud together with Marxist critique of modern consumerist capitalism. The combination of these two perspectives was ultimately aimed at explaining why the kind of revolution that was predicted by Marxists still had not happened in the early and mid 20th century and what forms this revolution could take in the future. In other words, it did not question the Marxist premise of history having its own logic as such. Therefore such notable members of the Frankfurt School as Max Horkheimer and Herbert Marcuse continuously discussed the issue of the looming, but as of now unfulfilled potential for social change.

Critical theory envisioned the future transformation not as a gradual or incremental change that carefully weighed benefits vs. trade-offs. Instead, it saw (or wanted to see) history move toward a radical shift that would make everyone doubt currently accepted rules of appropriate conduct, common sense and reason. According to the critical theory, the existing social system did not need to be preserved because it had been constructed by certain classes whose position in history propelled them to maintain their power. The current society was a product of history — it had been constructed by agents positioned in a certain historical place. As such, this social system could also be de-constructed by other groups of similarly decisive and historically driven agents.

Who would they be? According to critical theory, they were groups who saw that the existing system was an outcome of the capitalists' interests to own the world and to use war and oppression to accomplish this goal. The revolutionary groups were able to see that capital's power had created a social totality, which served its needs and was able to appear natural and common-sensical. The critical groups were those who could detect the constructed, historically specific and artificial nature of the world according to the capital and they would initiate a dramatic social change that would create a new society as a new historic phase (Horkheimer 1972).

Critical theorists advocated such dramatic social and political transformation because it would reveal the true nature of humanity that had been hidden behind the badly designed social structures of consumer capitalism. Thus, according to Herbert Marcuse, technological advancement had managed to eliminate all possibility for "independence of thought, autonomy, and the right to political opposition" (1964, 1). Under the conditions of constantly improving standards of living any search for alternatives, disagreements or non-conformity appeared like useless nuisances (2–3). This repressed people's natural creativity; destroyed their efforts at seeking personal uniqueness and suffocated their urge for change. To resist these tendencies, Marcuse advocated and predicted the coming of a revolution that would liberate sexual or libidinal senses and help people break out of capitalism's unfreedom and irrationalism of technology. The apathy of consumer in technological capitalism would be challenged when "instinctual revolt" would turn "into political rebellion" (Marcuse 1969, 9), that is, when "political radicalism" would become "moral radicalism," which could activate "the elementary, organic foundation of morality in the human being" (10). This moral-political change would be based on the disposition of the organism, more precisely, the erotic drive. Such instincts, according to Marcuse, would serve as the foundation for building a true solidarity among all human beings and reveal their ultimate essence. In sum, while capitalism had made people libidinally (erotically) attached to the commodities, the revolutionary morality would connect people to their true human nature thus accomplishing an authentic social and historical change (11).

Looking at these ideas from Popper's point of view, it is hard to miss their historicism. Critical theorists perceived the society as something that could be made and remade entirely historically, that is, according to the guidance of powerful historical forces such as the capital. It had created the existing society, while the historical change was going to form the liberated society of tomorrow.

In other words, critical theorists argued that history and its forces were the agents that determined social outcomes. In critical theory, people were not agents of history, and history was not driven by them. Instead, people were fulfilling a plan of history itself. Its blueprints could not be analyzed empirically because it had been generated by abstract and ultimately mystic forces.

The historicist aspects of critical theory became even more explicit when it turned to the discussion of nature and shape of the coming revolution. When Marcuse asserted that only a dramatic social and historical change could be truly liberating, he was speaking as a historicist. His hope was that a radical social and political change would affect the most basic and instinctual levels of human nature and reveal the most deep-seated and repressed features of human psyche. This would allow for the creation of an authentic society. As a historicist, he saw this revolution as the moment of truth that transcended the existing society. That is, change was the ultimate instrument for revealing the true nature of society and people. But again, as pointed out by Popper, such an understanding of history was not rational. Instead, it contained assumptions about mystic, instinctual and empirically unverifiable forces, which, as Popper would conclude, indicated that critical theory was not scientific in its conception of history. In sum, contrary to the claims of critical theorists themselves, their approach could not be used for the purposes of reliable social science research.

Conflict Theory

As explained by one of the most well-known representatives of the conflict theory, Ralf Dahrendorf (1958), this perspective assumed that change, rather than order and stability, was the most characteristic feature of any society. This change, according to Dahrendorf, was due to continuous power conflicts that existed in each and every society. Importantly, the theory of conflict did not focus on individuals as agents of change. Conflict theorists' central notion was "imperatively coordinated associations," that is, units of relations in which individuals were assigned places and acted according to the rules dictated by these associations. Individuals were granted authority only insofar as their position in the association possessed authority and social transformations were products of imbalance in power of social positions, not the people acting in them (1959).

Sociology was to analyze these associations and distribution of power, hierarchies, conflicts and change that they produced. In doing this, Dahrendorf claimed that sociology could be scientific and objective, however when seen through Popper's lens, it turns out to suffer from holism. Looking deeper at the conflict theory's view of society, one cannot help but notice that experiences of individuals in it were seen as entirely dependent on the whole of society. Social arrangements such as imperatively coordinated associations were attributed a tremendous amount of agency, while people had none because they were "representatives" of either the dominant or subordinate social positions. For conflict theorists, society was not a compounding result of numerous, complex and diverse individual actions (as it was according to Popper), but rather a system of abstract relations. Associations were networked and there was a possibility for individuals to travel from one to another, however the social nature of these relations was not derived from the fact that individuals participated in them. Imperatively coordinated associations were social by themselves, even without any people in them.

As a result, it was possible for conflict theorists to analyze society without mentioning actual people, which, according to Popper, was a notable feature of the holist, as opposed to a rational scientific, perspective. As noted earlier, holism emerged from the Platonic and Hegelian tradition of thinking about large social structures as superior in importance to individuals who participated in them. Popper warned that such views had serious repercussions because they could lead sociologists toward valuing and even actively supporting controlling institutions such as governments that may demand sacrifices of individual's rights in the name of idealistic, but repressive notions of common good. Popper's concern was that if individuals dropped out of the picture in sociological theories, sociologists could lose their critical ability to notice the growing power of government interventionism, which he perceived as anathema to individual freedom.

Another major contributor to conflict theory was C. Wright Mills. When analyzed from Popper's point of view, Mills' theory further exacerbated the previous problems. Mills made his name by arguing that political power over time had become increasingly concentrated in the hands of an ever-smaller group who occupied a social position from which they could modify the lives of many, if not most, other people. Mills identified this structural position as "the power elite" and claimed that it had more power than any other group in human history before (1958). The power elite derived its influence from the constellation of political, military and economic institutions. All other parts of the society had gradually lost their decision-making power and a chance for having impact on society as a whole.

When describing the power elite, Mills argued that there were certain social and even psychological similarities that developed because they all found themselves in positions that entitled them to power, not because they had accumulated their power through personal efforts. The power elite therefore, according to Mills, was an institutional product, not a result of direct struggles among competing groups or social actors. Moreover, Mills was convinced that any possibility for a public discussion, protest or opposition had been eliminated in contemporary social system. According to Mills, there was no force or group that could challenge the power position of the ruling elite because in modern society individuals were no longer agents of history. They were powerless, indifferent and apathetic.[2]

Mills' view of history was similarly bleak. He was convinced that history had moved into what he called the Fourth Epoch, which marked the end of the Modern Age (1963). The Fourth Epoch was a historical phase in which ideas of freedom and reason had disappeared, while increased rationality (such as the enlarged influence of technology, science and education) had failed to produce more liberty. People living under the Fourth Epoch performed highly rationalized functions as dictated by the social machinery, but they no longer made any decisions. They just followed what the rationally built and smoothly functioning social system was telling them to do, that is, they had become robots. Such a development, according to Mills, had not been determined by any specific actions of concrete groups or individuals. It was the next stage in the evolution of history that had began with Enlightenment and the subsequent over-emphasis on development, ever-expanding industrialization and increasingly efficient, but wasteful, commodity production. The death of true democracy, small associations, voluntary groups and freedom as opposed to the state, military and economic apparatus was historically unavoidable, according to Mills. The arrival of the Fourth Epoch was the path of history itself and everyday decisions of individuals did not matter. In other words, "history was made, behind man's backs" and it was "indeed fate" (Mills 1963, 208).

When analyzing Mills' theory using Popper's analytical tools, it becomes evident that the concept of the power elite was based on holism. Mills envisioned the elite as a collective position that possessed force to shape and determine everything including its members, but it was impossible to actually identify or study the power elite using empirical methods of research. It was an abstract and homogenizing power position, rather than a group consisting of real people with interests, needs and wills. According to Mills, power elite contained individuals who had ended up there rather accidentally and acted in unison because they were determined to do so by the collective nature of their social position. Therefore in Mills' theory individuals in the power elite did not actually possess authority personally. They could merely use it because of their structural placement within a social system that had formed this position over time. As Popper had warned us, Mills' sociology, just as that of Dahrendorf, ended up defining collective social arrangements as more real and influential than individuals inside of these structures. Thus Mills' theory of power elite suffered from a large dose of holism and led him to view people not as members of a society, but as dispensable plug-ins into the social whole.

It is particularly ironic because he tirelessly complained about the loss of individuality and freedom in modern society, while his sociological theory treated individual actors as representatives of social trends and outcomes of social positions. Due to this contradiction, whatever Mills accused the power elite of was indirectly affirmed by his own theory. While saying that the abstract, but omnipotent, power elite had disempowered the rest of the society, Mills also confirmed that he himself did not believe that individuals had any power to change their lives or to substantially alter the path of history.

Thus, Mills was a historicist, too. His historicist position was particularly clear in his discussion of the Fourth Epoch. He saw the Fourth Epoch as a historical phase that had arrived due to history's own evolution, not because of history having been pushed in that direction by individual agents. To him, history was a large scale process that followed its own rules. As pointed out by Popper, such a position lent itself to a totalitarian understanding of society and although Mills was critical of the Fourth Epoch, his theory reaffirmed the power of history over people and treated it as unavoidable. However, Mills was never aware of the contradiction that his historicist position generated. He did not admit that his sociological perspective not only caused him to pay attention only to grand movements of history, but it also led him to overstate and exaggerate them. Even if Mills was wrong about the Fourth Epoch, he would not have been able to detect this because, as a historicist, he assumed that history (without people) had omnipotent power. In sum, Mills was more of a true believer in historicism than a true researcher of history.

Feminist Theory

In the last forty years feminist theory has emerged as one of most important players on the scene of contemporary sociological theory. Examples of its writings are now discussed in most sociological theory textbooks where one of the most widely quoted feminist theorists is Dorothy Smith.

According to Smith, feminist sociology emerged as a radical critique of sociology as a whole. The particular target for feminists was sociology's claim that it was a pursuit of knowledge that existed separately from the social and physical characteristics of the people doing sociology (1990). Instead, as forcefully argued by Smith, sociology was not distanced from but fully involved in the relations of ruling. It was guided and controlled by the governing social institutions that gave more power to men than women. The alleged disconnection between researchers' everyday life and social position had worked only for men who were sociologists. Women sociologists experienced instead what Smith identified as bifurcated consciousness, where they had to consciously separate their scientific work from the daily responsibilities of taking care of others. According to Smith, men did not have this problem. They could afford to fully identify as sociologists-scientists since their private lives were taken care of by others, concretely, women. Meanwhile women who wanted to be taken seriously as scientists had to become non-women and men-like.

According to Smith, gender was a social position into which women were placed and which determined every aspect of their lives. Sociology had to realize, she demanded, that women had no choice but to bring their social position to bear on what they did as sociologists. Moreover, according to Smith, men had to become aware of the privileged position in which they were placed by their gender while working as sociologists-scientists. Consequently, according to Smith's version of feminist theory, none of the knowledge accumulated by sociology would be valid unless it was explicitly aware of the social position from which it was collected. Sociologists had to account for who they were as social and physical beings because no science was ever done from a neutral and intersubjective point of view. All science was socially located, historically determined, served the interests of the ruling relations and was shaped by the social position, including that of gender, of the researchers.

Moreover, the world around us, according to Smith, was socially constructed and it could be known only from within. The idea of studying society as something external to the individuals was socially constructed and reflected assumptions of a specific social and historical context such as men-dominated social sciences. In reality, all scientific theories were socially situated. The society determined who we were not only as people, but also as researchers. Therefore, according to the feminist sociology, we ought to take our everyday experiences as the starting point and analyze how the social world was organized for us and how it formed us. In sum, feminist sociology, as developed by Smith, demanded that social sciences study people as social products with methods that were acknowledged to be socially constructed as well.

Looking at this theory from Popper's point of view, Smith's approach represented a holistic view where individuals were seen as products or subordinates to the social collectivity. In fact, not only Smith's view of society, but also of sociology itself was holistic. According to Smith, sociology and its practice were controlled by interests of governing social institutions. In this sense Smith was consistent — not only individuals were products of social reality, but also everything they did, including practicing sociology, were outcomes of social conditions. As a holist, Smith attributed enormous power to the society. Neither sociologists nor the people whom sociologists studied could ever escape the collective power of the society. They were not seen as agents with will and rational capabilities of their own. Instead, their actions were interpreted as representative of the social whole from which they originated. Thus, the social and historical context was destiny although Smith also demanded a radical change, while at the same time reaffirming the helplessness of individual actors.

As Popper's analysis would point out, sociologists who believed that individuals were entirely constructed by their societies were also likely to support social transformations that would bring about new social institutions capable of constructing new individuals as long as the new societies followed their favorite values. And they applied the same logic to social sciences as well. According to Smith, if sociology of the past was a product of a society dominated by men, then the new sociology would be formed by a different society that acknowledged and questioned gender and gave preference to women's experiences. Smith would favor the second one based on her values and argue that this was not a problem because both the old and the new social sciences were pre-determined by the surrounding social conditions. Clearly, social science for feminist theorists was never about empirical facts and rational analysis. Instead, it was a symptom of social relations characteristic of a particular society and therefore value-based. According to Popper, such a view of sociology was irrational because it attributed mystically strong powers to the abstract notions of the social, while denigrating empirically observable facts about individuals.

Conclusion

What is the value of Karl Popper's ideas for today's sociology? Most of the past debates about Popper have concentrated on his theory of falsifiability and argument that methods of natural and social sciences should not be dramatically different. In contrast to this view, it was proposed here that an even more important contribution of Popper was his analysis of the internal limitations of sociology, particularly its treatment of history and view of society. Popper's criticism of sociology's sins of historicism and holism required practicing sociologists to look deeper into their assumptions and revealed dangerous tendencies that had never been fully addressed.

Popper was deeply concerned that due to its deep-seated historicism and holism, sociology was leading the study of society and its ideas of public policy toward totalitarian ends. It was historicism and holism that endangered sociology as a science and could turn it into an ideology that would blindly speak in favor of strong governments, powerful social controls and limitations to individual freedom and democracy in the name of grand historical trends and social collectivity. Popper warned us that irrationalism of historicism and holism could lead sociologists to give the wrong advice to the rest of the society. In order to find a remedy for this, Popper invited sociologists to have a rational discussion about their discipline's foundations and thus become an example for the creation of an open, as opposed to a closed society. However, sociologists have been reluctant to take on Popper's challenge and analyze the ideological nature of their assumptions. Popper wanted sociology to analyze and maybe cleanse some of its political presuppositions. Unfortunately, sociology has been more than happy to deny that and continue on its path of holism and historicism.

Notes

1. Friedrich Hayek (1899–1992) was a prominent Austrian economist and social thinker who criticized socialist economy and politics during and right after World War II. He argued on behalf of the free market economy (see the chapter by Josh McCabe and Brian Pitt on Hayek's ideas in this volume). Leo Strauss (1899–1973) was an émigré political philosopher

from Germany who taught political science and philosophy at the University of Chicago. He was a critic of modern liberalism and suggested bringing the classical authors such as Plato and Aristotle into the discussions of contemporary politics. He is also often mentioned as one of most discussed thinkers of the last quarter of the 20th century.

2. On the theoretical issues related to C. Wright Mills' contempt for the "plebeian" and hollow masses, see Abbott 2006.

References

Abbott, James R. 2006. Critical Sociologies and Ressentiment: The Examples of C. Wright Mills and Howard Becker. *The American Sociologist* 37(3): 15–31.

Aronowitz, Stanley, and Robert Ausch. 2000. A Critique of Methodological Reason. *The Sociological Quarterly* 41 (4): 699–719.

Brown, Richard, and Elizabeth Malone. 2004. Reason, Politics and the Politics of Truth: How Science Is Both Autonomous and Dependent. *Sociological Theory* 22 (1): 106–22.

Burawoy, Michael. 1989. Two Methods in Search of Science. *Theory and Society* 18 (6): 759–805.

Caldwell, Bruce. 1991. Clarifying Popper. *Journal of Economic Literature* 29 (1): 1–33.

Caputo, Richard. 2007. Social Theory and Its Relation to Social Problems: An Essay about Theory and Research with Social Justice in Mind. *Journal of Sociology and Social Welfare* 34 (1): 43–61.

Coates, Willson. 1958. Review of Karl Popper's "The Poverty of Historicism." *Annals of the American Academy of Political and Social Science* 319 (September): 210–11.

Cohen, Percy S. 1963. Review of Karl Popper's "The Poverty of Historicism." *The British Journal for the Philosophy of Science* 14 (55): 246–61.

Cook, Thomas. 1951. Review of Karl Popper's "The Open Society and Its Enemies." *Annals of the American Academy of Political and Social Science* 274 (March): 253–54.

Dahrendrof, Ralf. 1958. Toward a Theory of Social Conflict. *Journal of Conflict Resolution* 2 (2): 170–79.

_____. 1959. *Class and Class Conflict in Industrial Society.* Stanford: Stanford University Press.

Freeman, Michael. 1975. Sociology and Utopia: Some Reflections on the Social Philosophy of Karl Popper. *The British Journal of Sociology* 26 (1): 20–34.

Friedmann, John. 1978. The Epistemology of Social Science: A Critique of Objective Knowledge. *Theory and Society* 6 (1): 75–92.

Gluck, Samuel. 1960. Review of Karl Popper's "The Logic of Scientific Discovery." *Annals of the American Academy of Political and Social Science* 328 (March): 212–14.

_____. 1964. Review of Karl Popper's "Conjectures and Refutations: The Growth of Scientific Knowledge." *Annals of American Academic of Political and Social Science* 351 (January): 218–20.

Goldstone, Jack. 2004. Response: Reasoning about History, Sociologically.... *Sociological Methodology* 34: 35–61.

Gorski, Philip. 2004. The Poverty of Deductivism: A Constructive Realist Model of Sociological Explanation. *Sociological Methodology* 34: 1–33.

Horkheimer, Max. 1972. *Critical Theory.* New York: Continuum.

Jacobs, Struan. 1990. Popper, Weber and the Rationalist Approach to Social Explanation. *The British Journal of Sociology* 41 (4): 559–70.

Krige, John. 1978. Popper's Epistemology and the Autonomy of Science. *Social Studies of Science* 8 (3): 287–307.

Lynch, Michael, and David Bogen. 1997. Sociology's Asociological "Core": An Examination of Textbook Sociology in Light of the Sociology of Scientific Knowledge. *American Sociological Review* 62 (3): 481–93.

Lynd, Helen Merrell. 1951. Review of Karl Popper's "The Open Society and Its Enemies." *American Sociological Review* 16 (2): 268–69.

Marcuse, Herber. 1964. *One-Dimensional Man: Studies in the Ideology of Advanced Industrial Society.* Boston: Beacon Press.

_____. 1969. *An Essay on Liberation.* Boston: Beacon Press.

McDonald, Lynn. 1997. Review of Karl Popper "The Myth of the Framework: In Defense of Science and Rationality." *The Canadian Journal of Sociology* 22 (1): 142–44.

McLachlan, Hugh. 1980. Popper, Marxism and the Nature of Social Laws. *The British Journal of Sociology* 31 (1): 66–77.

Mills, C. Wright. 1958. The Structure of Power in American Society. *The British Journal of Sociology* 9 (1): 29–41.

_____. 1963. *Power, Politics, and People: The Collected Essays of C. Wright Mills.* New York: Oxford University Press.

Patnaik, Prabhat. 2004. Historicism and Revolution. *Social Scientist* 32 (1/2): 30–41.

Phillips, Derek. 1973. Paradigms, Falsification, and Sociology. *Acta Sociologica* 16 (1): 13–30.

Pickel, Andreas. 1989. Never Ask Who Should Rule: Karl Popper and Political Theory. *Canadian Journal of Political Science* 22 (1): 83–105.

Popper, Karl. 1963. *The Open Society and Its Enemies.* Vol. II. New York: Harper and Row.

Purkayastha, P. 1989. Science, Falsification and Ideology. *Social Scientist* 17 (3/4): 22–30.

Sica, Alan. 1987. Review of Hans Albert "Treatise on Critical Reason." *Contemporary Sociology* 16 (2): 246–49.

Smith, Dorothy. 1990. *The Conceptual Practices of Power: A Feminist Sociology of Knowledge.* Boston: Northeastern University Press.

Sorokin, Pitirim. 1958. Review of Karl Popper's "The Poverty of Historicism." *American Sociological Review* 23 (3): 344.

Tilley, Nicholas. 1980. Popper, Positivism and Ethnomethodology. *The British Journal of Sociology* 31 (1): 28–45.

Urbach, Peter. 1978. Is Any of Popper's Arguments Against Historicism Valid? *The British Journal of the Philosophy of Science* 29 (2): 117–30.

Vernon, Richard. 1976. The "Great Society" and the "Open Society": Liberalism in Hayek and Popper. *Canadian Journal of Political Science* 9 (2): 261–76.

Watkins, F.M. 1951. Review of Karl Popper's "The Open Society and Its Enemies." *The Canadian Journal of Economics and Political Science* 17 (4): 570–71.

Wetterstern, John. 2006. *How Do Institutions Steer Events? An Inquiry into the Limits and Possibilities of Rational Thought and Action.* Hampshire, UK: Ashgate.

4. CULTURE, AGENCY AND THE MEANS OF SIMULATION
Critical Assessment of Postmodernism

David Boyns

It cannot be that postmodernist culture is quite the thing that postmodern theory contends that it is, but this is not to say that the whole debate is without meaning or function.— Connor 1997, 9

The primary claims of postmodernist theory are cultural. From Jean Baudrillard's (1983) theory of simulations, to Fredric Jameson's (1984; 1991) conception of the postmodern as a "cultural logic," to Jean-Francois Lyotard's (1984) notion of the plurality of knowledge, to Linda Nicholson and Steven Seidman's (1995) idea of an identity-based "social postmodernism," culture is the dominant theme of the postmodern. This chapter explores the importance of culture in the theories of postmodernism, and in particular its role in the theories of simulations that have become their hallmark. It begins with a discussion of the contemporary revitalization of culture within postmodernism, and the trends and limitations that these "new" approaches bring to the study of culture. The focus is on Baudrillard's (1983) theory of simulations as a foundational statement of what is commonly called the "crisis of representation" within the theories of the postmodern. The postmodern conceptions of culture, however, are not to be taken as empirical or theoretical givens. A sociology of the theories of postmodern culture reveals some important limitations of the postmodern approach, first and foremost of which is the lack of any theoretical account of the means by which simulations are produced and subsequently reproduced through time. Postmodern theories assume the existence of simulations as a dominant and taken-for-granted component of everyday life in contemporary societies, but have very little to say about what I will call the *means of simulation*.

I argue that an understanding of the means of simulation involves an investigation of the technologies of mass media as the primary means by which simulations are produced, and the active engagement of these simulations by human beings at an experiential level. Because postmodern theories of culture have assumed the widespread existence and influence of simulations, they have abandoned the need for a theory of agency and, thereby, been able to preclude an investigation into the means by which simulations are incorporated into human experience. As a result, the postmodern conception of culture is one in which human agency is completely colonized by a free-floating culture of simulations. I will argue that this highly imaginative account of both culture and agency is clearly impossible and is based more upon science fiction-inspired models of reality than empirically based investigations. This chapter seeks to ground this account within a sociological investigation of postmodern culture in terms of the links between agency, culture, and the technologies of mass media.

The Postmodern Revivification of Culture

The development of a sociological interest in culture has been increasingly prominent for the past three decades (Alexander and Smith 2001; Lamont and Wuthnow 1990; Reed and Alexander 2009; Ritzer 1990; Smith 1998; Wuthnow and Witten 1988). There is no doubt that the emergence and influence of postmodern theories in the social sciences have largely been a byproduct of the growing fascination with the study of culture. In fact, it is commonly noted that postmodernism is part of a "cultural revival" within sociology (Smith 1998). This "revival" is probably not "news" for many sociologists, given the rise to prominence of the cultural studies of the British Birmingham School during the 1980s and 1990s (see During 1999; Grossberg, Nelson, and Treichler 1992) and the enormous influence of French cultural sociology since the 1970s (inspired by the works of Pierre Bourdieu, Henri Lefevbre, Michel de Certeau, and Roland Barthes). Postmodernism's "new" influence on the sociological study of culture, however, has been limited. Because postmodern theories highlight the centrality of culture in developing theories of contemporary society and, at the same time, reject outright the subject and subjectivity, they have done little toward advancing a theory of culture which incorporates human agency (Best and Kellner 1991, 283; Ritzer 1997, 248). In fact, many postmodernists (especially those, like Baudrillard, who are often identified as extreme, or skeptical, postmodernists) seem to be content to utterly dismiss the role of agency in their analyses of contemporary social life. This abandonment of agency is perhaps best illustrated by Baudrillard's (1988, 16) infamous conceptualization of individuals as no longer active "playwrights or actors" but, instead, as computer terminals passively wired to communication networks disseminating simulations.

Nonetheless, postmodern theories have had a significant impact on the contemporary study of culture in sociology, and their influence is twofold. First, they have been instrumental in the revivification of the interest in sociological theories of culture that had dramatically waned in the early post–Parsonsian era. Second, using semiotic analysis[1] they have conceptualized culture in a new way, reducing culture to autonomous systems of signs, codes and symbols, and excluding material dimensions of culture. This second point has perhaps had the most significant impact on the recent developments of cultural sociology. As postmodernists have proclaimed that all of social life has become an entirely cultural affair, they simultaneously have highlighted the prominence of the semiotic "sign" in contemporary culture, as well as the importance of the semiotic process in the interpretation of everyday life (Gottdiender 1995). However, under the postmodern transcendence of the sign, it is as if the material world has disappeared, eclipsed by the awesome and spectacular nature of the semiotic process.[2] This contention should be news to those of us who live in the material world and are restricted by the confines of the corporeal body, the physical limitations of space, and more fundamental encumbrances like gravity. Clearly, as Bauman (1992, 154) suggests, not every aspect of social or material life can be reduced to the symbolic hyperreality of the postmodern culture of simulations:

> Personal experiences can be enclosed by the frame of the television screen. One doubts whether the world can.... To many people, much in their life is anything but simulation. To many, reality remains what it always used to be: tough, solid, resistant and harsh. They need to sink their teeth into some quite real bread before they abandon themselves to munching images.

As Lenin remarked about automobiles many decades ago, if you doubt their material reality then just lie down in their path (cited in Gottdiener 1995, 24).[3]

Postmodern theories have been widely criticized for their exclusion of the real social problems of the material world, like economic inequality and poverty, global overpopulation and environmental degradation, and political conflict and violence (Best and Kellner 1991; Ritzer 1997). Despite the apparent absurdity of the postmodern elision of the material world, cultural sociology has been deeply affected by the emphasis on symbols in postmodern theory. Jameson's (1984; 1991) claim that the "logic" of contemporary societies is a "cultural dominant," where all of contemporary social, economic, and political life has been reduced to the semiotic interplay of signs and symbols, seems to have also become an *analytical* "dominant" in the contemporary study of culture. It is clear that postmodern theories have attempted to give a new face to the sociological study of culture and have been successful to a certain degree by suggesting that culture can be understood entirely as a regime of signification.

While it is provocative to assert that culture is a purely nonmaterial symbol system — especially given the predominant role that mass media does play in the production of the highly symbol-laden nature of contemporary cultures— I would argue that it is an inherently fallacious claim. Culture has both material use-values, as Marx (1978) has suggested, *and* the nonmaterial sign-values described by Baudrillard (1983). Even Alexander, who has recently argued (see

Alexander and Smith 2001) for the development of a cultural sociology which is premised upon the idea of an "autonomous" culture (much like that found in both functional and postmodern theories), has also maintained that material forms of culture, like technology, have been the "antisigns" of cultural analysis. In his discussion of the computer Alexander (1992, 299) writes that

> technology is a thing that can be touched, observed, interacted with, and calcu-lated in an objectively rational way. Analytically, however, technology is also part of the cultural system. It is a sign, both a signifier and a signified, in relation to which actors cannot entirely separate their subjective states of mind. Social sci-entists have not usually considered technology in this more subjective way. Indeed, they have not typically considered it a cultural object at all. It has appeared as the material variable par excellence ... as the most routine of the routine, not a sign, but an antisign, the essence of a modernity that has under-mined the very possibility for cultural understanding itself.

Alexander's argument highlights three very salient points. First, material technology, though it is often unrecognized as such, is a central aspect of cul-ture. Second, technology and other forms of material culture exist as material objects, but can also be heavily laden with symbolic meaning (e.g. clothing, food, architecture, automobiles, and cellular telephones), and both these mate-rial and symbolic dimensions are clearly interconnected. Finally, in cultural analysis technology is often taken for granted as a routinized aspect of the social world and is often ignored. This neglect is particularly true for postmodern theories that tend to obviate a discussion of technology in their analysis of con-temporary culture and emphasize the eclipse of material reality by signs and simulations. Postmodern theories tend to accept the existence of the technolo-gies of mass media as a given, as "the material variable par excellence," and then quickly move into an analysis of what they describe as a free-floating, and autonomous, symbolic culture. However, when assessing the claims made by postmodern theory it is essential to conceptualize the technologies that are used to produce culture as empirical variables, with different levels of influence, and distinct abilities to create symbolic codes. It is only by ascertaining the degree of exposure to mass media technologies, and subsequently the signs and sym-bols produced by these technologies, that the effects of mass media in the pro-duction of a "postmodern culture" can be delineated.

Let me explore this last point a bit further. It is clear that the postmodern conceptions of culture make a blanket assumption about the existence and importance of mass media technologies in contemporary societies. The mass media is *everywhere* in postmodern theory, though it is rarely treated with ana-lytical significance as a technologically grounded phenomenon derived from the material world. This omission represents a serious flaw in the theories of the postmodern, for I would contend that there is a *technological imperative* that underlies postmodern theories, and particularly their conceptions of cul-ture. It is also especially important given the reliance on mass media in the theories of the postmodern. As Luchmann (2000, 3) suggests, the process by which mass-mediated information, symbols and images are disseminated "is only possible on the basis of technologies. The way in which these technologies work structures and limits what is possible as mass communication. This has to be taken into account in any theory of the mass media." The emphasis on technology also has to be considered in postmodern theories that rely instrumentally on mass media.

Postmodern Culture: Signification, Fragmentation and Simulation

Perhaps the most provocative postmodern conception of culture is that which contends that a new culturally dominant logic has emerged within contemporary societies (Jameson, 1984, 1991) where signs and simulations have replaced the material world and confused the very idea of reality itself (Baudrillard, 1983), creating what postmodernists commonly call a "crisis in representation" (Bertens 1995, 238–48). While there are many descriptions of postmodern culture, it is this conception of culture that I will emphasize because I consider it to be the "ground-zero" of the postmodern argument. At the foundation of postmodern theory lies a conception of culture, which suggests that the dissociation of signs and symbols from objective and stable referents has become so extreme that cultural continuity has become a virtual impossibility, and the very idea of fixed meaning has become an absurd possibility. The "crisis of representation," according to postmodern theory, is first and foremost the result of the fragmented interplay of signs and symbols as they are produced by technologies of mass media. Baudrillard (1993) argues that beyond the raw fascination that human beings have with visual images, the new techniques of mass-mediated reproduction have served to destroy meaning, colonize reality and create what is commonly described as a "crisis of representation."

Postmodern Culture, Simulations, and the "Crisis of Representation"

The most influential discussion of the "crisis of representation" within postmodern theory has been that produced by Jean Baudrillard (1983) in his theory of simulations, and it is important to outline Baudrillard's argument in some detail. Baudrillard's well-known stage-model of the orders of simulacra (Baudrillard 1983) has perhaps become the most recognized conception of postmodern culture. Here, Baudrillard argues that the history of the Western world over the last five to six centuries can be described in terms of changes in the strategies with which human beings have come to represent reality, ultimately culminating in the emergence of reproductions of reality that are pure simulation, having little connection to reality but are instead experienced as reality itself. Baudrillard's stage model of the historical progression of simulacra has become widely influential, and is frequently recounted as a seminal statement on postmodern culture. Baudrillard's theory of simulations has had significant consequences for postmodern theories of culture, and has become the foundation for arguments that articulate the "crisis of representation" and attempt to dismantle any idea of a coherent and knowable reality (see, for example, Kroker and Cook 1991; Kroker and Kroker 1997).

While one can certainly be dubious about Baudrillard's model of the orders of simulacra, I do think it represents one of the most important insights of postmodern theory. With the issue of the historical plausibility of the model set aside, there is some evidence that contemporary cultural life is one of an increasing number of simulated events, encounters and experiences (Cubitt 2001; Turkle 2009). More important, however, is the fact that Baudrillard's theory of simulations has had several significant consequences (though not necessarily beneficial) for sociological theories of culture. First, it has been elaborated into a semiotic theory of both culture and meaning which suggests that an order of simulation has emerged where the self-referentiality of signs has created a "semiotic promiscuity." This free play of signs has rendered meaning, culture, and the process of meaning-making erratic and unstable (Jameson 1984; 1991).

Second, the theory of simulations has introduced another order of complexity to the long-standing sociological debates between structure/culture and agency (Archer 1996; Rubinstein 2001). Following Baudrillard, the possibility of human agency in the postmodern world is denied as a result of the determining forces of an unstable cultural network of simulations, which has become increasingly omnipotent in shaping the actions and ideas of individuals. Culture, however, as a self-referential semiotic code does not fare much better. It is conceptualized by Baudrillard as embodying incredible disjunction, incoherence, and fluidity, and cannot be said to exist with any stability, enduring only by virtue of its own emergent agency and self-reflexivity. In short, in the postmodern theory of simulations, the agency of actors is denied by a highly deterministic culture that itself has no inherent stability and seems to embody its own agency. Culture is theorized as a reality *sui generis*, in a Durkheimian (1982) sense, but it is also a reality that exists primarily for its own sake and with its own logic. Individuals and their experiences are merely epiphenomenon. Thus, for Baudrillard there is a refusal of both the determining force of a coherent culture, and the active efficacy of individual agency. The long-standing sociological tension between culture and agency is shattered as both are denied privilege, and even stable existence. The theory of simulations suggests that the semiotic codes of culture have their own self-referential agency that eclipses both the reality of culture and agency, as traditionally understood by sociologists, and pushes them into the background.

Finally, the "crisis of representation" derived largely from the theory of simulations has suggested that the totality of culture in contemporary societies has become something similar to a massive work of abstract, modern art. One of the central issues that concerns abstract art has been the idea of interpretation in relation to the absence of unambiguous, linear representation. The drip paintings by Jackson Pollock, the found-object sculptures of Marcel Duchamp, the pop art collages by Robert Rauschenberg and Jasper Johns, and even the cubist paintings of Pablo Picasso, all reflect a discontinuity of representation that seemingly renders linear interpretation impossible, or at least secondary. It is as if the aesthetic modernism of the modern era, as illustrated by the artistic *avant-garde*, has become the cultural basis of postmodern society. This fusion of aesthetic and social forms that is described in much of postmodern theory is a byproduct of the "crisis of representation," and has resulted in the analytical confusion of issues surrounding both the putatively new social forms of postmodernity and the contemporary cultural systems of postmodernism (see Kumar 1995, 101–102). The theory of simulations suggests that the cultural logic of postmodernism, inspired largely by aesthetic modernism, has become the guiding logic for both culture and social structure in the conditions of postmodernity.

Certainly, Baudrillard and the postmodernists following him have overstated the case of simulations. There is little empirical evidence to suggest that simulations have had the reality transforming effects that postmodernists claim. However, I do believe that postmodern theorists have captured something important, which is that a culture saturated by mass media does have the potential to produce a "crisis in representation" through the production of simulations that are foreign to the realm of everyday experience but can be, in some instances, seamlessly incorporated as a taken-for-granted component of everyday life. Yet, it is not only as a result of the simple presence of the mass-media that simulations come into existence. The existence of a technological imperative for the production of simulations is a necessary, but insufficient, condition for such a radical shift in both culture and social experience. It is only through interaction and engagement with these mass-mediated technologies that simulations, the "crisis of representation," and the whole of postmodern culture become a possibility.

Postmodern Culture and the Technological Imperative

While postmodern theories of culture deeply presuppose the exposure of individuals to mass-mediated technologies, as well as concomitant cultural transformations that stem from the interface of media technologies and human experience, it must be recognized that this is not altogether a new idea. Although, the postmodern theory of simulations is certainly a recent innovation

(Cubit 2001), one of its most important antecedents lie in the theories of Marshall McLuhan who argued decades ago that it is the interface between mass-mediated technologies and human experience that should be the focal point of media studies. His famous dictum, "the medium is the message" (McLuhan and Fiore 1967), is perhaps the most definitive statement of the importance of the human use of technology in the production of a culture that simulates and extends human experience. Baudrillard (1983) does acknowledge the importance of McLuhan's ideas for the theory of simulations. But, Baudrillard's emphasis is placed upon the "universe of communication" and its incorporation into the realm of human experience through both "*tactile* and *tactical* simulation*," where media communications arise to create a "tactile" substitute for social rapport by creating a "tactical," or strategic, system of communication that has its own logic and rules (123–24). In Baudrillard's analysis, the "tactical" goal of the simulation is to draw the individual into an imaginary universe of meaning, where the logic of the simulation is adopted and is reified as the boundary of sensory, social and "tactile" experience. McLuhan's theory, on the other hand, is firmly grounded in the interface between humans and technology, and the cultural consequences of the human use of technology. Baudrillard, though he admits a kinship with McLuhan, deviates from McLuhan's central point that the primary message of media is not its semiotic content but its technological form. Instead, Baudrillard celebrates a transcendence of media content over form, where the focus on technological engagement recedes into the distance as an ontological given, and the contents of (technologically produced) free-floating culture becomes the dominant determining force of contemporary societies.

McLuhan and Baudrillard on the
Interface of Technology and Flesh

Much of McLuhan's work is directed towards interrogating the significance of technology in shaping human perception and experience. For example, in *The Gutenberg Galaxy: The Making of Typographic Man* (1962), McLuhan argues that the invention of the printing press opened a new realm of experience for human beings. Here, the development of a "print culture" resulted in the emergence of a linear and rationalized system of visual communication that would ultimately come to compete with the aural, and collective culture of oral communication. Print would not only construct new modes of communication, but it would also create novel forms of time and space that could be rationalized and individualized. While McLuhan's theory of the form of media would begin with an analysis of print, his ideas would ultimately develop into a technological determinism that conceptualized the technologies of media themselves as extensions of the human nervous system, as strict reticulations of technology and flesh.

The idea of technology as an extension of the human organism would be theoretically developed by McLuhan in *Understanding Media: The Extensions of Man* (1964). Here, McLuhan distinguishes between "hot" media, like print, which require a very little user participation and interpretation, and "cool" media, like radio and television, which require higher levels of human involvement and rely heavily on interpretive processes. Thus, for McLuhan the "cooler" the medium the more likely that medium is to interface with the human body simply because humans are required to interact with it on a more complex and imaginative level. As Stevenson (1995, 120) writes,

> The most obvious example of a cool medium is the telephone. The telephone is a dialogic medium that normally requires at least two people to participate in communication. Conversely, print culture remains a hot medium in that the activity of reading makes fewer demands upon the subject in terms of shaping the flow of information.

"Cool" media require high levels of human involvement and because of this are much more likely to be experienced as extensions of the human senses. McLuhan sees the development of television as the pinnacle of this process, a medium that "completes the cycle of the human sensorium. With the omnipresent ear and the moving eye.... Television demands participation and involvement in the depth of the whole being.... It will not work as a background. It engages you" (McLuhan and Fiore 1967, 125).

McLuhan's theory of the unification of technology and flesh has taken on contemporary expressions in the analysis of what Featherstone and Burrows (1995) call the "cultures of technological embodiment," as expressed in the ideas of the "posthuman" (Halberstam and Livingston, 1995), and the "cyborg" (Gibson 1984; Haraway 1991; Zylinska 2002). In these more recent conceptions of the integration of human and machine, there is an obvious reliance upon the potential of mass media as "virtual reality" creating technologies. Of course, McLuhan was historically excluded from an analysis of these technologies but with great prescience he unquestionably anticipated them (see Levinson 1999). Certainly, the idea of the cyborg is clearly a product of the imaginations of science fiction writers and filmmakers and is typically described as such even by its most fervent advocates (see, for example, Haraway 1991). But, McLuhan takes the idea of the technologically "extended" human being very seriously, suggesting that it is a seemingly natural and inevitable step in the evolution of the human being, one which will ultimately result in what McLuhan refers to as the "discarnate man" (Levinson 1999, 55–64). However, McLuhan does not describe the interface of technology and flesh as having variable effects on human beings; but instead makes a series of blanket assumptions, guided obviously by his technological determinism, about the impact of media technologies on individuals. For McLuhan, there is a rather simplistic relationship between technology and the human being: the development of, and exposure to, technology inevitably creates a necessary symbiosis between machine and flesh.

Baudrillard's theory of simulations seems to embrace the essence of McLuhan's argument but takes the discussion to another level. While he describes the emergence of what he calls the "automaton," and the "mechanical and clock-like man" (Baudrillard 1983, 92), he does not conceptualize the cyborg as a pure simulation. For Baudrillard, the cyborg represents a lower-level of simulation (he includes it as an example of the counterfeit simulations of the second-order), because it can be deconstructed into its constituent elements, of technology and flesh, respectively. His is especially the case if it is obvious that there is an ersatz integration of "artificial" technologies with "real" flesh. The cyborg, in this respect, still has independent agency, with real human motivations, desires, and sociality; only now these faculties are simply channeled through both human flesh and robotic technology. True simulation, on the other hand, is achieved when both machine and flesh become indistinct, and what emerges is a cultural context for social experience in which technology becomes a completely taken-for-granted and intrinsic component of everyday life, and even of the body. Here, it is not necessary for technology to be directly integrated into human flesh, as the science fiction model of the cyborg suggests. Instead, the cyborg needs to merely be understood as a metaphor for the human-machine interface such that the human conditions that emerge from "extensions" of technology becomes irreducible from basic human experiences themselves. For Baudrillard, pure simulation emerges in the world beyond the cyborg, where there is a taken-for-granted and unrecognized interface between technology and flesh. What develops from this condition is a transcendent world that is created through the emergence of simulated "events" and "experiences" that are disassociated from the "real" world, but yet are reified and exist as if they are real. Following McLuhan, Baudrillard assumes that human beings have already become cyborgs, that a metaphorical synthesis of technology and flesh in the postmodern condition is a pre-existing given, and that the emergence of a truly simulated cultural world has developed as the inevitable result.

In constructing his argument in this manner, Baudrillard moves the analysis away from both embodied reality and material technology and focuses instead upon the imagined product of the combination of technology and flesh. He envisions a cultural world in which human beings, as posthuman cyborgs, are so integrally "wired" to mass-mediated technologies that practices like television viewing can no longer be seen simply as "extensions" of human senses. Instead, the integration of technology and human flesh has become accelerated to the degree that mass-mediated experiences are indistinguishable from those of a non-mediated nature. The symbolic world of the mass media, as well as the technologies that are responsible for its production, become reifications and are experienced as if they were natural facts. Thus, for Baudrillard the power of both simulations and simulation-producing machines stems from their ability to become seamlessly integrated into everyday experience.

The assumption of the cyborg-like human who is unable to differentiate between the "virtual" experiences created by mass-mediated technologies and "real" experiences has had important consequences for conceptions of post-modern culture. Not only has it created a conceptualization of human beings as intimately tied to technology, but it has also helped to obscure the need for an analysis of technologies, and in particular the mass media, in the shaping of human experience and the ability to substitute simulations for reality (Kellner 2006). Because theorists of postmodern culture accept as a given the interface between technology and human flesh, they are able to obviate the need for a discussion of mass media and its potential to create simulations. This is an enormous assumption, and one of its primary implications has been to atten-uate the need for empirical and theoretical investigations into human interac-tion with mass-mediated technologies and the simulated reality that is the putative result. With the presence of this theoretical gap, it is clear that post-modern culture cannot simply be present as it is described by postmodern the-ory.

The Means of Simulation: Toward a Sociological Analysis of Postmodern Culture

As Connor (1997, 9) has argued, culture cannot exist in the way that it has been imagined by postmodern theory. The idea of postmodern culture is premised upon a series of speculative assumptions about both the determining force of an increasingly fragmented culture and the impotence of human agency. It is important to summarize the limitations of some of these assumptions.

First, on a sociological level it is questionable to propose that a simulated cultural reality can be produced and maintained without the participation of human agency. In fact, I would argue that it is impossible for any form of cul-ture, especially that of a symbolic nature, to exist and persist without some force of human agency. I do not intend this to mean, however, that individual human agency should be conceptualized as the sole author of human cultural life. Individuals can be "dupes" of their cultural world and in terms of post-modernism they can be oblivious to fact that their reality is one permeated by simulations. But, as sociologists (Blumer 1969; Garfinkel 1967; Wrong 1961) have argued for decades, individuals are never mere "dupes" of their society and culture.

However, in order for the postmodern theory of culture to have any merit, there must be some conceptualization of the means by which simulations are incorporated into the active experience of everyday life. The practical engage-ment of simulations is essential in order for them to exist for human beings and have any potential efficacy. In short, if the claims of postmodern theory are to have any validity there must be some *means of simulation* by which the hyperreal world of postmodernism is imbedded into the flow of everyday life. Such a process needs to involve some margin of human agency, for simulations by themselves, do not do anything. I argue that it is the individual engagement in the technologies of mass media that produce a cultural framework for a *means of simulation*. The mass media are the primary simulation producing technologies, but in order for simulations to have any social influence they cannot merely be "produced"; they must also be "consumed" and incorporated into the domain of everyday interaction.

Second, a view of humans as computer terminals passively wired to a cultural network that circulates signs and symbols is also untenable. Such a perspective merely requires a very crude and unsophisticated conception of human agency, one which revisits not only the limitations of Parsonsian functionalism but, also, of the depersonalized theories of structural Marxists like Louis Althusser (1977) and Nicos Poulantzas (1975). In short, agency cannot be reduced to the simple tourism of the passive spectator. Instead, individuals need to be conceptualized as playing some active role in the production of cultural reality, even if it is a reality composed of cultural simulations. A model of simulations that includes both culture and agency must be developed if the theories of postmodern culture are to have any relevance for serious sociological investigation. Additionally, if there is to be a means by which simulations are both produced and consumed, this *means of simulation* must involve two interrelated components: the production of simulations as artifacts of culture, and their acceptance and employment within everyday social interaction.

A Theoretical Analysis of Postmodern Culture

I want to propose two lines of sociological theory that can be useful in framing the theories of postmodern culture and teasing-out both their central limitations and insights. The first theory is the morphogenetic approach developed by Margaret Archer (1996) in her analysis of the respective roles of culture and agency in social theory. The second is that of the social construction of reality thesis developed by Peter Berger and Thomas Luckmann (1967). While both approaches confront the central issue of the relationship between culture as an objective social fact and agency as the constructive capacity of human actors, their outcomes are very different. On the one hand, Berger and Luckmann develop a model of agency linked with culture that is based upon a dialectical relationship between subjective and objective social domains. On the other hand, Archer's theory emphasizes agency and culture as separate, but interrelated, levels of social reality that have distinct constitutions, and that require unique modes of analysis.

Archer's (1996) morphogenetic theory establishes itself as a critique of various attempts to reconcile the agency vs. structure/culture debate in sociology. Archer argues that two basic levels of analysis are important in assessing the theories of the agency vs. structure/culture debate: the Cultural System level (the domain of culture and social structure) and the Socio-Cultural level (composed of groups and individuals). She outlines several resolutions to this debate, each with its own inherent limitations. Among these resolutions are theoretical projects that emphasize the conflation of culture and agency in either "downwards" or "upwards" directions. The tendency towards "downwards conflation" is expressed by those approaches which emphasize the primacy of the Cultural System over the Socio-Cultural level. Upwards conflation occurs as a result of the domination of the Cultural System by key individuals or groups within the Socio-Cultural System. Archer (1996, 97) sums up the distinction between these two approaches, writing that

> in the downwards version, Cultural Systems engulfed the Socio-Cultural domain through the basic processes of regulation and socialization, while in the upwards version, the Socio-Cultural level swallowed up the Cultural System as the result of domination and manipulation. In brief, both versions treated one level as an epiphenomenon of the other level — they differed about which of the levels was held to be epiphenomenal.

The postmodern theories of cultural simulations are primarily those which commit what Archer calls the fallacy of "downwards conflation." These theories focus almost entirely upon the Cultural System composed of series of signs, images, and symbols, leaving aside any substantive discussion of the potential for agency to be derived from the Socio-Cultural System of interpersonal interaction. In fact, in the theories of simulations the Socio-Cultural System is entirely epiphenomenal of the Cultural System. This downwards epiphenomenalism is one of the primary limitations of the theories of postmodern culture.

Archer develops a meta-theoretical model which is premised upon four "propositions" about the interrelationships between the Cultural System and the Socio-Cultural System (1996, 106). She argues:

1. Logical relationships exist between components of the Cultural System.
2. The Cultural System exerts causal influence upon the Socio-Cultural Level.
3. Causal relationships exist among the elements at the Socio-Cultural Level.
4. The elaboration of the Cultural System is a result of modifications made at the Socio-Cultural Level.

The first two propositions describe the dynamics of the Cultural System and its ability to act upon the Socio-Cultural System. The second two propositions describe the independence of the Socio-Cultural System from the Cultural System, and the influence that the former may exert upon the latter.

The strength of Archer's set of propositions is that they are multidimensional, providing a clear means by which culture and agency as distinct dimensions of social life can be both separately studied and analytically linked. As I have argued, this analytical distinction is essential for any analysis of the postmodern theories of simulations. Because postmodern theories of culture focus almost entirely upon what Archer calls the Cultural System, to the exclusion of the Socio-Cultural System, their approach is not comprehensive and has inherent limitations. Only the first two of Archer's propositions, which describe the Cultural System, can be applied to the postmodernist investigations of culture. The second two propositions, which describe the micro-level agency of the Socio-Cultural System, are almost completely unrelated to the postmodern analysis of culture, thereby exposing the shortcomings of the postmodern approaches. Because of this self-limiting nature of postmodern theory, the post-modern models of culture are unable to answer a very basic question: How do the contents of mass-mediated simulations (as elements of the Cultural System) become internalized into human experience (at the Socio-Cultural System), animating a world of simulations, and resulting in the conditions described by postmodern culture? This internalization and animation of simulations is a fundamental assumption of postmodern theories; yet, they have almost nothing to say about how it occurs.

It is here that the social constructionist perspective developed by Peter Berger and Thomas Luckmann (1967) is able to provide some insight. In their phenomenologically inspired model of what they call the social construction of reality they argue that emergent properties, like those, which characterize Archer's Cultural System, become elements of social reality through a threefold process of externalization, objectification, and internalization (129). Berger and Luckmann argue that in some fundamental capacity, social reality is initially the product of interpersonal negotiations among members of a society. These negotiations result in a series of socially constructed habituations that become externalized through human interaction and practice. Eventually, these social constructions are objectified as institutions becoming reified as legitimate and taken-for-granted components of the human experience. In time, these objectified externalizations are internalized by members as a reality through socialization into the world of natural social facts. Finally, this process of internalization results in a further externalization and objectification of these social facts through time, as individuals adopt and enact the social constructions as a taken-for-granted social reality.

Berger and Luckmann's perspective describes a cyclical process of social reproduction that provides a useful theoretical model for understanding the historical change in culture. If we follow the social constructionist argument to explore the constitution of culture the following dynamics are revealed. An externalized and objectified culture cannot persist through time unless social agents internalize it. It is only through the reproduction of culture by the active process of human agency that culture is able to persist through time. New externalized cultural elements, like the simulations celebrated by many postmodernists, only become an aspect of everyday life if individuals subsequently internalize them. Thus, a change, or a disruption, in culture is only "legitimized" on a social level if individuals adopt it. This does not mean that the internalization of culture must occur at a conscious level. As Berger and Luckmann (1967, 53) point out, the internalization of the objective world of social facts occurs most effectively at a non-conscious, routine, and habitual level because it allows for the reproduction of social patterns as taken-for-granted.

Postmodern theory assumes that culture has become objectified in a viral like state, where it is able to reproduce itself with its own agency. Culture is an emergent property that exists as an animated reification that is separate from human influence, self-programmed and autonomous, like a self-sustaining cybernetic machine. However, the theory of the social construction of reality tells us that this cannot be. Behind any apparently objectified, or reified, emergent property there must exist a sociological process that is not only its source, but also continually reaffirms it as an objectified reality.

It is the cyclical nature of Berger and Luckmann's theory that distinguishes it from Archer's more structural and linear model, and provides a more processually-based insight into the limitations of the postmodern descriptions of simulations. While Archer's model describes two distinct, yet static, levels of analysis (i.e. the objective Cultural System, and the more subjective Socio-Cultural level), the social constructionist strategy emphasizes the importance of both objective and subjective dimensions of social reality as dialectically interrelated social processes. As Berger and Luckmann describe them, externalization and objectification are more objective processes, internalization is more subjective, and all three are essential in the reproduction of society. The processes of externalization and objectification occur primarily at the level of Archer's Cultural System, whereas the internalization that leads to the reproduction and externalization of reified social facts is primarily a Socio-Cultural phenomenon.

Berger and Luckmann's model also provides an analysis of the interrelations between agency and culture as social processes that is helpful in exposing the limits of the postmodern theory of culture. Postmodern theory has a very coarse conception of what the social constructionist perspective describes as externalization and internalization. The theory of simulations presupposes the existence of simulations as objectifications and emphasizes simulations as objective elements of culture. However, in this approach there is a very limited analysis of the externalization of simulations (one assumes that it occurs through mass-mediated technologies) and an overly-simplistic discussion of the internalization of simulations (as the existence of both agency and self-directed individuals are obscured). It is as if the putative objective existence of simulations is simply good enough, and there is no need to detail their social production and reproduction in the quotidian experience.

The postmodern theory of simulations, however, does assume the means by which simulations are produced and externalized, but little effort is given over to elaborating this issue as a theoretical concern. As I have argued, there must be some means of simulation by which simulations are manufactured. It is not sufficient to simply assert that simulations exist. Simulations must come from somewhere, and once produced they must be incorporated into social experience and reproduced through time. The means of simulation by which this occurs must have two dimensions. First, simulations—as hyperreal cultural symbols, representations, and events—are externalized and achieve widespread circulation throughout society. Second, simulations are internalized by individuals, incorporated into everyday human experience, and reproduced within the practical activities of individuals. Such a process involves theoretical conceptualization not only at both levels of Archer's model (the Cultural System and the Socio-Cultural Level), but also must account for all three processes described by Berger and Luckmann (externalization, objectification, and internalization). For example, if a postmodern culture of simulations can be said to exist as an objectified reality, there must be some means by which it is externalized and reified as a component of the Cultural System. This point highlights the importance of an understanding of the technological imperative that underlies postmodern theory. Mass-mediated technologies are the primary means by which simulations are created, externalized, and objectified as elements of the Cultural System.

However, the process cannot end here. Simulations must be further integrated into human experience at the Socio-Cultural level, and internalized by human beings if they are to have any efficacy, for simulations are inert without the active participation of human beings. In addition, in order for simulations to persist through time they must be re-externalized through human practice and interaction. A simulation, or any element of culture for that matter, that does not achieve further externalization is an inanimate element of culture and will remain as such until it is reactivated. The re-externalization of simulations occurs primarily without technological mediation and, instead, occurs through human practice and interaction on an interpersonal level. This process of re-externalization through the human engagement of simulations is necessary for the simulations described by postmodern theories to become aspects of culture in the first place, and is instrumental in their subsequent reproduction as social facts of society.

Conclusion

In many ways the theorists of postmodern culture take as a given what Samuel Taylor Coleridge (1965) once described as our ability to engage in the willing suspension of disbelief. Postmodern theories articulate models of social reality that seem to be more inspired by science fiction than by empirical experience. Much like the popular film *The Matrix* the theories of postmodern culture presume that mass-mediated simulations of reality have become the new models of social reality, and a bewildered human population has accepted them all too willingly and unreflectively (Lawrence 2004; Lutzka 2006; Thomas 2002).

Nonetheless, I remain convinced that the theories of postmodern culture are useful tools for the further development of sociological theories of contemporary societies. For example, it is clear that in the contemporary social world technology has become incorporated into human experience as an extension of the physical body. The technological enhancement of the human body is a social phenomenon that exists in present societies at a level that makes its study fundamental to an understanding of everyday human experience. Given this, it is astonishing that among sociologists very little theoretical or empirical consideration has been granted to the study of the everyday engagement of mass-mediated technologies, and the means through which these technologies create a sense of a simulated world. The postmodern theory of simulations has not presented much of a sociological advance in this respect, as it has not articulated the means by which technology extends the human body, or creates a simulated cultural experience. What the theory of simulations has accomplished, however, is to make problematic the taken-for-granted nature of the technological embeddedness of everyday life, especially with respect to mass-mediated technologies. Sociological theory cannot ignore the role of technology in changing, enhancing, and perhaps distorting the social experience. Postmodern theories have made this notion a *fait accompli.*

Postmodernism assumes that simulations do indeed exist, and that they have been seamlessly incorporated into everyday social experience. However, a more relevant line of questioning should be directed towards the degree to which the mass media is able to produce simulations, and the means by which this production of simulations has been able to produce a distortion of everyday experience. Instead of accepting the premise of the unabated existence of simulations, a more fundamental series of questions involves whether or not simulations do exist, to what degree they are able to create a "crisis of representation," and to what extent they are able to become embedded in the taken-for-granted nature of everyday experience. In this respect, the most appropriate task of sociological investigations is to develop a sociology of postmodern culture, by which the primary objects of postmodern culture (e.g. simulations, the fragmentation of culture and meaning, the dissolution of agency, etc.) can be studied as possibilities, instead of assumed as empirical givens.

While theories of postmodern culture have emphasized the symbolic and non-material dimensions of culture, an analysis of the theoretical premises of postmodern culture reveals a set of assumptions concerning the role of material technologies (primarily those of the mass media) in creating the conditions for the production a simulated sociological world. In short, technologies for the production of simulations are a precondition for postmodern culture; as such, the possibility of a postmodern culture is guided by a technological imperative that is the driving force behind the proliferation of signs and results in the

"crisis of representation." It is only through the human engagement and interaction with mass-mediated technologies that cultural conditions can be produced that approximate those described by postmodern theory.

While the postmodern theories of simulation are provocative, and have
no doubt been influential, they cannot be the end of the discussion. A new sociology of postmodern culture must be grounded in an analysis of what I have
called the means of simulation—the process through which simulations are
created, adopted, and engaged within human cultural experience. This notion
highlights an important weakness in the postmodern conception of culture and
its assumption of a significant, if not absolute, interface between human beings
and mass media technologies. This is not to say that the postmodern argument
is without merit or substance. In a contemporary era, where individuals are
routinely wired into a cultural world of mediated interactions and spectacles,
it is clear that the postmodern interest in simulated worlds is of relevance. Postmodern theories, however, have only begun to help develop an understanding
of the increasingly mass-mediated world. It is our task to continue the discussion.

Notes

1. Semiotic analysis is a mode of investigation that examines the meaning of signs and
symbols that are used to carry meaning through forms of communication. Semiotics examines
both complex systems of meaning, like written and spoken language, as well as less systematic
conventions of meaning like fashion, art and food. In its approach to the investigation of the
meaning, semiotics is distinct from the analysis of syntax, which emphasizes the structural
rules of language and other forms of expression.

2. In fact, Baudrillard (1983, 44, italics in original) addresses this issue directly when he
writes that "*contemporary 'material' production is itself hyperreal*. It retains all the features,
the whole discourse of traditional production, but it is nothing more than its scaled-down
refraction."

3. It is also perhaps because of the need to demonstrate, beyond exception, that symbolic
culture is more powerful than physical reality that the editors of the postmodern-inspired
journal *Social Text* chose to publish a paper written by a theoretical physicist who made the
absurd claim the laws of physics were in essence semiotic phenomena. In fact, Sokal's (1996)
parodic synthesis of postmodern theory and theoretical physics no doubt captured the attention of the editors primarily because it asserted that physical reality, including the forces
which govern the physical universe, were nothing more than linguistic constructions. For a
more detailed treatment of this hoax see Alan Sokal and Jean Bricmont (1998).

References

Alexander, Jeffrey. 1992. The Promise of a Cultural Sociology: Technological Discourse and
    the Sacred and Profane Information Machine. In *Theory of Culture*, ed. Richard Munch
    and Neil J. Smelser, 293–323. Berkeley: University of California Press.
Alexander, Jeffrey, and Philip Smith. 2001. The Strong Program in Cultural Theory: Elements
    of a Structural Hermeneutics. In *Handbook of Sociological Theory*, ed. Jonathan Turner,
    135–150. New York: Kluwer Academic/Plenum Publishers.

Althusser, Louis. 1977. *Politics and History.* London: NLB.
Archer, Margaret S. 1996. *Culture and Agency: The Place of Culture in Social Theory.* Cambridge: Cambridge University Press.
Baudrillard, Jean. 1983. *Simulations.* New York: Semiotext(e).
_____. 1988. *The Ecstasy of Communication.* New York: Semiotext(e).
_____. 1994. *The Illusion of the End.* Stanford: Stanford University Press.
Bauman, Zygmunt. 1992. *Intimations of Postmodernity.* New York: Routledge.
Berger, Peter, and Thomas Luckmann. 1967. *The Social Construction of Reality: A Treatise in the Sociology of Knowledge.* New York: Doubleday.
Bertens, Hans. 1995. *The Idea of the Postmodern: A History.* London: Routledge.
Best, Steven, and Douglas Kellner. 1991. *Postmodern Theory.* New York: The Guilford Press.
Blumer, Herbert. 1969. *Symbolic Interaction: Perspective and Method.* Englewood Cliffs, NJ: Prentice Hall.
Coleridge, Samuel Taylor. 1965. *Biographia literaria.* London: Oxford University Press.
Connor, Stephen. 1997. *Postmodernist Culture: An Introduction to Theories of the Contemporary.* Cambridge, MA: Blackwell.
Cubitt, Sean. 2001. *Simulation and Social Theory.* London: Sage Publications.
During, Simon, ed. 1999. *The Cultural Studies Reader.* London: Routledge.
Durkheim, Emile. 1982. *The Rules of Sociological Method.* New York: Free Press.
Featherstone, Michael, and Roger Burrows. 1995. *Cyberspace, Cyberbodies, Cyberpunk: Cultures of Technological Embodiment.* London: Sage Publications.
Garkfinkel, Harold. 1967. *Studies in Ethnomethodology.* Englewood Cliffs, NJ: Prentice Hall.
Gibson, William. 1984. *Neuromancer.* New York: Berkeley Books.
Giddens, Anthony. 1984. *The Constitution of Society: Outline of the Theory of Structuration.* Berkeley: University of California Press.
Gottdiener, Mark. 1995. *Postmodern Semiotics: Material Culture and the Forms of Postmodern Life.* Oxford: Blackwell.
Grossberg, Lawrence, Cary Nelson, and Paula Treichler, eds. 1992. *Cultural Studies.* New York: Routledge.
Halberstam, Judith, and Ira Livingston, eds. 1995. *Posthuman Bodies.* Bloomington: Indiana University Press.
Haraway, Donna J. 1991. *Simians, Cyborgs, and Women: The Reinvention of Nature.* New York: Routledge.
Jameson, Fredric. 1984. Postmodern, or, the Cultural Logic of Late Capitalism. *New Left Review,* 146 (July–August): 59–92.
_____. 1991. *Postmodernism, Or, The Cultural Logic of Late Capitalism.* Durham: Duke University Press.
Kellner, Douglas. 1989. *Jean Baudrillard: From Marxism to Postmodernism and Beyond.* Stanford: Stanford University Press.
_____. 2006. Jean Baudrillard after Modern Philosophy: Provocations on a Provocateur and Challenger. *The International Journal of Baudrillard Studies* 3(1). http://www.ubishops.ca/baudrillardstudies/vol3_1/kellner.htm.
Kroker, Arthur, and David Cook. 1991. *The Postmodern Scene: Excremental Culture and Hyper-Aesthetics.* New York: St. Martin's Press.
Kroker, Arthur, and Marilouise Kroker, eds. 1997. *Digital Delirium.* New York: St. Martin's Press.
Kumar, Krishan. 1995. *From Post-Industrial to Post-Modern Society: New Theories of the Contemporary World.* Cambridge, MA: Blackwell.
Lamont, Michele, and Robert Wuthnow. 1990. Betwixt and Between: Recent Cultural Sociology in Europe and the United States. In *Frontiers of Sociological Theory: The New Syntheses,* ed. George Ritzer, 287–315. New York: Columbia University Press.
Lawrence, Matt. 2004. *Like a Splinter in Your Mind: The Philosophy behind the Matrix Trilogy.* New York: Blackwell.
Levinson, Paul. 1999. *Digital McLuhan: A Guide to the Information Millennium.* London: Routledge.
Luchmann, Niklas. 2000. *The Reality of the Mass Media.* Stanford: Stanford University Press.

Lutzka, Sven. 2006. Simulacra, Simulation and The Matrix. *Critical Studies* 29(1): 113–129.
Lyotard, Jean-Francois. 1984. *The Postmodern Condition: A Report on Knowledge*. Minneapolis: University of Minneapolis Press.
Marx, Karl. 1978. *The Marx-Engels Reader*. New York: W.W. Norton.
McLuhan, Marshall. 1962. *The Gutenberg Galaxy: The Making of Typographic Man*. London: Routledge.
_____. 1964. *Understanding Media: The Extensions of Man*. New York: McGraw Hill.
McLuhan, Marshall, and Quentin Fiore. 1967. *The Medium Is the Massage*. New York: Bantam Books.
Poulantzas, Nicos. 1975. *Classes and Contemporary Capitalism*. London: NLB.
Reed, Isaac, and Jeffrey Alexander. 2009. *Meaning and Method: The Cultural Approach to Sociology*. Boulder: Paradigm.
Ritzer, George. 1997. *Postmodern Social Theory*. New York: McGraw-Hill.
Rubenstein, David. 2001. *Culture, Structure and Agency: Toward a Truly Multidimensional Society*. Thousand Oaks, CA: Sage Publications.
Smith, Philip, ed. 1998. The New American Cultural Sociology: An Introduction. In *The New American Cultural Sociology*, 1–14. Cambridge: Cambridge University Press.
Sokal, Alan. 1996. Transgressing the Boundaries: Toward a Transformative Hermeneutics of Quantum Gravity. *Social Text* 46/47 (Spring/Summer): 217–252.
Sokal, Alan, and Jean Bricmont. 1998. *Fashionable Nonsense: Postmodern Intellectuals' Abuse of Science*. New York: Picador USA.
Stevenson, Nick. 1995. *Understanding Media Cultures: Social Theory and Mass Communication*. Thousand Oaks, CA: Sage Publications.
Thomas, William Irwin. 2002. *The Matrix and Philosophy: Welcome to the Desert of the Real*. Chicago: Open Court.
Turkle, Sherry, ed. 2009. *Simulation and Its Discontents*. Cambridge: MIT Press.
Wrong, Dennis. 1961. The Oversocialized Conception of Man. *American Sociological Review* 26 (2): 183–193.
Wuthnow, Robert, and Marsha Witten. 1988. New Directions in the Study of Culture. *Annual Review of Sociology*, 14: 49–67.
Zylinska, Joanna. 2002. *The Cyborg Experiments: The Extensions of the Body in the Media Age*. New York: Continuum.

5. CONSEQUENCES OF EXPERIENCE
The Place of Life Course and Biography in Theory Formulation

Keith Kerr

Theory can oftentimes be overly abstract and therefore, to borrow a phrase from William James, difficult from which to find a perch to begin to understand and translate its flow. This can especially be true for non-specialists and students just entering its exciting, yet difficult to navigate waters. However, one such perch that can begin to direct us down the currents various theories follow is a theoretician's biography. As will be discussed below, biographical examinations of theorists themselves, and especially their early childhood experiences, give great insight into the theoretical interests and concerns they focus on in their adult writings. As Alice Miller ([1979] 1997; 1991; 1986) tells us, to understand the child is to understand the adult, and to fully understand the adult, is to understand the psychological traumas suffered as a child. Just as psychoanalysis first demonstrated the revealing truths about artists and how almost as if by magic, their unconscious struggles "slip" into their art, to understand the theorist's biographical experiences is to understand the theories which stand in part as refractions of these very events. Such an approach is new in that it compliments existing tracts within the sociology of knowledge that look to understand knowledge development as a sociological outcome of historical and structural forces. Our current approach does not discount or deny these causative areas, but looks to integrate these with recognition of the unique place that individual experience and socialization plays underneath macro-level historical trajectories. Drawing off pragmatic influences within sociology, most notably William James and his influence on C. Wright Mills's methodology of sociological imagination, the following pages will argue that authors' experiences and life course matter in understanding their theory formulation.

This chapter will cover pertinent literature that lends itself to this conclusion, and then critically examine Karl Marx's and Max Weber's major theoretical contributions through early biographical experiences. To do an adequate job of demonstrating the causative mechanisms of theory formulation within early biography would require a book-length study. Space here does not permit for such depth. At the very least we can cover biographical vignettes and link major theoretical concerns to important events in a theorist's life. We can thus at least point a direction so as to begin to understand particular theories as an outgrowth of psychological traumas experienced by a given theorist.

Biography's Place in Theory Formation

For some time, the social sciences have widely recognized that childhood experiences impact later life outcomes and character formation (see especially Erikson [1950] 1986 and Riesman [1950] 1961). In more recent years, the link between biography and theory has gained some traction. John D. Brewer, in addition to exploring C. Wright Mills's biography as "a medium into understanding his whole vision of sociology," (Brewer 2005, 661; see also Brewer 2004; Kerr 2008) also pointed the direction for tying biography to theory formulation. According to Brewer, sociological research that centered on backstage/front-stage, private/public dichotomy and reflexivity while not speaking directly to the causative nature of biography, still provided the framework to connect the theoreticians' private life with their public work, and went a long way to demonstrate the link between the private and public self. More specific discussions about the causative nature of biography could be found in Alvin Gouldner's work on reflexivity in *The Coming Crisis of Western Sociology* (1971). He demonstrated biography's importance to understanding knowledge production, with his discussion of reflexivity as a needed component in sociological studies. Gouldner's formulation of reflexivity demonstrated that while it is easy to fall into the trap of believing that academics and intellectuals stand as detached objective observers of social reality, such observers also are affected by the very mechanisms they attempt to understand (Kerr 2008). Gouldner's position has strong connections to Bourdieu's (1992) discussions on reflexivity as a quasi-methodology to locate and expose contradictions and self-biases as they are projected onto one's academic work. To reverse this proposition was to state that the biases and contradictions found in an intellectual's work reflect the biases and contradictions within their selves.

The roots of these contradictions and biases could often found in childhood confusions. Social scientific literature has demonstrated that childhood experiences impact later life events. Perhaps one of the most prolific writers in this area, Alice Miller ([1979] 1997; 1991; 1986), has done much to show the causative connection between early childhood traumas and subsequent biographical trajectories, including intellectual work. Likewise, the entire psychoanalytic tradition demonstrated the importance of childhood experiences on the totality of the child's adult life.

While not a Freudian or psychoanalytical theorist proper, even C. Wright

Mills recognized the contributive link between early childhood experiences and the eventual adult. He wrote at the closing of his psychologically focused biographical essay on Max Weber, "Surely Weber's life illuminates the manner in which a man's relation to political authority may be modeled upon his relation to family disciplines" (Gerth and Mills [1946] 1958, 31).

But perhaps the most definitive and important sociological statement on biography's impact on later theoretical work comes from Mills's *The Sociological Imagination* ([1959] 1967). This still widely read treatise on sociological practice was on the forefront of the public-private debate within sociology. In demonstrating the link between "private troubles" and "public issues" Mills's work did much in tearing down the false dichotomy between the two arenas. It was Mills's proposition that sociological practice and the "quality of mind" it produced, existed at the causative and dynamic intersection of structure, history and biography.

This work stands as an important contribution for its refocus on individual biographies in knowledge production. As had been previously established by Karl Marx, Karl Mannheim and later Thomas Kuhn, knowledge and intellectual developments were largely outcomes of their contextual time and place. In other words, knowledge emerged in large part because it could not have emerged at another point in history. Yet Mills's writing on the sociological imagination posited the existential and less determinative biographical arena as equally important. It is not enough to understand the culture, social structure and historical currents as causative agents of order and action. Any number of individuals experience the pull and tug of what Emile Durkheim ([1895] 1982) called "social facts." Yet, within this shared milieu, new insights, new thoughts and new theories are developed, studied and focused on by a particular individual, while never imagined, much less cultivated, by others.

Mills contended that living within similar historical currents, and bending under the weight of shared structures, the unique and irreproducible arena of biographical experiences is a variable ignored at a great price. In his oft-overlooked appendix to *The Sociological Imagination* ([1959] 1967, 195) he writes,

> The most admirable thinkers within the scholarly community you have chosen to join do not split their work from their lives. They seem to not allow such dissociation, and they want to use each for the enrichment of the other.

He goes on to say (1967, 196):

> [Y]ou must learn to use your life experiences in your intellectual work.... To say that you can have "past experience" means, for one thing, that your past plays into and affects your present, and that it defines your capacity for future experience. As a social scientist, you have to control this rather elaborate interplay, to capture what you experience and sort it out.

If there was ever any question as to the causative nature of biography on subsequent intellectual work, Mills indicates otherwise, "[perhaps] everything you

write ... isn't about anything at all but your own god damned self" (quoted
from Gillam 1981, 43).

We now turn to specific theorists and the relationship between their early
childhood traumas and subsequent theories developed as adults. From at least
the time of Freud, we have known of the struggle that children endure in choos-
ing a life path vis-à-vis conflicts in their earliest relationships, namely with
their parents. This is ultimately at the heart of the Oedipus complex, and speaks
to the tension and contradiction all children face in both attempting to succumb
to their familial wishes and obligations and reject these at the same time in
order to claim an identity of their own.

Literature within cultural and personality studies have identified just such
psychological and cultural contradictions as the central place of self as process.
Thus David Riesman ([1950] 1961) wrote of being lonely in a crowd; Georg
Simmel ([1904] 1984) wrote of fashion's ability to both make one stand out and
fit in simultaneously; Erik Erikson ([1950] 1986) wrote of the child's need to
separate from the parental control vis-à-vis the parent's need to merge and
unite with the child; Karen Horney ([1937] 1964) wrote of ideologies of freedom
bound up with the American dream coupled against a competitive ethos that
demanded a loser, and Carl Jung ([1957] 1959) wrote of the multiple dualities
in self. Theoreticians, as do all children, struggle with the contradictions, tensions and traumas enacted within their earliest familial relationships. And it is
often the case that the choices these children make as adults, the ideas and pas-
sions that consume them, that is, their theories reveal both rejections of their
parents' life (a needed step for psychological maturity and health) as well as an
infantile attempt to reclaim the very life they are attempting to reject.

Thus for Karl Marx, destined to follow in his long line of rabbinical fore-
fathers and feeling a strong desire to please his father who converted to Christianity, we see both a rejection of religion coupled with secular writings that
are striking in both their religious overtones and Judeo-Christian themes. Likewise for Max Weber, the very relationship he endured with his overprotective
mother and his arguably overbearing and abusive father is found at the heart
of rationalizing theories he spent his life working out. As we will see, neither
overcomes the tension and contradiction between themselves and their early
parental relations. While their theories certainly stand on their own, the imprint
of their struggle to both break free and reclaim their earliest relationships are
still solidly anchored at the heart of their writings.

Karl Marx

Little is known about Karl Marx's earliest years, and for this reason, biographers have relied heavily on the larger body of knowledge revolving around
the immediate familial environment in which he was socialized. Karl Marx was

born in 1818 in the Catholic city of Trier to a Protestant father, descended from a long line of Jewish rabbis, the earliest of whom had taken up the rabbinical post in 1723, nearly a century before Marx was born. The post had been the family's ever since. Marx's grandfather and great-grandfather as well as his father's brother practiced the family vocation. Such was also the case on the mother's side of the family. His maternal grandfather was a rabbi, too (Berlin [1939] 1973; Kamenka 1983; Wheen 1999).

Despite the strong familial pull to follow in the family tradition, Herschel Levi Marx, Karl Marx's father, not only failed to continue his family tradition of rabbinical training, but also outright rejected it, becoming the first in the family to receive a secular education at his own expense. He later converted to Protestant Christianity when anti–Jewish laws went into effect in Trier. Some biographers indicate that his religious leanings were best summed up as "deistic" and his true conversion was away from religious mysticism of any brand, and into the rationalism sweeping through with the Enlightenment (Spargo 1910). However, as will briefly be discussed below, there is some disagreement on this point. Heinrich Marx, strongly attracted to the thrown of rationality which seemed to offer a path to equality, cut ties with his family, trained himself in the secular vocation of law, changed his surname to Marx and did what he could to assimilate into the dominant German culture, including becoming a member of the Casino-Club where members congregated to engage in political and intellectual debate (Berlin [1939] 1973; Wheen 1999).

One could surmise that such a conversion on the part of the father, especially when considered in the context of the family's rabbinical legacy and the larger social and religious forces at the center of the politics at the time, would have had an impact on the young Marx. But perhaps more convincing is the seeming struggle that played out within the family on this very issue. While Marx's father was baptized into the Evangelical church a year before Karl Marx's birth, Henriette, Marx's mother, did not make such a conversion at that time. Curiously, she did not even attend the ceremony. With Jewish lineage traced through the mother's side, Marx was born to a converted Christian father and a Jewish mother who had also come from a long line of rabbi's, and remained formally Jewish through the first seven years of Marx's life. It was not until 1824 that Karl Marx was baptized into the Evangelical church. Again, his mother resisted leaving the Jewish faith. It was not until 1825 that Henriette joined the rest of her family as a Christian of Jewish descent (Kamenka 1983).

Biographers of Marx seem to be in agreement that the struggles Marx's father and mother had with religion almost certainly had some lasting impact on the young Karl Marx, though what that impact was is in disagreement. With religious identity having perhaps even greater importance in one's life during the 1800s than it does at the present (especially in the context of Germany and the Jewish history there), Karl Marx was born to a father who attempted to skirt this social force as if it were clothes that could be changed for impression management purposes. His mother, conversely, resisted such a conversion for many years. Thus, Marx was born to a deist father who was attempting to "pass" or play down his Jewish and rabbinical roots to a Christian community dominated by Catholics, and to a Jewish mother who would not convert until some years later. Yet he was also living amongst and interacting daily with rabbi's who were also his family members.

Liebknecht (1901) as well as Dawson (1888) in both of their biographical accounts of Marx's life argue that the conversion by the father and eventually the rest of his family was one of necessity considering the plight of Jews in their home city of Trier. The young Marx, according to their accounts, was so offended by the forced conversion that his life must be understood as a revolt against the anti–Semitism that made him and his family to denounce their Jewish tradition (Liebknecht 1901; Dawson 1888). Conversely, Spargo (1910, 20) concludes differently, in that he saw Marx as thankful to his parents for "freeing him from the yoke of Judaism." What is of importance in the context of our current discussion, however, is not the disagreement but the agreement amongst biographers that Marx must be understood in the religious context of his family and early years.

Likewise, and recognizing the gap between what is known of the familial-religious context in which Marx was raised and actual events in Marx's early years, some biographers and most notably Kamenka (1983) and Berlin (1939) have attempted to draw more distinct connections between the Marx family's religious environment and its influence on the young Marx. These investigations have characterized Marx as being "aloof," "ambitious," "sharp-tongue," "unusual and difficult," and "intransigent." Kamenka (1983, xv) finds such traits as "evidence of an underlying insecurity and distress, so frequently linked with equivocal status." In close alliance to this position, Berlin (1939, 27) writes, "[Marx's] hostility to everything connected with religion ... may well be partly due to the peculiar and embarrassed situation in which such converts sometimes find themselves. Some escaped by becoming devout and even fanatical Christians, others by rebelling against all established religion. They suffered in proportion to their sensitiveness and intelligence."

Wheen (1999, 9) summed it up as such: "Marx's determined efforts to cut loose from the influence of his family, religion, class and nationality were never wholly successful.... Even in ripe maturity Marx insisted that that human beings cannot be isolated or abstracted from their social forebears." Marx was weighed down by generations before him; born a Jew to a Jewish mother and an heir to the rabbinical post at Trier, confronted with a father torn between a Judaic past, deist beliefs, and his increasing allegiance with rational and Enlightened thought he associated with the Protestant church (Kamenka 1983). As a child growing-up amidst this contradiction and confusion, it is little wonder that we would see his family's struggles reappearing in Marx's adult ideas.

Regarding the influence that Marx's father played in his life, Berlin writes ([1939] 1973, 35):

It seems certain that the father had a definite influence on his son's intellectual development. The elder Marx believed ... that man is by nature both good and rational, and that all that is needed to ensure the triumph of these qualities is the removal of unnatural obstacles from his path.... [W]ith their disappearance a new day would dawn for the human race, when all men would be equal.... Elements of this belief are clearly apparent in his son's social doctrine.... There is a definitive sense in which he remained both a rationalist and a perfectibilian to the end of his life.... [T]he principles of philosophical rationalism, which were planted in him by his father and his father's friends, performed a definitive work of inoculation, so that when later he encountered the metaphysical systems developed by the romantic school, he was saved from the total surrender to their fascination which undid so many of his contemporaries.

Although there is much truth to what Berlin states, there is also an over emphasis in his writing on Marx's eventual reliance on rationality. I would like to stress that Marxist and neo–Marxist intellectuals in their attempt to crown rationality as the ruler and savior of humanity failed to account for or even recognize the power that the irrational counter-current had in shaping social action (most notably their own ideological and dogmatic underpinnings). While Berlin was correct in the place and power that rational thought played in what I would call Marx's *faith* in progress, so too are Marx's biographers correct in the importance they find in Marx's early religious environment. As will be discussed below, irrational and religious undertones are clearly present alongside Marx's manifestly rational thought. Further, an over emphasis on the father's embrace of rationality against irrational mysticism and religion, does not account for the confused, yet important religious milieu in which Marx lived out his early years. The father certainly influenced him, but so did the century-old rabbinical legacy and his family's struggles with religious allegiance.

At the very least, if we are to accept Berlin's proposition, Marx's early interactions with his father strongly shaped a rationalistic and positivistic undertone to Marx's thought. It is likely that Marx's under-estimation of non-rational forces such as religious and ethnic-solidarity can be tied directly to his father's imprint on his life. His father, and as a consequence Marx himself, likely never saw this because of the lack of religious and ethnic solidarity felt by the father in changing religion in order to move up the social class ladder. Class becomes the driving force in his father's life at the expense of the "old" irrational religion and ethnic order of his father and father's father. As a consequence, we see Marx over-emphasize this in his own theories.

There is no doubt that on the surface, Marx had issues with the irrational force of religion. For Marx, the spectres he saw haunting Europe were very different from the spectres of past generations that Marx tells us about in *The Eighteenth Brumaire of Louis Bonaparte* that were haunting him. As he wrote, "the tradition of all the dead generations weighs like a mountain on the mind of the living" (quoted from Wheen 1999, 9). The struggle that was passed down to Marx from past generations and then from his father, the struggle between religious training and understanding of the world in an increasingly secular age plays itself out within Marx's thought and can be found in the religious undertones and illusions present within Marx's doggedly rational writings. Marx may have been an open atheist, but the past generations haunting him made their way into his writings none the less. Marx became a secular preacher to the down trodden with a secular message containing strong theological undertones and Judeo-Christian structures.

In the image and heritage of Abraham, Marx was attempting to lead the secular slaves of another era to a new land of milk and honey, that is, the secular land of communism. Certainly the Hegelian (and its associated mystical) undertones must have spoken to Marx on some level. For just as he rejected his father's religion and deism, his mother's religion, and the religion of his father's father while simultaneously taking up their themes, Marx accepted and rejected Hegelian dialectics. Marx both rejected his family's religious mysticism as embodied in beliefs in a more perfected afterlife — a belief system built into the Christian doctrine he and his immediate family were baptized into, and Hegel's mysticism as embodied in dialectical progression toward pure Being. Yet, Marx carves out his own secular brand of mysticism with the positing of a Utopian communist state at the end of History. In the end, despite what Marx proclaims to reject in spirit, he attempts to recreate in substance.

Perhaps the most evident and straightforward place where Marx attempts to reconcile the contradiction between his Judeo-Christian family and is atheist leanings, between his rabbinical heritage and his father's seemingly evangelical embrace of rationality, is in Marx's writings on alienation. In many ways the crux of Marx's theory rests on the problematic psychological outcomes of alienation. In very broad terms, Marx contended that capitalism was problematic in large part because it took free and autonomous humans and made them separated, estranged, apart from, and alien not only to each other and nature, but even to themselves (Marx [1844] 1983). This was the trajectory of human existence that Marx posited—from a perfected state of nature, to a problematic world where toil and estrangement dogged the human. It was Marx's fervent belief in what psychiatrists today would likely call narcissistic magical thinking, that the Dialectic's invisible hand (along with Marx's own writings) would eventually lead us out of an alienated existence and return us to the Utopian world he saw as the inevitable outcome of History.

Yet this story that he tells of going from Harmony to alienation and back again to Utopia, is not a new one. Joseph Campbell ([1949] 1973, 12) famously writes, "Full circle, from the tomb of the womb to the womb of the tomb, we come." Marx's story is what Campbell has identified as the root of all mythology (and mythology is only an antiquated religion). It is the story of ourselves: we are in a perfected state found in the womb only to be torn away to suffer the slings and arrows that life throws at us as we suffer individuation and the psychological turmoil that ensues, followed by an heroic attempt to enter back into the state of perfected union from which we came.

According to the Judeo-Christian story, humans originally find themselves in a womb-like existence void of form, in darkness and with only fluid. From there God carved out a perfected state for Man and eventually Woman. There, all is good. At one with nature, with each other and with God, humans live in world without want, without need, and without suffering. The story also reminds that there was only one rule — not to eat from the Tree of Knowledge. Yet, Man and Woman did, and in doing so, they set the stage for the endemic state of alienation we now find ourselves enduring. Suddenly recognizing their nudity and attempting to hide from God, they were cast from the Garden. Alienated from each other, from God, from nature and forced to toil upon the land, they were alienated from product and labor and barred from ever re-entering the Garden again.

For Marx, this lost Garden is no longer in the present. It is in the future, in another place and another time. It is still the hope of many, and was certainly the belief of Marx, that to the Garden we would return. From the Garden to an alienating world of sin and the promise of a perfected and holy state to come, Marx goes full circle. In his fervent embrace of rationality, and equally fervent rejection of religion, Marx gives us a mythical and religious story cloaked in secular language. In doing so, we see that Marx and his theories are still being driven by the early tension present in his childhood. His rabbinical heritage and his father's strong rational imprint coupled with the Christian influence are never quite overcome for Marx. Like his mother before him, Marx, symbolically and unconsciously, seems to be resisting conversion. In many ways, Marx's writings can be read as the workings of a young boy trying to make sense of his impulse to both separate and reconnect with a family. This is the essential and underlying tension that acts as a driving force through his writings.

As Marx famously writes in *Critique of Hegel's Philosophy of Right*, "Religious suffering is at one and the same time the *expression* of real suffering and a protest against real suffering. Religion is the *sigh* of the oppressed creature, the heart of a heartless world and the soul of soulless conditions. It is the *opium* of the people" (Marx [1844b] 1983, 60). There is little doubt that the story of alienation is the story of religion and mythology. In Marx's attack on and rejection of religion he was also embracing his early traumatic and confusing relationship with the very subject. In his writings' straddling of rationality and irrational religious undertones, we see playing out before us the attempts of a young Marx to make sense of a family history that pulled him in opposite directions—one toward the Judaic mysticism of his rabbinical heritage, and the other toward the rational and reasoned thought that was the legacy left to him by the father.

Those who have taken up the banner of communism have often done so out of altruism, fraternity and ideals of equality. The seeming promise of a way to a classless and free society and a perfected world is a strong one and a noble calling. However, just as was the case with the crusades of many religious movements, the callings of our better angels often become the callings of our darkest demons. The promise of Marx and communism to lead the slaves of capitalism to a Utopian paradise on earth gave birth to the Stalins and the Maos of the world. Just as the crusaders for Christ, Allah or Yahweh often had turned into instruments of nefarious doings at the hands of those best understood as devils, so too has communism followed the same trajectory. In this way, the religious undertones found within Marx's writings are not so hidden after all. Obscured, defended and symbolically cloaked, they have not altogether disappeared. Still visible to our unconscious, the power and fervor of the latently irrational spectre within the human psyche and human culture that religion represents, maintains its powerful force within Marx's manifestly secular writings.

Max Weber

The link between Weber's biography and his later intellectual work has previously been noted even if downplayed by at least some biographical statements. Lewis Coser (1971, 234) noted that "[Weber's] ambivalence toward authority ... and his fascination with the topic in his writings, his double concern with rationality and the ethic of responsibility, his attraction to inner-worldly asceticism and his partial identification with the heroic lifestyles of charismatic leader — these and many other themes in his work have their source in his biography." Mills more succinctly makes the same point in his biographical essay when he tells us "if we are to understand Weber's biography as a whole, we must examine his tensions and his repeated psychic disturbances" (Gerth and Mills, [1946] 1958, 26).

Weber was born in Germany on April 21, 1864. He is the seemingly rare theorist who did not have close family ties to a religious leader. This does not mean that religion did not play a role in his early life and had some influence on his later writing. Weber was born and raised by a successful Protestant family who, on his father's side descended from a line of entrepreneur refugees of Catholic persecution. His mother's side was of similar stock, that is, prosperous merchant Protestants (Weber [1926] 2007). There are strong connections between his family history and his work in *The Protestant Ethic and the Spirit of Capitalism* ([1904] 2001) that looked at the development of capitalism and acquisition of wealth as tied to an emerging Protestant culture and break from the Catholic Church.

In relation to our current aim, however, a more direct tie can be seen between his relationship to his estranged parents and his attempts to work through this. The emotional struggle their relationship posed for him played itself out in his later theories. Weber's father was not an emotional man in his interactions with his family, nor was he religious. A romantic intellectual, he worked as a teacher and later a civil servant. Weber's father has been described as "domineering" (Gerth and Mills [1946] 1958, 28), an "inflexible disciplinarian" and "authoritarian" (Coser 1971, 236). Though Weber identified in his college years with his father, it was the mother whom he would eventually be drawn to.

Contrasted against the father, Weber's mother was devoted, if not over-bearing, and took great care of the physical, emotional and spiritual lives of her offspring. She suffered the deaths of two children, and with seeming little emotional support or even recognition of this loss from her "hedonistic" (235) husband. This only heightened her sense of duty to Weber and his surviving siblings. With a husband who likely shared none of her religious sentiments, she was both faithful and pious in her Protestant Christian convictions (Weber [1926] 2007), and partly as a result, learned to dutifully endure under the heavy hand and absent heart of Weber's father.

Weber's wife perhaps best sums up the parental situation facing the young Weber ([1926] 2007, 62):

> In those years it was not clear whether [Weber] would decide in favor of his father's or his mother's type. *He already had an obscure feeling that such a choice would have to be made someday....* There was his mother, in whom the powers of the gospel were active, to whom loving service and self-sacrifice to the last were second nature, but who lived in accordance with burdensome heroic principles, performed her ... daily tasks with ... moral energy ... and quietly placed every significant event in the context of eternity. She was dynamic in all she did, energetic in coping with her every day chores, joyously open to everything beautiful in life, and had a liberating laugh. But, every day she plunged into the depths and was anchored to the supernatural.

By contrast, Weber's wife described the father as such (2007, 63):

> [He] was not good at being a "good companion" to [young Weber]. He was too much the traditional, patriarchal paterfamilias, too convinced of his own superiority and his inalienable right to respect and authority. Some of his peculiarities—such as the way he let his wife wait on him — drew criticism.

These two extremes and Weber's alternating association with each were an important emotional struggle in Weber's development, and a struggle he almost certainly never overcame. A sickly and weak child described as a "delicate" "mother's boy" (Weber [1926] 2007, 63 and Gerth and Mills [1946] 1958, 29), Weber attempted to compensate for his feminine tendencies by adopting an uber-masculine, machismo-like persona once at college. In less than a year Weber grew in size from an inordinate amount of beer drinking, and returned home for his first visit with a scar across his face — a result of one of the several duels he engaged in. The resulting shock to his mother upon his appearance resulted in a sharp slap to his face. As depicted in C. Wright Mills's biographical essay on Weber, "The two models of identification and their associated values, rooted in the mother and father, never disappeared from Max Weber's inner life" (Gerth and Mills, [1946] 1958, 28–9). Nor did they disappear from his outward academic work.

Weber's biography is infused and his theory of rationalization is propelled by a dualistic construction that is a projection of his childhood traumas: the masculine ideal of rationality coming to dominate and consume the feminine ideals of the irrational, charismatic and subjective component of the social human. In terms borrowed from Talcott Parsons, this is the dominance of the instrumental over the expressive. For Parsons, the expressive role was associated with the "feminine" and was geared toward emotional support, care giving and mothering; whereas the instrumental was associated with "masculine," rational and goal-oriented action (Parsons 1937; 1951; Parsons and Bales 1955). Within Weber's theories of rationalization then we see the re-creation and compulsion to repeat the family dramas of Weber's "domineering" and non-religious civil-servant father and his emotional, if not literal enslavement of the house-bound, religious, sensitive and emotional mother.

Undoubtedly, the most evident theme central to most Weberian pieces is rationalization. Best understood as the tendency for rational thought, often in the form of rules, methods and procedures, coming to dominate all aspects of social life at the expense of irrational motivators of action (tradition, emotion, etc.), Weber dealt with this theme in most of his major writings. Amongst several main themes, *The Protestant Ethic and the Spirit of Capitalism* ([1904] 2001) looks at the rationalizing trajectory of spiritual life and its conversion to rigid and rationalized procedures that led to the acquisition of wealth and the foundation of economic principles surrounding capitalism.

In the discussion on authority types Weber ([1925] 1978) analyzed the increasing rationalization of legitimate authority from the religious and subjectively oriented charismatic and traditional type, to the rational-legal type present in contemporary Western culture. This type of authority is marked by impersonality, strict rules and regulations. In a direct reflection of the dominant and strict style of his father-bureaucrat, we see the dramas of a youthful home played out here. The emotionally overbearing and religiously obsessed mother who refused to allow the paid help to do chores or work around the house so as she could take a break ran the household during the day only to have her authority supplanted each evening with the return of the strict, non-religious bureaucrat-father who biographers tell us was an unemotional disciplinarian. We see the same theme existing and paralleled in both Weber's early life and his later writings: irrational motivation of action guiding legitimate authority (charismatic and traditional) only to be replaced and surpassed in power by the unstoppable rationalization of authority into rational-legal structures. What Weber recognized in the overarching power trajectory within Western culture was achieved by the recognition and struggle with just such a trajectory in his own young home-life.

Likewise, in his discussions on bureaucracy (Weber [1925] 1978) we see an emphasis on the growing dominance of rationalized institutions with a hierarchical and goal-oriented focus, at the expense of value-oriented organization centered on religion, charisma and tradition. It is here that we see Weber finally choose sides in the rift between his mother and father. For it were his assessment and his fear that despite the power and dominance of the rational, instrumental components within culture and the efficiency thus resulting, this came at an expense. Trapped and imprisoned in a cold and impersonal world of rules and regulation that he famously describes as a "polar night of icy darkness" Weber seems to almost mourn this very entrapment as a proxy for his mother's imprisonment in her equally impersonal, hierarchical and controlling marriage.

It need be noted here that just as in his writings in his life, too, he was concerned with the emotional toil such a situation would wrack. At the age of 31, Weber confronted his father regarding his controlling and cold treatment of his mother. In a near violent clash, Weber threw his father out of his house and threatened to cut ties with him completely unless he allowed Weber's mother the freedom to travel and visit Weber alone in the future. The father died just weeks after this confrontation. Consumed with guilt, it would be five years before Weber recovered from the resulting psychological breakdown (Weber [1926] 2007; Gerth and Mills [1946] 1958; Coser 1971). We see clear parallels to this play themselves out in his later theoretical writings with his concern for the instrumental and rational growth coming to create an "iron cage" that killed off the emotional, religious and culturally symbolic feminine expressive motivators of action.

Conclusion

While our discussion has hinted at the causative biographical factors in theory development, undoubtedly macro-social and historical forces are also of utmost importance. Of late, however, and in a fit of revisionist-led historical hindsight, sociology has re-written many of its "greats" to be macro-level theorists. Most were not. Durkheim we are told focused on collectives, order, cohesion or lack thereof. Yet he also spoke of anomie, which when wrestled from its widely misunderstood interpretation as a state of normlessness (and hence something located in the social), we find an internally and psychologically located "infinity of desires" located within the individual (Mestrovic 1992; [1988] 1993). Likewise, while Marx wrote extensively on political-economy, superstructures and other macro-level systems, he too was concerned with psychological repercussions within the individual, such as alienation from self. Weber too, despite sociology's overemphasis on his macro-level works dealing with religion, economics, bureaucracy and rationalizing tendencies warned us to not lose our understanding of the unique and non-rational individuals existing under such structures.

While undoubtedly sociology and especially American sociology has moved toward micro-level studies over the last several decades, this does not erase the fact that we are re-focusing our theorists of old in exactly the opposite direction. Studies within Symbolic Interactionism still heavily influenced by Erving Goffman's (1959; 1963) work often times paint a seeming narcissistic false self that acts out, role-plays, manipulates and seems to be constructed with a plasticity tied to the social environment of the present, that has no tie to an authentic and biographically anchored self. Postmodern theories have begun in denying the self's existence altogether.

But biography matters. For biography is the direct result of social and historical milieus as filtered and interpreted through socialization process and imprinted within us as the uniqueness of self. We face the world anew at each moment, but we do so with baggage. Just as our place in history, various structural positions and culture filter, weigh down and direct our actions and ideas, so too do our unique past. Theorists and intellectuals, despite many claims to stand as detached and "objective" observers, are not exempt from shaping mechanisms. They too are influenced by their experiences and subjective interpretations of their biography. Theoretical ideas emerge from the lives of particular theorists because as such they could not have emerged from any other biographical life. To sum up — experience has intellectual consequences.

References

Berlin, Isaiah. [1939] 1973. *Karl Marx: His Life and Environment.* Oxford: Oxford University Press.

Bourdieu, Pierre, and Loïc JD Wacquant. 1992. *An Invitation to Reflexive Sociology.* Chicago: University of Chicago Press.

Brewer, John. 2004. Imagining the Sociological Imagination: The Biographical Context of a Sociological Classic. *The British Journal of Sociology* 55(3): 317–34.

_____. 2005. The Public and Private in C. Wright Mill's Life and Work. *Sociology* 39 (4): 661–77.

Campbell, Joseph. [1949] 1973. *The Hero with a Thousand Faces.* Princeton: Princeton University Press.

Coser, Lewis. 1971. *Masters of Sociological Thought: Ideas in Historical and Social Context.* New York: Harcourt Brace Jovanovich.

Dawson, William. 1888. *German Socialism and Ferdinand Lassalle: A Biographical History of German Socialistic Movements During this Century.* London: Swan Sonnenschein and Co.

Durkheim, Emile. [1895] 1982. *Durkheim: The Rules of Sociological Method and Selected Texts on Sociology and its Method.* New York: Free Press.

Erikson, Erik. [1950] 1986. *Childhood and Society.* New York: W.W. Norton.

Gerth, Hans, and C. Wright Mills. [1946] 1958. *From Max Weber: Essays in Sociology.* New York: Oxford University Press.

Goffman, Erving. 1959. *The Presentation of Self in Everyday Life.* New York: Anchor Books.

_____. 1963. *Behavior in Public Places: Notes on the Social Organization of Gatherings.* New York: Free Press.

Gouldner, Alvin. 1971. *The Coming Crisis of Western Sociology*. New York: Avon.

Horney, Karen. [1937] 1964. *The Neurotic Personality of Our Time*. New York: W.W. Norton.

Jung, Carl. [1957] 1959. *The Undiscovered Self*. Translated by R.F.C. Hull. New York: Mentor Books.

Kamenka, Eugene, ed. 1983. Introduction. In *The Portable Karl Marx*, xlvi–li. New York: Penguin Books.

Kerr, Keith. 2008. *Postmodern Cowboy: C. Wright Mills and New 21st-Century Sociology*. Boulder: Paradigm.

Liebknecht, Wilhelm. 1901. *Karl Marx: Biographical Memoirs*. Chicago: Charles H. Kerr and Company.

Marx, Karl. [1844a] 1983. Alienated Labour. In *The Portable Karl Marx*, ed. Eugene Kamenka, 131–46. New York: Penguin Books.

_____. [1844b] 1983. Contribution to the Critique of Hegel's Philosophy of Right: Introduction. In *The Portable Karl Marx,* ed. Eugene Kamenka, 115–124. New York: Penguin Books.

Mestrovic, Stjepan. 1992. *Durkheim and Postmodern Culture*. New York: Aldine de Gruyter.

_____. [1988] 1993. *Emile Durkheim and the Reformation of Sociology*. Lanham, MD: Rowman and Littlefield.

Miller, Alice. 1986. *Thou Shalt Not Be Aware: Society's Betrayal of the Child*. Ontario, Canada: Meridian Books.

_____. 1991. *The Untouched Key: Tracing Childhood Trauma in Creativity and Destructiveness*. New York: Anchor Books.

_____. [1979] 1997. *The Drama of the Gifted Child: The Search for the True Self*. New York: Perennial.

Mills, C. Wright. [1959] 1967. *The Sociological Imagination*. New York: Oxford University Press.

Parsons, Talcott. 1937. *The Structure of Social Action*. Glencoe, IL: Dorsey Press.

_____. 1951. *The Social System*. Glencoe, IL: Free Press.

Parsons, Talcott, and Robert Bales. 1955. *Family, Socialization and Interaction*. Glencoe, IL: Free Press.

Riesman, Daniel. [1950] 1961. *The Lonely Crowd: A Study of the Changing American Character*. New Haven: Yale University Press.

Simmel, Georg. [1904] 1984. *Georg Simmel on Individuality and Social Forms*. Chicago: University of Chicago Press.

Spargo, John. 1910. *Karl Marx: His Life and Work*. New York: B. W. Huebsch.

Weber, Marianne. [1926] 2007. *Max Weber: A Biography*. New Brunswick, NJ: Transaction Press.

Weber, Max. [1925] 1978. *Economy and Society*. Berkeley: University of California Press.

_____. [1904] 2001. *The Protestant Ethic and the Spirit of Capitalism*. London: Routledge Classics.

Wheen, Francis. 1999. *Karl Marx: A Life*. New York: W.W. Norton.

6. CRITICAL SPACE
Divisions, Ambiguities, and Conceptions
of Space in Social Theory
Patricia Snell

The boundary is not a spatial fact with sociological consequences, but a sociological fact that forms itself spatially. — Simmel 1903, 143

What is sociological about spatial context? This is a question which the original founders of sociology attempted to answer in multiple ways and which many prominent social thinkers continue to ponder. However, much of contemporary sociological empirical work is either implicitly aspatial or lacks adequate attention to the spatial patterning present in the data. Andrew Abbott (2001) argues that space and time are critical to sociological pursuits because context is generally where the conventions of societal activity can be examined. He conceptualizes space and time as interrelated tools to understanding society and states that context is always inherent to sociological studies, and it can either be studied in the foreground or background, depending on the analysis. He argues that sociological analyses are balanced when they foreground and background various aspects over time, but the field becomes unbalanced when a level of analysis is continuously only foregrounded or backgrounded. Andrew Sayer (2000) states that many social scientists fail to recognize the extent of abstraction from space in current analysis and equates this to taking apart a machine and putting the parts back together incorrectly. He specifies a divide between, on the one hand, an assumption of aspatial social process and, on the other hand, a spatial fetishism. The former ignores the level of space as an important aspect of social phenomenon, operating under the assumption that space has no involvement in what constitutes it or what is constituted by it. The latter focuses entirely on the level of space, with an assumption that space has some sort of societal power regardless of what constitutes it. Sayer argues that space is most commonly mentioned but never accounted for, inadvertently studied, or simply not addressed. He states that space, time, and matter cannot be abstracted from one without unknowingly abstracting from the others. Sayer argues that time has recently begun to be added back in to current social scientific pursuits, while space yet remains a problematic abstraction that causes a reduction in the complexity of society.

Despite arguments for the importance of accounting for space in social theory and research, and despite the fact that the typical social scientist would not deny the importance of space, it is unclear what it means to adequately account for space and what constitutes spatially-based sociology. This chapter explores how space has been conceptualized in social science. It includes a formulation of what space is, what it is constituted by, what it helps to form, and how it matters for the study of society. I use a critical realist approach to construct a more coherent theory of space that helps to clarify how social science can employ a critical conception of space.

Fragmentation and Ambiguities in Conceptions of Space

A survey of relatively current conceptions of space turns up a fragmented approach to understandings of space both within and across the areas of current social theory and empirical investigations. A recent symposium on the concept of the "ghetto" published in *City & Community* in 2008, for example, reveals a dizzying jumble of perspectives on how to conceive of this spatially-based concept. Some of the authors attribute the origination of the term "ghetto" with the Chicago school, others to an Italian origin. Some state that the ghetto is about involuntary segregation, others that barrios— involving voluntary segregation — are similar to the ghetto. Some talk about neighborhood effects, while others state that neighborhoods are imagined communities. Some say the concept of a ghetto is U.S.–centric, others that it applies beyond the United States. Some argue that a ghetto is defined by poverty levels reaching a certain threshold, while others state it is an ideal type that never fully exists in reality. Some state that the concept of the ghetto is a helpful sociological tool, others that it reduces non-processes, actors and choices, while yet others say it represents precisely those concepts. The one element that all of these authors seem to agree on is that the ghetto represents some sort of concentration, which is an inherently spatial concept. Despite this fundamental conceptual thread, there is very little agreement on the way to employ and investigate this spatial concept. What explains this fragmentation in conceptions of space?

There currently exists a divide in approaches to understanding spatiality as (1) discrete, absolute, and purely material, or (2) relational, symbolic, and ideational (Del Casino and Jones 2007). Two extreme versions of spatial conceptions focus either exclusively on space as *only* material or *only* ideational. Primarily material orientations are exampled by the type of neighborhood effects literature summarized by Lee et al. (2008) which reduces space to census tract variables and drops them into standard regression analysis. These approaches take space seriously as an important element of social investigation but have developed from a political economy type of perspective, which reduces space to merely the material configurations of production. The extreme version of the ideational approach is exemplified in the types of human geography that emphasize the importance of culture and perception to the point of morphing into studies of identity (see chapters in Benko and Strohmayer 1997). These studies take meaning and interaction seriously but have lost the importance of history and, ironically, geography in their conception of "existential spatiality."

Less extreme conceptions of space do not explicitly articulate space as only material or only ideational. However, the ambiguities inherent in these approaches, and the dialogues between them, highlight the lack of balance between the two elements of space. Such ambiguities are evidenced in the literature on social exclusion and segregation. Gough, Eisenschitz, and McCulloch (2006, xxi) state that there is an "active role of space, place, scale and distance in creating exclusion." They describe a locational disadvantage as composed of a new underclass who, in addition to living in poverty, are excluded from many social activities and live in concentrations of social problems. The inequality embedded in social exclusionary spaces is then one of inferior environments which disproportionately affect the life outcomes of residents. Wilson and Taub (2006, 161) state that "national racial tensions cannot be disassociated from tensions originating in neighborhood social dynamics." They argue that neighborhood contact over time leads to distinctions in traditions, values, beliefs, worldviews, language, and skills. This in turn causes lower chances for economic and social advancement.

Though this view seems to incorporate some elements of both material and ideational conceptions of space, Wilson argued in previous work (1978; 1996) that the concentrations of destitution found in African American segregation are the product of out-migration of middle class African Americans and the disappearance of work from these areas. Thus, Wilson highlights the importance of economic factors causing the importance of spatial configurations. Massey and Denton (1993) conceptualize Wilson as focusing only on the economics, or material, to the neglect of segregation as a matter of racism. And in fact, Wilson seemingly struggles with some ambiguity around this when he writes (quoted in Massey and Denton 1993, 140),

> Despite the fact that racial friction is more a symptom than a cause of the declining central city, the urban crisis and the proposed solutions advanced in different quarters (for example, black political control of the city, school desegregation, and residential integration) are often directed at altering the patterns of racial interaction or dominance. Nonetheless, the way that urban families are affected by or are responding to the problems of urban living are more a function of their economic class position that of their racial status.

Before the writing of Wilson, Taeuber and Taeuber (1965, 95) stated, "Clearly, residential segregation is a more tenacious social problem than economic discrimination. Improving the economic status of Negroes is unlikely by itself to alter prevailing patters of racial segregation." Thus, space-interested researchers can generally be seen as taking one of the two extremes of ideational versus material conceptions of space or as existing in some ambiguity in between the two conceptions. Though many space-interested scholars do not take one of the two extreme positions, the existence of the extremes confuses important elements of a theory of space and thereby creates prevalent and persistent ambiguities in accounts of space. To better formulate a theory of space, we thus must turn further back in time to examine more classic approaches.

Chicago School's Spatial Innovations

The Chicago school of sociology is often credited with creating what became the subfield of urban sociology (e.g. Tonkiss 2005). Their focus on investigating the city is frequently touted as providing one of the first explicitly spatial explorations in sociology. Martin Bulmer (1984) described the scholars of the Chicago school as exploring the city as a social laboratory. Their investigations relied heavily on the use of maps, and they charted natural environments and measured the clustering of social patterns. Providing the impetus for the later segregation studies, the Chicago school sociologists showed that slums were the products of processes of social disorganization and therefore were more a result of structural rather than individual-level attributes. In the time period in which the scholars were writing, this was an important finding to establish the existence of social pathologies and inferior situations, rather than inferior people (Faris 1967).

The direct connection between the work of the Chicago sociologists and the discussion carried forward through segregation scholars, such as Taeuber & Taeuber, Wilson, and Massey & Denton, can be seen in a study conducted by Albert Hunter (1971), which extended the data analyzed by the early Chicago school scholars forward. After examining Census data through 1960, he concluded that "family status as a factor decreases in its explanatory power while racial-ethnic status becomes a more powerful factor in explaining variations in the composition of Chicago's local communities. Economic status as the principal factor remains relatively constant in the degree of variability which it explains, but its position relative to the other two increases due to their shifting explanatory power" (Hunter 1971, 443). He conducted the study to determine whether the ecological patterns that the earlier Chicago school scholars found still held thirty years later. His findings indicate that the ecological pattern is much more varied at any particular time than it is over the course of many years. Thus, while scholars could discredit ecological theorizing with empirical evidence if they looked at any particular decade, the pattern was true over the longer term.

The Chicago school scholars are often remembered for creating ecological research (e.g. York and Mancus 2009). Robert Faris (1967, 51) stated that there was an "unprecedented surge of highly original research in urban ecology. The scholarly output in these fields was in fact so abundant that the department unintentionally and perhaps unwillingly acquired the reputation of almost exclusively concentrating on spatial distributions." Ecological research became known as the hallmark approach of the school. This approach to understanding space was based on a biological conceptualization of the city as an organism which contained particular parts that functioned in various ways in order to maintain the larger whole (Levine 2004). This allowed social phenomenon, such as attitudes and beliefs, to be investigated in the same way a biologist would understand the function of organs within an organism. They were seen as having a purpose and a function that could only be understood within the larger whole. The organism metaphor is seen as having developed also due to the discovery of natural selection, and the idea of "metabolism" meant that certain societal occurrences, such as ghettos and slums, were the city's way of absorbing and processing social groups.

Park and Burgess often wrote about the idea of the city as an organism (e.g. Park 1921). Park (1925) described it as originating from the discovery of plant communities which led first to ecological studies and then to the idea of human ecology. Social scientists and theorists since Park and Burgess have thus mostly understood them as articulating a specifically material version of space that strongly emphasized structural processes and did not adequately account for the more ideational aspects of culture, identity, and perception. However, the organism was meant by the Chicago school sociologists to merely be a metaphor of social life (Gross 2004). And as Morris Janowitz (1967) explained, much of the contemporary arguments regarding urban sociology involve over-simplifications of the Chicago school, due to a reading of secondary interpretations of the scholars and not the original texts from the scholars themselves. In original text, Park (1925), for instance, stated that human ecology was to be considered separate from geography or even human geography. In a footnote, he (1925, 3) specified:

> Geographers are probably not greatly interested in social morphology as such. On the other hand, sociologists are. Geographers, like historians, have been traditionally interested in the actual rather than the typical. Where are things actually located? What did actually happen? These are the questions that geography and history have sought to answer.

This quote highlights the fact that one of the main scholars attributed with taking a materialist approach to space is in fact setting human ecology apart from a purely material study.

In *The City*, Park and Burgess (1925) described spatial proximity and neighborhood contact as constituting the most basic forms of association, which are founded in local sentiments. They stated, "Physical and sentimental differ-

ences reinforce each other" (Park and Burgess 1925, 10). They described the
spatial locality of the city as consisting of processes, human nature, transporta-
tion, geographical, ecological, communication, habits and customs, and moral
organization. Even one of the self-identified human ecologists, R. D. McKenzie
(1925) specifically stated that conceiving of location as place on the earth is a
geographical explanation, while recognizing it as a position within interacting
human beings and institutions is an ecological perspective. Therefore, space
was constantly in a state of change because of the forces of both the environment
and cultures. Burgess (1925) himself stated that while the Chicago scholars
used to be more focused on an organism metaphor, they had increasingly led
away from this conceptualization to more heavily emphasize the role of the
economy and culture. And Park (1925) also discussed how space cannot be simply quantified as in the natural sciences and needs instead to account for change
that can occur through communication across space which forms new habits
and memories. Physical distance is only important, then, insofar as it causes
social distance.

Less recognized was a component of the Chicago school investigations
which explored space as also associational (Tonkiss 2005). In *A Social Philosophy
of the City*, Nicholas Spykman (1925) described the connection between spatial
proximity and social distance as an outcome of the increasing move to city life.
The fact that people need to relate to each other in closer physical distances
begins to decrease the level of moral and aesthetic values that still hold true.
Park (1925) described this by stating that segregation establishes "moral distances." He described space as therefore enabling individual action while simultaneously at times acting as a barrier to communication. He saw struggles
over space as ultimately struggles for status. Even the concentric circles view
advanced by Park and Burgess (1925) was not meant by them to be taken literally
as exact mapping of material processes. Rather, they meant the circles to represent ideal types that would never be fully seen in any particular city (Bulmer
1984).

Andrew Abbott (1997) described the Chicago school as emphasizing context to the point of creating a "contextualist paradigm." The goal was to examine
social phenomenon in relation to each other in physical space. Though there
were some tendencies present to investigate space as purely a physical environment and as equivalent to the natural sciences, there was also a strong tendency
toward ideational approaches to space as communication and association. They
saw individuals as both participating in constructing, and being constructed
by, their social environments. As North (1925, 233) stated,

> If it is true that the city is the most characteristic phenomenon of modern life it
> is because in the city the outstanding forces of present-day society are working
> out their logical consequences in more complete form than elsewhere. Here the
> operations of capitalism, mobility of population, democracy, individualism, and
> group action are all found in full swing. And here are displayed their end results

in the extremes of luxury and poverty, of civic virtue and crime, of stable social organization and appalling disorganization.

Thus, the Chicago school researchers in fact had two differing conceptualizations of space. Some focused on purely material conceptualizations, some on more ideational, and many saw important combinations of both. But again, this lack of a clear and explicitly articulated theory of space caused confusion of how to understand the various approaches.

Conceptions of Space in Classical Sociological Theory

Though they often tended to focus more on time dimensions than spatial, many of the classical theorists either specifically explicated space in their theories or had spatial elements implicit throughout their work (York and Mancus 2009; Lobao, Hooks, and Tickamyer 2007). The most popular work of Max Weber, for example, is dedicated to understanding what social processes differentiate the development of one global region, the West, from another, the Occident (Weber 2002). And Karl Marx focused on the nation as a unit of analysis and theorized modes of production, which inherently had a geographical component to it during industrialization (Marx 1978). Emile Durkheim also had spatial elements to his work, by explicating divisions of labor and comparing cultural practices of indigenous societies with those of industrialized societies (Durkheim 1997; 1995). And, as described further below, Simmel and Tönnies both explicitly conceptualized spatial dimensions in their work (Simmel 1971; Tönnies 2002). The classical social theorists also articulated conceptions of space that often accounted for both material and ideational elements. Though Marx is typically characterized as focusing only on materialism, he viewed it in the form of labor, as a dialectical movement with thinking and representation (Fracchia 1991). Durkheim's concept of social morphology contained both material/geographical and ideational/metaphorical conceptions of space (Ethington 1997).

The Chicago school of sociologists drew heavily from the work of Georg Simmel (Ethington 1997; Tonkiss 2005). Prior to the Chicago school Simmel articulated space as a reflection of and basis for social relations. He thought of space as a condition, on the one hand, and as a symbol on the other. To Simmel, space and time were inextricably linked. Space was not some abstract force which is removed from people but is inherently constituted by people and their choices, interactions, and perceptions. It is the across-time element of space, in that it exists beyond the lifespan of any particular person, which causes people to inherit spatial configurations that were not created by them and yet influence them. Simmel conceptualized space in a way that drew attention to the tension between social space that occurs in the external physical environment and that which occurs internally to bodies and minds. He saw the process of connection across space as part of the same process which also creates separation across space, and did not believe one was possible without the other.

As Andrez Zieleniec (2007) described it, space for Simmel was important to understanding human experience because it was the "where" in which social activities and interactions occur. Simmel saw space as both determining of and constructed by social relations. All social interactions therefore have a spatial dimension, and space is a necessary but not sufficient condition for what he called "sociation." The uniqueness of places, the fact that boundaries of space are both real/fixed and socially constructed, as well as the fact that social forms can become fixed in space through meaning and emotional attachment, all specifies space as both real/material and imagined/ideational. "Cities in this sense are one of the best examples of the idea that things which are real are also imagined. Social structures, realities and practices are linked in sometimes complicated ways to symbolic urban forms. Cities, after all, are dense material realities which also take their shape in memory and perception" (Tonkiss 2005, 2). To Simmel, space was important to study precisely because it was the location of the interaction between the material and ideational.

This idea was expressed perfectly in the metaphors of a door and a bridge (Simmel 1909). The irony of the bridge is that it symbolizes the human desire to connect two natural environments to each other, and yet in determining that two areas need to be connected to one another their separation must first be identified and recognized. Thus, the bridge automatically symbolizes both connection and separation. This is a human idea — things are separated and therefore need to be connected — which becomes manifested in physical reality. From then on, the physical reality of the bridge is no longer an idea that is up to any one individual to have or not, but is a reality which confronts any individual who sees or crosses the bridge with the notion that that which the bridge connects was formerly separated. Simmel described path-building as a process specific to humans. Animals travel across their own paths, but the idea of creating and "freezing" a set path for others to follow is only seen in humans.

The door also symbolizes the interaction between the imagined and the real, as well as the human desire to separate and connect. The door links the space between the inside, which is designated as for human beings, and the outside, which is designated as for all the rest of nature. The door becomes a physical reality that causes this separation (from outer) and connection (within), and it also retains its symbolism as transcending the space within and the space without. Precisely because it can be opened, it has a different symbolism than a wall and communicates a stronger sense of isolation from what is without. For Simmel (1909, 174) space is inextricably a form (material) and a symbol (ideational).

Simmel also theorized the importance of space through a focus on proximity and distance (e.g. Simmel 1901; 1903; 1909; Frisby & Featherstone 1997; Simmel & Levine 1971). This type of "external circumstances" describes where people

stand in relation to one another. He stated that convictions, character, and relationships are shaped by the configurations of their spatial contact. Simmel conceived of communication as having the capacity to cross social distance, and
therefore reduce the effect of geographical distance or proximity. But because
social unity occurs through regularities, institutions, and written communication, spatial locations facilitate and act as barriers to the ability of communication
to cross spatial distance. It is the interaction of spatial proximity or distance and
the extent of communication that creates the quality of social relationships.

Thus, if individuals are based near to each other but do not regularly converse, as is often the case in work environments, then their relationship to each
other will be abstract. The more the individuals converse, the more they will
have a consciousness of unity that is not abstract but strongly unique and personal. Their experience of closeness through their senses creates the ability to
recollect communication within their bodily experiences of hearing, speaking,
smelling, and seeing. Thus, spatial proximity and distance is experienced
through the senses, and the nearness or farness of the contact is translated into
the level and number of senses that are affected by the presence of another.

The Chicago school sociologists inherited from Simmel a focus on the city
in sociological investigations. Simmel (Frisby & Featherston 1997) thought of
city life as fundamentally about geographical proximity and simultaneously
social disassociation. In a reaction to an overload of the senses in compacted
city environments, he theorized that people draw distinctions in such a way
that they are left with a blasé attitude and indifference of strangers. He saw this
as both liberating, in that there was a freedom from constraint, but also iso-
lating, in that there was a loneliness that came with constantly being in crowds.
Aversion to people and events became a defense mechanism of sorts that allowed
individuals to preserve psychological private space. In this way, individuals
located in a city were less likely to experience a unity consciousness with those
who were located in spatial proximity to them, and were more likely to experience a social closeness to individuals who were based further apart in space.
This, Simmel thought, creates a daily sense of alienation that allows for an
expression of individuality in a sea of indifference.

This ambiguity in the effect of space is primarily due to the fact that Simmel
was responding to a rapidly changing environment in which configurations of
space were playing a new role in social life than had previously been observed.
He described the tension between the individual and the collectivity and wrote
about the city as representing the change in modernity from a society organized
around the collectivity to one focused on the individual (Tonkiss 2005). In *The
Metropolis and Mental Life* (1903, 185) he stated, "The carrier of man's values is
no longer the 'general human being' in every individual, but rather man's qualitative uniqueness and irreplaceability." In this way, Simmel was responding to
a process that nearly all the classical social theorists addressed, namely, the shift
in societal configurations accompanying the industrial revolution. His concep-

tion of a shift from a society focused on collectivity to one centered around individuality drew most heavily from the work of Ferdinand Tönnies.

The bulk of Tönnies' scholarship focused on one central idea, which was to theorize the causes and effects of a shift from a community (gemeinschaft) to a society (gesellschaft) (Tönnies and Loomis 2002). His theory pits two ideal types in tension with one another. One is communal and collectively focused, and the other is individually oriented. These are driven by two types of will and come to be represented spatially over time in their configurations of society. Tönnies (2002, 62) wrote,

> Whatever its empirical origin, the existing town must be regarded as a whole on which the individual fellowships and families constituting it are necessarily dependent. Thus, with its language, its customs, and its creed as well as with its land, its buildings, and its treasures, it represents something enduring which outlasts the sequence of generations and forever reproduces essentially the same intellectual attitude, partly from itself, partly through heredity and through the education of its burghers.

This is a description of a more community-oriented configuration, in which the neighborhood is the basis of connection. As the configuration moves toward a societal orientation, this connection lessens and relationships between people become more focused on laws and justice rather than association and trust. Tönnies' clear influence upon Simmel points to his as the true original theory of space. Like Simmel, to Tönnies, space is important for understanding social activity because it is where values, beliefs, and associations become configured in ways that structure the reality of individual lived experience. Thus, Tönnies and Simmel both had a conceptualization of space that combined the material and the ideational.

Space has a long history of being studied in the social sciences, and many social scientists generally recognize the importance of context in social processes. Classical social theorists accounted for space either explicitly as a focus of theory, as in the cases of Tönnies and Simmel, or implicitly in accounting for space and time through the study of historical change and differences across cultures, as in the cases of Marx, Durkheim, and Weber. Despite this rich history in social theoretical conceptions of space, accounts of space in current social theory and research are mostly fragmented and ambiguous. What accounts for the disconnects and ambiguities that have occurred in spatial conceptualizations since these theorists?

Critical Space: A Neo-Classical and Critical Realist Approach

The disconnect between the past and the present approaches to space is due to a trend over time in social science becoming pervaded with a positivist approach to social science research (Smith 2010; York and Mancus 2009; Banister 1987; Held 1980). Positivism is an approach to conducting science which has varied from an explicit philosophy of science to a de facto mode of operation (e.g. Benton and Craib 2001; Smith 2010; Ron 1999). The end goal of this approach to social science is to reveal the social laws that cause events to occur by showing the "constant conjunctions" of factors, meaning identifying that certain events nearly always occur with certain other events and therefore can be presumed to be in a causal relationship. Critiques of positivism argue that in order to make positivist claims about the world, much of the complexity of reality must be simplified (Benton and Craib 2001; Smith 2010; Ron 1999; Porpora 2008; Goldthorpe 2007). Deterministic critiques highlight that positivism assumes that every event has an antecedent cause which explains and predicts that event's occurrence. In what is often called "variables sociology" (e.g. Esser 1996; Blumer 1956) or large-scale survey research that focuses on the statistical analysis of relationships between variables, this positivist approach to social science is often carried out in the background through a probabilistic analysis which seeks to show that specified outcomes have a high probability of occurring given a specified model which posits specifiable causes. The result of this philosophy of science foundation, as it relates to spatial theory, is that it caused space to either be ignored altogether, undertheorized, or reduced to overly deterministic conceptualizations.

Critical realism was designed to address the problems of positivism through careful clarification of terms and approaches (Bhaskar 1978). Most centrally, critical realists focus on the role of causation in social science (e.g. Porpora 2008; Smith 2010; Benton and Craib 2001). Rather than viewing causation as primarily about revealing regularly occurring social laws and predicting future events, critical realism views social science as needing to investigate the rich complexity of social life and not seek to reduce it to predictable models.

The primary vehicle through which critical realists intend to study social life is through the concept of "social mechanisms" (Gorski 2009; Hedstrom and Swedberg 1998; Smith 2010). Social mechanisms are conceived of as natural tendencies or propensities embedded in social life which can be activated or obstructed, based on all the complex conditions of social life, to cause various outcomes. Agents, according to a critical realist perspective, can be mechanisms of social change, as can their unobservable beliefs and motivations. Likewise, social structures are also important for understanding social life (e.g. Sayer 1992; Smith 2010), and critical realists view social structures as in a dialectical relationship with agents, in which each can have causal influence on the other. This process occurs through "emergence," which is the notion that different levels exist within society, and people and structures exist at different levels. Through a process of "upward causation," people can influence the broader structure of which they are a part, but by nature of the structural existing at an "upper" level, this interaction does not meld the upper level into the lower level, and the upper level retains its own characteristics and causal propensities, at the same time that it can be changed by the lower level. Through "downward causation," social structures can also act backward upon the people who compose them and have causal influences upon this lower level of reality in ways that can influence, but does not determine, the actions of societal actors.

In this way, many critical realists seek to resolve the structure-agency, or voluntary-mechanistic, debates which have pervaded much of social science. These debates are characterized by many contemporary social theorists (e.g. Giddens 1979) as reducing social life to a mechanism carrying out the social structure. That is, people are essentially pushed around by the social factors that existed before they were born and will continue to exist long after they are gone, or a reduction in the opposite direction by positing people as free to carry out their wishes with little to no societal constraints. Margaret Archer (1996) argues that critical realism resolves these age-old debates by looking at the ways in which the material and the ideal, the social structure and the meanings and values held by agents within the social structure, can combine and affect one another over time. Critical realism was also described by Sean Creaven (2000) as coherently combining materialism and idealism insofar as ideal elements cannot be reduced to material structures but are dependent upon them. This is made possible through the notion of emergence where ideal elements—beliefs and meanings—emerge from their material basis, such as human bodies and geographical locations, and have new powers in the social system. Thus, social structures develop out of and form the material and the ideational (Smith 2010).

Peter Manicas (2006) explained that social science based in critical realism is not about prediction and control but rather an understanding of outcomes and the processes that produce them. People are the primary agents in history, and causes are conceived of as mechanisms that produce various outcomes in particular places and times. There is an ongoing process of activity which is based in, and can only be understood as, context dependent. The goal of critical realist social science is to draw on already established knowledge of enduring structures and mechanisms to identify the specific combination that generated the event of interest (Archer et al. 1998).

In critical realism, social reality is seen as consisting of *both* a pre-existing society which acts upon individuals *and* individual agents who act upon their social structures, or structure and agency. From a critical realist perspective, society is composed of both structures which impose themselves upon individuals and intentional individuals who consciously enact change in social structures and unconsciously reproduce them (Bhaskar 1998). Social contexts are important for understanding the connection between structure and agency, and conceptualizations of social space are crucial for adequate representations of the role that context plays in the creation, change, and reproduction of social systems by individual actors.

Applied to a theory of social space, critical realism implies that context is important to all social realities and should be conceptualized as a level with its own properties, which acts upon and is acted upon by social actors. Space entails both the material elements of physical geographical locatedness and the ideational elements of perception, memory, meaning, and social interaction. There are social mechanisms which operate to create certain configurations of space, and configurations of space can create differences in experiences for the actors who live in or travel through them. From a critical realist perspective, some elements of the importance of space in social life may be observable at any given moment and some may not. The effect of space on individuals can vary over time and locations, and likewise for the effect of individuals on space. A critical realist approach to conceptualizing space allows us to adequately account for its multidimensional, complex, and emergent properties. Space can then be conceived as both an outcome of social processes, insofar as it is constructed of socioeconomic, gendered, and racial dynamics, and as a mechanism of social processes, via contextual and neighborhood effects. It is important to account for both the observable aspects of space, such as visual representations of class, and unobservable, such as symbolic meanings attached to contexts.

Thus, an adequate conception of space in social theory must incorporate both the material — e.g. physical locations, natural environments, and geographical proximities— and the ideational elements of social configurations and locations— meaning and interpretation of places, experience in locations, solidarity, exclusion, and social proximity (Campbell 2000; and similar to a critical human ecological perspective in York and Mancus 2009). As stated by the critical realist Andrew Sayer (2000, 114), "The spatio-temporal situation of people and resources affects the very natures of social phenomenon. In turn, the effects of actions are influenced by the content and form of their external settings or contexts. The constitutive property of space can work in two ways, often in conjunction: in terms of material pre-conditions of actions, and in terms of their constitutive meanings." This is largely due to the fact that spatial configurations are inherited and therefore can precede the life of any one individual, while at the same time there exists a spatial flexibility in which individuals are not determined by their social settings.

So the conceptualization of space that I propose here draws from a historical lineage of sociological theory and combines formerly divergent strains of thought into a more comprehensive approach to studying space. I incorporate critical-realist principles in order to create a theory that accounts for space's material and ideational aspects and generates a structure *and* agency-based concept of space. Here social space includes natural environments, social constructions and human perceptions, boundaries, limitations, relations, networks, embodied ideas and emotions, socioeconomic patterns of production and relative status, residential and commercial buildings, and neighborhoods, communities, cities, and nation-states. A great deal of what is abstracted in social scientific analysis in to social relations is better understood as located in a contextual reality that combines and divides social bodies in physical and communicative proximity and distance. Social space is a meaningful physical environment which, under specifiable circumstances, may serve to either exclude or connect people, objects, and events in specific configurations in a three-dimensional field.

Without implementing the theory of space articulated here, sociological pursuits remain inherently divided and fragmented over a concept that is critical to any accurate pursuit of sociological investigation. The conceptualization of space offered here points to the importance of both geographical and symbolic elements of space. Ignoring spatial influences means excluding from study a bundle of social processes such as connections across space, exclusion from access to space, and concentrations of sets of social processes within the same place. At the very least then, it is important to recognize space as a potential influence or outcome. Attempts to control for space will need to find complex ways of accounting for the autocorrelation of spatial influence (on this see, for example, Kapoor, Kelejian, and Prucha 2007; Goodchild, Anselin, Appelbaum, and Harthorn 2007; Anselin 1988).

Foregrounding space by implementing the theory of space proposed here has the potential to improve studies in a number of fields and sociological subfields. Community and urban studies in particular can benefit from implementing this theory of space. Over the last several decades, urban sociology has actually lost a focus on anything specifically urban to study and in this regard has become "all limbs and no head" (Zukin 1980, 575). The fact that new forms of technology span urban centers and increasingly connect people across space has led to confusion within the field of what the topic of study should be. This theory of space helps to remedy that by pointing to concentrations and bundles of social processes within and across urban spaces as still worthy of pursuit. The complex nature of space does not undermine its investigation but rather specifically justifies an area of study dedicated to foregrounding its complexity and investigating it from many directions. Class-based spatial contexts are also important for the study of stratification and social reproduction of inequality (Adkins and Vaisey 2009). Spatial inequality has ramifications for studies of disorganization, delinquency, criminology, organizations, medicine, education, religious congregations, families, and nearly all of sociology. And this is mainly because, undeniably, all of social life occurs in spatial locations and contexts.

Acknowledgments

I thank Omar Lizardo, Christian Smith, and Meredith Whitnah for their feedback on previous drafts of this chapter.

References

Abbott, Andrew. 1997. Of Time and Space: The Contemporary Relevance of the Chicago School. *Social Forces* 75(4): 1149–82.
_____. 2001. *Time Matters: On Theory and Method.* Chicago: University of Chicago Press.
Adkins, Daniel E., and Stephen Vaisey. 2007. Toward a Unified Stratification Theory: Structure, Genome, and Status Across Human Societies. *Sociological Theory* 27(2): 99–121.
Anselin, Luc. 1988. *Spatial Econometrics: Methods and Models.* Dordrecht: Kluwer Academic Publishers.
Archer, Margaret, Roy Bhaskar, Andrew Collier, Tony Lawson, and Alan Norrie, eds. 1998. *Critical Realism: Essential Readings.* New York: Routledge.
Benko, Georges, and Ulf Strohmayer. 1997. *Space and Social Theory: Interpreting Modernity and Postmodernity.* Oxford: Blackwell.
Benton, Ted, and Ian Craib. 2001. *Philosophy of Social Science: Philosophical Issues in Social Thought.* New York: Palgrave Macmillan.
Beveridge, Andrew A. 2008. A Century of Harlem in New York City: Some Notes on Migration, Consolidation, Segregation, and Recent Developments. *City & Community* 7(4): 358–65.
Bhaskar, Roy. 1998. Societies. In *Critical Realism: Essential Readings,* ed. Margaret Archer, Roy Bhaskar, Andrew Collier, Tony Lawson, and Alan Norrie, 206–57. New York: Routledge.
Blokland, Talja. 2008. From the Outside Looking In: A European Perspective on the *Ghetto. City & Community* 7(4): 372–77.
Blumer, Herbert. 1956. Sociological Analysis and the "Variable." *American Sociological Review* 21(6): 683–90.
Bulmer, Martin. 1984. *The Chicago School of Sociology: Institutionalization, Diversity, and the Rise of Sociological Research.* Chicago: University of Chicago Press.
Burgess, Ernest W., ed. 1925. *The Urban Community: Selected Papers from the Proceedings of the American Sociological Society.* New York: Greenwood Press.
Campbell, Christopher D. 2000. Social Structure, Space, and Sentiment: Searching for Common Ground in Sociological Conceptions of Community. In *Community Structure and Dynamics at the Dawn of the New Millennium,* ed. Dan A. Chekki, 21–57. Stamford: JAI Press.
Chadda, Anmol, and William J. Wilson. 2008. Reconsidering the "Ghetto." *City & Community* 7(4): 384–387.
Creaven, Sean. 2000. *Marxism and Realism: A Materialistic Application of Realism in the Social Sciences.* New York: Routledge.
Danermark, Berth, Mats Ekstrom, Liselotte Jakobsen, and Jan C. Karlsson. 1997. *Explaining Society: An Introduction to Critical Realism in the Social Sciences.* New York: Routledge.
Del Casino Jr., Vincent J., and John P. Jones III. 2007. Space for Social Inequality Researchers: A View from Geography. In *The Sociology of Spatial Inequality,* ed. Linda Lobao, Gregory Hooks, Ann Tickamyer, 233–252. New York: State University of New York Press.
Durkheim, Emile. 1997. *The Division of Labor in Society.* New York: Free Press.
Dukheim, Emile, and Karen E. Fields. 1995. *The Elementary Forms of Religious Life.* New York: Free Press.
Esser, Hartmut. 1996. What Is Wrong with "Variable Sociology"? *European Sociological Review,* 12(2): 159–66.
Ethington, Philip J. 1997. The Intellectual Construction of "Social Distance": Toward a Recovery of Georg Simmel's Social Geometry. Epistémologie, Historie de la Géographie, Didactique, 30. http://www.cybergeo.eu/index227.html.
Faris, Robert E. 1967. *Chicago Sociology, 1920–1932.* San Francisco: Chandler Publishing Company.
Fine, Gary A. 1995. *A Second Chicago School? The Development of a Postwar American Sociology.* Chicago: University of Chicago Press.

Fracchia, Joseph. 1991. Marx's Aufhebung of Philosophy and the Foundations of a Materialist Science of History. *History and Theory* 30(2): 153–79.

Frisby, David P., and Mike Featherstone. 1997. *Simmel on Culture: Selected Writings*. Thousand Oaks, CA: Sage Publications.

Gans, Herbert J. 2008. Involuntary Segregation and the *Ghetto*: Disconnecting Process and Place. *City & Community* 7(4): 353–57.

Giddens, Anthony. 1979. *Central Problems in Social Theory: Action, Structure, and Contradiction in Social Analysis*. Berkeley: University of California Press.

Gieryn, Thomas F. 2000. A Space for Place in Sociology. *Annual Review of Sociology*, 26: 463–96.

Goldthorpe, John. 2007. *On Sociology*. Stanford: Stanford University Press.

Goodchild, Michael F., Luc Anselin, Richard P. Abbelbaum, and Barbara H. Harthorn. 2000. Toward Spatially Integrated Social Science. *International Regional Science Review* 23(2): 139–59.

Gough, Jamie, Aram Eisenschitz, with Andrew McCulloch. 2006. *Spaces of Social Exclusion*. New York: Routledge.

Gross, Matthias. 2004. Human Geography and Ecological Sociology: The Unfolding of a Human Ecology, 1890 to 1930 and Beyond. *Social Science History* 28(4): 575–605.

Hartwig, Mervyn. 2007. *Dictionary of Critical Realism*. New York: Routledge.

Haynes, Bruce, and Ray Hutchison. 2008. The *Ghetto*: Origins, History, Discourse. *City & Community* 7(4): 347–52.

Held, David. 1980. *Introduction to Critical Theory: Horkheimer to Habermas*. Berkeley: University of California Press.

Hunter, Albert. 1971. The Ecology of Chicago: Persistence and Change, 1930–1960. *American Journal of Sociology* 77(3): 425–44.

Janowitz, Morris. 1967. *Community Press in an Urban Setting: The Social Elements of Urbanism*. Chicago: University of Chicago Press.

Kapoor, Mudit, Harry H. Kelejian, Ingmar R. Prucha. 2007. Panel Data Models with Spatially Correlated Error Components. *Journal of Econometrics* 140(1): 97–130.

Lee, Barrett A., Sean F. Reardon, Glenn Firebaugh, Chad R. Farrell, Stephen A. Matthews, and David O'Sullivan. 2008. Beyond the Census Tract: Patterns and Determinants of Racial Segregation at Multiple Geographic Scales. *American Sociological Review* 73(5): 766–91.

Lefebvre, Henri. 1991. *The Production of Space*. Cambridge, MA: Wiley-Blackwell.

Levine, Donald N. 2004. The Organism Metaphor in Sociology. *Social Research* 62(2): 239–65.

Lobao, Linda M., and Gregory Hooks. 2007. Advancing the Sociology of Spatial Inequality: Spaces, Places, and the Subnational Scale. In *The Sociology of Spatial Inequality*, ed. Linda Lobao, Gregory Hooks, Ann Tickamyer, 29–62. New York: State University of New York Press.

Lobao, Linda M., Gregory Hooks, and Ann R. Tickamyer, eds. 2007. *The Sociology of Spatial Inequality*. New York: State University of New York Press.

Manicas, Peter T. 2006. *A Realist Philosophy of Social Science: Explanation and Understanding*. Cambridge: Cambridge University Press.

Massey, Douglas S., and Nancy A. Denton. 1993. *American Apartheid: Segregation and the Making of the Underclass*. Cambridge: Harvard University Press.

Monteiro, Circe. 2008. Enclaves, Condominiums, and Favelas: Where Are the *Ghettos* in Brazil? *City & Community* 7(4): 378–83.

Natter, Wolfgang, and John P. Jones. 1997. Identity, Space, and other Uncertainties. In *Space and Social Theory: Interpreting Modernity and Postmodernity*, ed. Georges Benko and Ulf Strohmayer, 141–61. Oxford: Blackwell.

Marx, Karl. 1978. *Marx-Engels Reader*. Scranton, PA: W.W. Norton.

Park, Robert E., 1921. Sociology and the Social Sciences: The Social Organism and the Collective Mind. *American Journal of Sociology* 27(1): 1–21.

Park, Robert E. and Ernest W. Burgess. 1965. *The City: Suggestions for Investigation of Human Behavior in the Urban Environment*. Chicago: University of Chicago Press.

Porpora, Douglas. 2008. Recovering Causality: Realist Methods in Sociology. In *Realismo*

Sociologico, ed. Andrea Maccarini, Emmanuele Morandi and Riccardo Prandini, 183–220. Genova-Milano: Marietti.

Pred, Allan. 1997. Re-Presenting the Extended Moment of Danger: A Meditation on Hyper-modernity, Identity and the Montage Form. In *Space and Social Theory: Interpreting Modernity and Postmodernity*, ed. Georges Benko and Ulf Strohmayer, 117–140. Oxford: Blackwell.

Ron, Amit. 1999. Regression Analysis and the Philosophy of Social Sciences— A Critical Realist View. *Journal of Critical Realism* 1(1): 119–42.

Sayer, Andrew. 2000. *Realism and Social Science*. Thousand Oaks, CA: Sage Publications.

Simmel, Georg. 1971. *Georg Simmel on Individuality and Social Forms*. Chicago: University of Chicago Press.

Small, Mario L. 2008. Four Reasons to Abandon the Idea of "The Ghetto." *City & Community* 7(4): 389–98.

Smith, Christian. 2010. *What Is a Human Person? Rethinking Humanity, Social Life, and Morality from the Person Up*. Chicago: University of Chicago Press.

Strohmayer, Ulf. 1997. Belonging: Spaces of Meandering Desire. In *Space and Social Theory: Interpreting Modernity and Postmodernity*, ed. Georges Benko and Ulf Strohmayer, 162–185. Oxford: Blackwell.

Taeuber, Karl E., and Alma F. Taeuber. 1965. *Residential Segregation and Neighborhood Change*. Edison, NJ: Transaction Publishers.

Tonkiss, Fran. 2005. *Space, the City and Social Theory: Social Relations and Urban Forms*. Malden, MA: Polity Press.

Tönnies, Ferdinand, and C. P. Loomis. 2002. *Community and Society*. Mineola, NY: Dover.

Vigil, Diego. 2008. Barrio Genealogy. *City & Community* 7(4): 366–71.

Weber, Max. 2002. *The Protestant Ethics and the Spirit of Capitalism*. New York: Penguin Books.

Wilson, William J. 1978. *The Declining Significance of Race: Blacks and Changing American Institutions*. Chicago: University of Chicago Press.

_____. 1996. *When Work Disappears: The World of the New Urban Poor*. New York: Random House.

Wilson, William J., and Richard P. Taub. 2006. *There Goes the Neighborhood*. New York: Random House.

York, Richard, and Philip Mancus. 2009. Critical Human Ecology: Historical Materialism and Natural Laws. *Sociological Theory* 27(2): 122–149.

Zieleniec, Andrzej. 2007. *Space and Social Theory*. Newbury Park, CA: Sage Publications.

Zukin, Sharon. 1980. A Decade of the New Urban Sociology. *Theory and Society* 9(4): 575–601.

7. FINDING COHERENCE IN SOCIOLOGY
(Finally!) A Foundational Theory

Debbie Kasper

The compulsion to better understand human social life — in all its countless manifestations— is what drew me to sociology as a college student, and what kept me there ever since. There is overwhelming evidence, however, that the discipline, as it exists in textbooks, undergraduate majors, and graduate programs does not provide a consistent and reliable basis for fulfilling the promise that so many students sense in it. While I had the good fortune to be exposed to a combination of ideas and authors that set me on a path toward better understanding, I had to do a good bit of off-roading along the way. The result is largely the product of an unpredictable combination of personal inclinations and dumb luck, not a recipe for a sound discipline.

This state of affairs has led to the widely shared conclusions that sociology is incoherent, without consistent organizing principles, lacking anything resembling a real theory, and in the midst of an ongoing identity crisis— recurring themes across generations of sociologists. These problems and their persistence are due, at least in part, to the fact that, despite the warnings of attentive scholars, they are not adequately addressed (or even mentioned, in many cases) in the primary channels through which the discipline is perpetuated: sociology courses and textbooks. When sociologists-in-training are kept ignorant of the challenges of their work, they and therefore the discipline remain ill-equipped to deal with them.

Having been in high school when the infamous closings of some sociology departments caused such a stir, I had not yet heard of sociology. I was in college (having recently declared sociology as a major) when Stephen Cole, as editor of *Sociological Forum*, solicited and published responses to the question: what is wrong with sociology? Even if I *had* been aware of that publication, I would have had no idea what the question meant or what the answer might be. And I gained no further insights, at least not through any formal means, during subsequent years in graduate school. When, as a working sociologist, I finally discovered the question and its meaning, I felt certain that competent people must be on the job by now. To the contrary, whenever I raised questions about sociology's problems (in casual conversations, formal discussions, and in papers) sociologists of the baby boom cohort tended to respond in the same way, with the equivalent of "yawn, boring, old news," and a swift change of subject. It may be old news to some, but it remains news, and disconcerting news at that, for each generation of sociologists alerted to it for the first time.

Fortunately, there is also plenty of good news. For starters, sociology continues to attract significant numbers of students, nearly all of whom are drawn to its "interesting concepts." These students also appreciate gaining a better understanding of the relationship between social forces and individuals, social change, and their own lives (Spalter-Roth and Van Vooren 2008). Second, given the complexity of human social life today and the global nature of the problems demanding attention, the need for sociologically informed understanding and action is greater than ever, and will only continue to grow. Finally, we already have the makings of a more coherent sociology via a foundational theory to guide our thinking and empirical research. This is the good news I focus on here, but in order to realize this potential, we must recognize, understand, and ultimately get beyond some of the primary obstacles that have blocked advancement so far.

In order to save students (and the future sociologists that derive from them) from having to discover these problems on their own — or worse, remain ignorant of them — I discuss some of them here. In particular, I address current manifestations of sociology's incoherence; its origins in the dualism that developed in modern western thought; and sociology's isolation from other disciplines, especially the sciences. The persistence of these problems and their consequences is not due to a lack of sociological insights over the years. Though not widely recognized as such, there *is* a salient category of efforts to overcome them and advance the discipline in necessary ways. Of them, I find the works of Norbert Elias and Pierre Bourdieu to be particularly valuable. In synthesizing some of their most important contributions, I derive a foundational theory for sociology. Here I present its core concepts, propose a model to help visualize and convey it, and suggest practical ways to use it for understanding and studying social phenomena.

Reproducing Incoherence

At a 2009 Eastern Sociological Society session devoted to C.W. Mills and the 50th anniversary of the *Sociological Imagination*, presider and panelist Craig Calhoun expressed great pride about what he saw as one of the greatest achievements of his generation of sociologists. Along with the many other things his cohort rebelled against, they widely rejected the conservatism they saw in the reigning sociology of the time, especially that espoused by superstars like Parsons (at Harvard) and Lazarsfeld and Merton (at Columbia). In establishing the "three theoretical perspectives," Calhoun continued, these young sociologists managed to topple the status quo *and* bring Marx in the form of "conflict theory" squarely into the canon.

While the inclusion of Marx may have been a coup for the "disobedient generation,"[1] instituting the three perspectives as dogma did nothing to promote useable theory or genuine coherence in sociology. Decades of assessments agree that sociology is incoherent in that it lacks a core of organizing principles and anything resembling a foundational theory (just a few examples include Becker and Rau 1992; Cole 1994; Davis 1994; Huber 1995; Kalberg 2004; Keith 2000; Phillips 1999; Rule 1994; Stinchcombe 1994; Turner and Turner 1990; Turner 2004). Without these, they conclude, sociology is not a sustainable enterprise. While valuable for providing a clearer sense of the problems, such assessments have had little effect on the day to day business of sociology, which just keeps chugging along as if nothing were amiss. It is not difficult to imagine the consequences of such problems for any discipline, but of interest here are the effects on efforts to convey the essentials of what sociology is and how to do it.

Introducing Sociology

Sociologists, and students studying sociology, quickly become accustomed to the question from friends, relatives, and strangers to the effect of: "what is sociology?" In my own experience, which concurs with that of friends and colleagues, people most often equate sociology with psychology or some kind of social work. This confusion is understandable. Sociology is not taught in most high schools—less than 40 percent nationwide—and even when it is offered, subject matter tends to be distinctively non-sociological, with primary emphases on uncritical civic education and social problems (DeCesare 2007; 2005). As a consequence, some have a tenuous understanding of what sociology is, and many others may have no understanding at all. While we may not expect the average citizen to be able to answer this question, we should expect to find an informative response in a book intended to acquaint students with the discipline's subject matter — its foundational concepts, theories, methods, and historical contributions.

In the absence of agreement about core subject matter, however, one wonders how a textbook can effectively introduce a discipline in such a position. Even in a discipline like biology, in which there are (relative to sociology) very high levels of agreement about such things, introductory textbooks can reinforce general misunderstandings of fundamental ideas like evolution and foster faulty mental models of its place in the biological sciences merely through the conventional, yet problematic, organization of their contents (Nehm et al. 2008). How much more likely it must be, in a discipline that exhibits far less agreement about what it is and does, that sociology textbooks unwittingly perpetuate confusion about sociology! This is not trivial because in many ways, as Dandaneau (2009, 16) puts it, "textbooks reproduce (the) discipline."

So what is sociology? The meaning of our Latin-Greek hybrid is not immediately intuitive (the study of allies, friends, companions?). Twelve recently published texts I happen to have define sociology as primarily "the study of" either society (7) or human social behavior (4); one book indicates both.[2] Other elements of definitions variously include the study of social change, social interaction, and organizations. This inconsistency betrays a lack of clarity about sociology's primary units of analysis— portrayed as either a collective entity or individual traits and behaviors.

Similarities in topics and structure among introductory texts create the illusion of consensus about sociology's core, and there *is* a somewhat stronger common knowledge base than there was a half-century ago. However, data show that, despite appearances, there is little commonality among the concepts used by textbook authors to define and frame the discipline (Babchuk and Keith 1995; Keith and Ender 2004). In fact, the "vast majority [of concepts] are referenced by only one text, with fewer than three percent of all concepts shared in common" (Keith and Ender 2004, 19). One consequence of this has been a proliferation of vocabulary words in introductory texts and courses and an over-emphasis on teaching students to use them (Eckstein, Schoenike, and Delaney 1995; Leming 1990). Another is that students in introductory courses taught by different instructors are likely to get very different versions of the discipline (Keith and Ender 2004; Keith 2000).

One of the most important agreed-upon concepts appears to be the "sociological perspective" or "imagination." But there is evidence that introductory sociology students are failing to develop even that (Bengston and Hazzard 1990; Dandaneau 2009; de Silva 2003; Eckstein, Schoenike, and Delaney 1995). Nor do they exhibit critical sociological thinking at all (Grauerholz and Bouma-Holtrop 2003). How could they? Without any foundational theories or unifying principles that sociologists actually agree upon and use, there is little hope for coherence among the hundreds of concepts introduced, or for cultivating a sense of sociology's place among other kinds of inquiry and why it is important.

Theories of Human Social Life

The absence of coherence in sociological theory has long been viewed as an indicator and an important source of incoherence in the discipline. The state of contemporary theory is most frequently characterized as a "Tower of Babel" (Mouzelis 1995; Phillips 1999, 2001; Turner 2004) and hopeless evaluations abound, as in: "Nobody today knows what sociological theory is, or even if there is any such thing at all" (Lopreato and Crippen 1999, 19); "Today there is no such thing as sociological theory" (Davis 1994, 104); and that we have seen the end of sociological theory (Seidman 1991). Oblivious to all of this, introductory books are shockingly sanguine about theory in their presentations of it. Most striking is the texts' automatic and uncomplicated invocation of functionalism, conflict theory, and symbolic interactionism as sociology's "three theoretical perspectives."

As a prominent theorist put it in a recent conversation with me, "Everybody knows those categories are meaningless and have been for 40 years; introductory textbooks are the only places they exist." But even at that elementary level, they remain a source of confusion and almost completely useless. Authors assure readers that each theory "is right in its own way" (Thio 2005, 15), that "each makes a contribution to our understanding" (Ballantine and Roberts 2009, 57), and that "we need to use all three" (Henslin 2009, 20). At the same time, the theories are portrayed as distinct specializations which are not compatible, as in "Both [micro and macro approaches] are needed," but the "micro level ... would not interest functionalists and conflict theorists" (Henslin 2009, 86 and 19) or that these approaches are "competing" and "completely different" (Alexander and Thompson 2008, 409–10). Even authors' efforts to show how certain phenomena can be understood through each perspective (which they increasingly go to great lengths to do) are not all that helpful. What students take away is that one can view a situation from different perspectives. True enough, but they remain understandably confused about *what* sociological theory is, what to do with it, and how. As a result, the prospect of a theory class inspires fear and dread in most students (and many teachers).

In the effort to seem inclusive and up to date, some texts add feminist, postmodern, rational choice, race-conflict, queer, and other theories to the list of essentials. This only confuses matters more. The distinct tendency in contemporary sociological theory to focus on difference stifles possibilities for recognizing fruitful similarities and creates a cycle of ever-expanding pluralism. Teachers are urged to "be more responsible than ever in recognizing and presenting theoretical diversity" (Deflem 1999, 7). Not only do they have little basis for making any practical sense of the growing assortment of seemingly unrelated theories, but there are more of them than can be packed into a semester-long course. Teachers must select among them as they see fit, resulting in blatant inconsistencies in how sociological theory is taught and learned, particularly problematic at the graduate level (Sica 1998; Zald 1991).

The widely accepted claim that theory is the backbone of a discipline is certainly at odds with the reality of sociological theory's current disarray. In light of this, it seems that our options are: (1) to deny that there are problems and continue to go about our business as if all were well, (2) to give up on the prospect of sociology altogether, or (3) to take steps toward establishing greater coherence in our theories of human social life. I opt for the third. Before we can take such steps, we need to first appreciate the origins of some of sociology's biggest problems.

A World Divided

At the heart of sociology's inability to settle on a foundational theory are assumptions about the incompatibility between micro or macro approaches, emphases on agency or structure, the focus on individuals or societies, and the longstanding stalemate between these positions. Underlying this seemingly fundamental disagreement is the modern Western view of the world as divided neatly between subjects and objects. Certain developments in this strand of social thought over the past few centuries have contributed to the sense, taken for granted by most of us, that the self exists inside a person and in opposition to the external world (including other selves). Not only does this idea pervade the history of philosophical and scientific thinking that has shaped contemporary Western worldviews, but also this modern conceptual wrong turn is cited as the basis of some of the most persistent obstacles to advancement in social science. Some have devoted their life's work to debunking this dualism and to equipping sociology with the tools to better think about, talk about, and study human social life. Three prominent examples include Norbert Elias, Pierre Bourdieu, and Anthony Giddens. Their common point of departure is an assessment of subject/object dualism as sociology's most fundamental problem (Bourdieu 1988, 78; 1990, 25; Elias 1987a, 12 and 49; Elias 1991b, 6–7; Giddens 1979, 120; 1984, xx).

Through a dualistic lens the social world is misconstrued as an assortment of separate entities; and social change appears to be the result of classical physics-like interactions among them. This view gives rise to seemingly impossible questions about *how* these unconnected entities are related to and affect one another. By what mechanisms do people "internalize the external" or "objectivize the internal"? Which is the real causal agent: the individual or a collective entity? And which came first?

These and other enduring questions have led to the widely accepted premise that the relationship between the individual and society — and their conceptual equivalents — is the driving question of contemporary sociology (Calhoun 2007, 4; Elliott 1999, 7; Elliott and Ray 2003, xiii–xiv; Ritzer 2008, 500). The ongoing consequence of sociology's apparent inability to answer it has been the development of opposing theories about voluntarism versus determinism, structuralism versus subjectivism, functionalism versus interpretivism, and so on. Despite the obvious inadequacy of these options, they tend to force a choice of one over the other, as if we get to decide how the world works. Being dislocated from reality, none of these views (nor the theories they inspire) are empirically justifiable and we are stuck at, what appears to be, an impasse. Happily, there is an alternative.

A Turn Toward Relations

Instead of beginning with (what are presumed to be) substantial entities—whether individual or collective — there is a category of efforts that strives to shift the focus toward relations. In addition to my early observations of this in the works of Elias, Bourdieu, and Giddens, Wacquant identifies relational tendencies in Piaget, Jakobson, Lévi-Strauss, Braudel, Durkheim, and Marx (Bourdieu and Wacquant 1992); Emirbayer (1997) adds Dewey, Bentley, Foucault, and others to the list of relational thinkers. But with the current and dominant focus on difference, this important common ground has gone largely unnoticed. And in the context of ever-expanding pluralism, it is unlikely that students will even be exposed to many of these efforts and the continuing dialogue of which they are part, much less recognize their similarities. In any case, putting that kind of sociology into practice has thus far proved difficult.

Questions about how to study dynamic relations persist: What are the units of analysis? How can we conceptualize process? How should we redefine familiar concepts as relational processes, rather than static entities (Emirbayer 1997; Kaspersen and Gabriel 2008)? These questions endure, in part, because of sociology's failure to ground itself within current scientific knowledge about humans, without which such problems cannot be solved. A necessary first step, then, is to more clearly situate sociology's subject matter in and among that of other sciences. In doing so, we find abundant evidence of humans' inherent relationality.

Situating Sociology

At present, sociology appears to exist in isolation from other disciplines, especially the human sciences. Most introductory and theory texts conspicuously lack serious attention to, or even a demonstrated understanding of, what is known about the bodies and brains from which human social life arises. This is likely the reason why discussions of socialization in almost all intro books rely on cursory discussions of "nature vs. nurture" and well-worn anecdotes about unsocialized children and identical twins separated at birth, rather than empirically-based discussions of the fundamental conditions that make socialization both possible and necessary. Stories about feral and isolated children (included in 11 of my 12 books), for example, are offered as "proof" of nurture's greater importance, and that nature alone cannot do the job. While most books rightly acknowledge that the two interact, they perpetuate the belief that natural and social influences are totally distinct; many adopt a competitive stance and imply that "nurture matters more" (Macionis 2007, 119).

All this is misleading, for assertions that "what makes humans unique is not our biological heritage but our ability to learn the complex social arrangements of our culture" (Ballantine and Roberts 2009, 101) are simply wrong in their incompleteness. As a species, our biological heritage is unique in that it gives us not only an extraordinary capacity, but also a need, for social learning. As individuals, our genetic composition, life experiences, and the ongoing interactions between them render each of us completely unique. Uninformed discussions of nature vs. nurture obscure the undeniable fact that human biology and social learning are utterly inseparable.

Our understanding of human social life could not but be enhanced by a better understanding of the conditions that make it possible. The basics of the neural and biological processes that contribute to our humanity, for instance, should be fundamental to sociological training. This reasonable prospect is analogous to the expectation that, for example, chemistry students know some physics or that biology students understand chemistry. While a few significant efforts in this direction stand out (e.g., Lenski 2005; Massey 2005), it has in no way become standard in sociology.

Whether sociology's isolation is motivated by the desire to resist the science label *or* to establish its autonomy from other sciences, it has been criticized for promoting a view of human life that is uninformed by, or at least grossly neglectful of, the biophysical foundations of that which it studies. Unflatteringly characterized as the "standard social science model" (Tooby and Cosmides 1992) and the "blank slate" (Pinker 2002), the ongoing neglect of people as organisms has impeded sociology's advancement. Most notably, it precludes the development of a coherent and foundational theory. Without an understanding of the relationships between sociology's subject matter and the underlying conditions of its existence, Elias (1991b, 43) observes that the former is left "without ontological status, without anchorage in the observable world ... left hanging in the air." This is an impossible starting point for explaining the existence and workings of human social life.

Understood within the context of the biophysical world, on the other hand, there is no need to posit unobservable entities or quasi-magical links between individuals and societies. The first fact to grasp is that human persons are always also organisms; a fact that is explicit in Elias' work. Our very existence depends upon the physical, chemical, and biological processes constantly at work within and between each of us and the world and, like all organisms, we have a particular evolutionary history which has conferred upon us certain characteristics. Like several other species, we have evolved as social organisms. As such, we are "made for a life with each other, a life which, seen realistically, includes interpersonal and inter-group struggles and their management" (Elias 1991b, 91). This simple observation helps to loosen the grip of the popular modern idea that individuals exist in opposition to the social entities they perceive as antagonistic. In actuality, social bonds are essential to the creation, survival, and normal development of all human individuals.

The capacity to learn, store, and communicate information is part of what makes us unique among other living things. As Elias (1987b) appreciates, our evolutionary history is distinguished by the gradual shift toward the prominence of learned over unlearned behaviors, mostly due to changes in the brain. Not only is it the case that humans *can* learn, but we *must* learn from other people. One remains capable of learning throughout life, but is particularly malleable as a child, who "*needs* to be adapted by others ... needs society in order to become physically adult" (Elias 1991a, 26). These learning processes are not separate from but are intertwined with instinctual tendencies and biological maturation; children must learn certain things at certain periods in their physiological and neurological development. Though learning processes are biologically based, the content of what is taught and learned is almost infinitely variable. That content makes up what we call culture, one of the features that enable humans to "evolve" more rapidly than other organisms, independent of the processes of genetic change and natural selection.

An appreciation of the contexts and processes underlying human life highlights a number of important conclusions: (1) humans are always involved in and shaped by interdependent relations, both with the world and other people; (2) individuals, and the figurations they form, are dynamic and contingent processes; (3) as such, they exhibit stability while remaining always open to change; and (4) human social relations, among the most complex of phenomena, are not reducible to or predictable from their "parts." While such statements could be elaborated on at length, I mention them here merely to suggest some core principles around which sociology could be more effectively organized. The articulation of such principles encourages a clearer understanding of sociology's subject matter and highlights the need for a more adequate and consistent means of engaging in sociological inquiry.

Core Concepts of a Foundational Theory

One could cite any number of authors who have contributed to developing better ways to think about and do sociology. Here I focus on the particularly valuable contributions of Elias and Bourdieu, especially their use of two concepts that embody the above principles. *Figuration* (introduced by Elias) and *habitus* (used by Elias and Bourdieu) are the core concepts and key units of analysis in the relational process theory outlined below.[3]

Figuration

Figurations are the dynamic patterns that interdependent people form with, and in response to, each other. The term supplies an alternative concept for thinking and talking about social phenomena, as well as a more adequate means for investigating and communicating the "compelling force which this form of interdependence" exercises upon people bound to each other in this manner (Elias 1987a, 85). Unlike conventional group concepts (e.g., society, institution) that connote ideas about pre-existing and static entities, relations and process are implicit in the concept of figuration and need not be "added."

When we think of people as a collection of independent and closed entities (what Elias calls *Homo clausus*), we cannot properly see what binds them together. The fact is that, as social organisms, humans have countless valencies: the capacities to combine with other individuals and groups. Viewed as such, their inherent relationality and specific bonds of functional interdependence become apparent.[4] These interdependent bonds encompass not only "practical" bonds (like those we familiarly call the "division of labor," for example), but also, and no less natural, the "emotional valencies which bind people together ... whether directly by face-to-face relationships or indirectly by their attachment to common symbols" (Elias 1978, 137). Figurations are the result of the totality of participants' dealings in their relationships with each other. Elias compared figurations to games in that the continuing outcomes of people embedded in relations of interdependence can never be controlled or planned by any one individual, nor understood via the examination of individual behaviors alone. They are the ongoing products of decisions and actions that are necessarily made in relation to those of others.

Among the diverse kinds of interdependent bonds observable across societies, Elias identifies the sexual, survival and development, and emotional functions humans serve for one another as universal forms; bonds serving the function of group survival (particularly those of attack and defense) tend to be most prominent. Bringing dynamic interdependent relations to the forefront, the concept of figuration represents significant advancement in sociology. The term makes explicit that actual and active people comprise figurations, thereby avoiding the reification toward which conventional concepts tend. Remaining aware that, as attributes of relationships, functions are always multi-perspectival, we can better comprehend the meanings of other important sociological concepts. Power, for example, ceases to be a thing that one *has* and is more easily recognized as a structural characteristic of all human relationships, which must always be viewed in the context of a *relative* balance of power. Discouraged from incorrectly viewing social functions from the single perspective of either a collective or an individual, we better understand what we are *really* talking about when we talk about institutions like family, economy, and government.

Beyond the conceptual advantages, the concept of figuration also illuminates distinct possibilities for empirical research, lending itself to identification and observation in ways that concepts like "social structure" do not. Pointing us to the observable relations that bind particular people at a given time, the concept of figuration does not require us to imagine pre-existing entities and then hypothesize about their origins. Figurations of all sizes are observable. Small groups make up relatively comprehensible figurations with each other.

Larger figurations cannot be perceived directly because the chains of interdependence linking people together are longer, tighter, and more differentiated, in which case they must be perceived indirectly, through an analysis of the various bonds.

Devising a map of such bonds would be a big job, depending on the degree of detail desired. The point, however, is not to represent the entire figurational universe but to be able to characterize and compare figurations by key traits, like their degrees of integration and differentiation, and changes in them over time. As an indicator of integration, Elias suggests the number of levels of coordination within which people are bound together in units (e.g., family, neighborhood, city, county, state, regional, national, international). Accounting for the number of types of bonds within each level (e.g., personal, professional, governmental, corporate, and more) would further enhance this measure. And something as simple as "the number of occupations for which a society has distinct names" and its rate of change over a given time period (Elias 1978, 144) could effectively indicate differentiation.[5]

Whatever the topic of research, the concept of figuration reminds us that changes in interdependence mean changes for actual people and their ways of being in the world. As such, it remains necessary to focus on people as individuals as well as figurations. An understanding of either level of observation suffers unless we constantly consider both. On that note, I shift the discussion to the similar ways of being in the world that interdependent individuals develop, also known as habitus.

Habitus

In short, habitus refers to our "second nature," that is, the perceptions, dispositions, practices, and overall lifestyle that are recognizably similar to others in similar sociohistorical conditions. Elias and Bourdieu both employ the concept to transcend dualism, avoid connotations of "individual" as passive recipient of social influence *or* independent actor, and make the inherent sociality of individuals explicit. Bourdieu's use of the term is far more self-conscious and technical than Elias', and continues to evoke charges of determinism (see Bourdieu and Wacquant 1992, 79, 135; Crossley 2001; King 2000; Lemert 2004; Sewell 1992). Bourdieu cannot comprehend "why this notion, in a sense very banal (everyone will readily grant that social beings are at least partly the product of social conditionings), has triggered such reactions of hostility, if not rage" (Bourdieu and Wacquant 1992, 132). At the same time as habitus helps to shatter the "illusion of spontaneous generation" of people's dispositions and reveals how they "vary in a necessary way according to their ... conditions of production" (Bourdieu 1984, 99–101), it also highlights the human capacity for novelty, spontaneity, and change. And in a scientifically-grounded sociology, this is not at all paradoxical.

Individuals differ in their natural constitutions (via genetics, conditions of development, and their interactions) as well as their unique positions within webs of relationships and personal experiences. While this distinctive makeup certainly has an ineradicable influence on one's entire fate, the undeniable fact is that how the malleable features of a child gradually take firmer shape as he grows "*never* depends solely on his constitution and always on the nature of the relations between him and other people" (Elias 1991a, 22). As inherently social beings, individuals always develop within and are influenced by social (and other) contexts. And people in similar social contexts manifest and express those influences in similar ways, but each does so uniquely.

When we recognize human persons as processes, it becomes clear that individuality and social relatedness are not only not antithetical, but that it is only possible for one to achieve individuality growing up in a social group. Whatever illusions one might have about being completely autonomous and in control of self-development, it is the case that "the whole structure of ... self-control, both conscious and unconscious, is a network product formed in a continuous interplay of relationships to other people, and that the individual form of the adult is *a society-specific form*" (Elias 1991a, 26–7, emphasis added). Habitus is this society-specific form.

In a sociology cut off from other sciences, habitus appears to have a transcendental existence, to be a "black box." Questions about where habitus is, what it is made of, how it is created seem terminally unanswerable. But habitus development and social reproduction are not unsolvable mysteries when human social life is viewed as inseparable from, and an emergent product of, the processes that underlie phenomena in other levels of human and non-human nature, rather than an alien event requiring a wholly different kind of explanation. Though not reducible to biological, neurological, and other processes, understanding the interactions in and among them greatly enhances our ability to grasp the basic meaning of habitus as "an *open system of dispositions* that is constantly subjected to experiences, and therefore constantly affected by them" (Bourdieu and Wacquant 1992, 132–3).

The tremendous advances made in the neuro and cognitive sciences provide an empirical basis for, and enrich our understanding of, habitus. Accumulating evidence in research on brain plasticity and mirror neurons, for example, suggests answers to questions about which an isolated sociology can only speculate. As part of the basis of our capacities for imitation, empathy, and other aspects of learning from others, mirror neurons are rapidly becoming central to our understanding of social learning processes and the evolution of culture (Colapinto 2009; Ramachandran 2000; 2004). Mirror neuron circuitry is crucial to the systems that enable modeling behaviors and seeing things from another's point of view. At the level of neural networks, scientists are beginning to understand better how social learning involves an ongoing process of "wiring" and re-wiring the brain, to which *all* experiences and interactions contribute. Through this process, culture becomes "second nature" and seems as natural as one's own innate human instincts (Doidge 2007). Important here is that much of this "wiring" is neither given, nor fixed. Human brains, and thus human learning, are plastic to an extraordinary degree. Paradoxically, this plasticity is implicated in the creation of stable and sometimes rigid patterns, because "even when we do the same behavior day after day, the neuronal connections responsible are slightly different each time because of what we have done in the intervening time" (Doidge 2007, 208). What manifests as relative stability at one level involves constant change at another.

Brief mention of these examples can only hint at how research in other sciences can contribute to a better understanding of social phenomena, but the crucial point is that they show how the latter is not reducible to the activity in individual brains and bodies alone. The activation of certain neurons and the configurations of neural networks depend on and are shaped by one's relations with other people and the world. It is decidedly not the case that the uniqueness of individuals is a fatal blow to sociality nor are social influences an affront to individual freedom.

They are facts of nature, which decrees that human individuals be simultaneously unique and conditioned within specific social contexts. Habitus develops through a process, which begins naturally from birth (or even before) and continues throughout life. Dramatic transformations are possible — Bourdieu likens these to a "second birth" (1990, 68) — but are not simply a matter of rational decision or wish. I cannot, for example, conjure up the habitus of a Dutch peasant in 1900 or even that of my own grandmother. This is not because humans are incapable of experiencing different conditions and adopting new habits and perceptions; that is what being human enables us to do. But it is only through the constraints of interdependence within certain figurations that we develop and embody a habitus at all, and thus the capacity for agency.

As the level at which the perceptions, dispositions, and practices are generated, expressed, and constitute an overall lifestyle, habitus serves not only as a central concept but also an important unit of analysis. In observing the activities that comprise lifestyle (including those which are only accessible through indirect methods of observation, see Elias 1987b, 115–6n), there are limitless possibilities for studying habitus, both in what to study and how. The concept's greatest value, however, lies in the way that it makes the inherently relational and processual nature of human social life the object of sociological inquiry.

Modeling Relational Process Theory

For all that Elias and Bourdieu have provided in the way of more adequate sociological concepts and examples of their use, without a concise summary of the resulting theory it remains difficult to convey the importance of their contributions and to how to apply them. Adapting Bourdieu's (1984, 171) habitus diagram, I propose a general model of the relationships between individual people and their expressions of habitus, the figurations of which they are part, and the contexts within which these develop and occur (see Figure 1). The model is meant to be more comprehensive than Bourdieu's (which focuses solely on habitus) while at the same time being more comprehensible. Still, as an unfamiliar theory with unfamiliar concepts, it may take some time to make sense of it. The theory depicted here is not intended as a means for predicting particular outcomes. It is, rather, a theory in the sense that it can provide one "at the foot of a mountain a bird's eye view of routes and relationships that he cannot see for himself" (Elias 1978, 160).

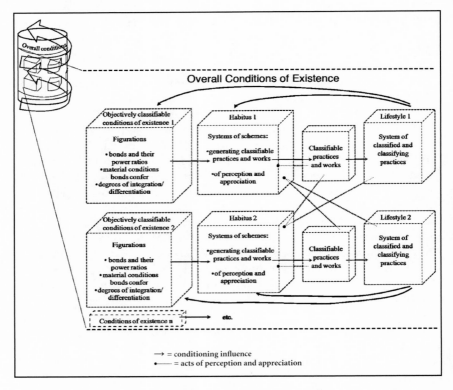

Figure 1. Model of Relational Process Theory

The model portrays five-dimensions of human social life, the familiar four dimensions of space-time and, in Elias' words, the fifth dimension: "that of symbols, which serve humans as a means of communication and identification" from which they derive meaning (1991b, 47). Conveying the processual nature of human social life, the model has no one correct point of entry. For simplicity's sake, I follow the model from left to right in briefly defining the components below.

Overall conditions of existence indicate the broader contexts in which all social life necessarily occurs, including the ecological and biophysical contexts that condition each other as well as the objectively classifiable conditions of existence in which people develop. They include, for example, climate, terrain, water, the built environment, population density, and other environmental conditions that affect and are affected by societal developments. The conditions of interest to researchers will vary according to the demands of particular projects, but their inclusion in the model makes the relationships between humans and non-human nature, and their histories, explicit — which has not always been the case in sociological models. If we think about food, just *one* aspect of social and cultural life, it is easy to imagine how these overall conditions influence the kinds of foods procured and produced as well as the means of procuring and producing them in a given place and time.

Objectively classifiable conditions of existence are the observable sociological conditions affecting habitus development (excluding universal human conditions like the necessity of food, shelter, and other basic needs). In the model below, they refer to the figurations of which people are part and the qualities and quantities of bonds of functional interdependence that condition the development of habitus. In particular, these include the overall patterns of bonds (especially their degrees of integration and differentiation) and changes in them over time, the various bonds of interdependence, their power ratios, and the general material conditions these confer upon different participants. Staying with the food example, if we map out the relations that we (in a modern industrialized society) depend on to procure food, we would see a very long and complicated relational chain. As eaters, we would be linked to: growers; researchers, developers and providers of seeds, chemicals, and farm equipment; processors; corporations; advertisers and their media; products and brand names; shippers; sellers; coordinators and regulators of these processes; employees involved in these activities; and more. At the same time, we can easily imagine contrasts with eaters involved in different figurational circumstances whose food-related bonds are fewer, less functionally differentiated, involve fewer levels of integration, are less stratified, and produce very different material conditions.

Habitus refers to the group-specific — observable at varying levels of generality — system of schemes (i.e., an orderly combination of elements) that organizes perception and generates classifiable practices and works. The capacity of habitus to engender such products is endless, but habitus is limited in that it reflects the historical and social conditions in which it develops. As a "system of schemes" involving countless processes at chemical, biological, neurological, and social levels, habitus underlies the development of society-specific dispositions. While sociologists cannot directly observe these simultaneous processes, we can observe habitus indirectly through the practices and works it generates.

Classifiable practices and works refer to the stuff we make and do via a certain kind of habitus. These include, but are not limited to, thoughts, perceptions, expressions, actions, and ways of doing, perceiving, and classifying. Integrated together in a particular way, they constitute a lifestyle. The overall system within which what we make and do fits, lifestyle involves the recognition and use of distinctive signs by which we perceive and classify others and are perceived and classified by others. In the process of doing lifestyle, we condition (or influence the development of) habitus of our existence on an ongoing basis, via reinforcement, change, or both.[6]

Again, using food to illustrate and summarize, we can understand that it is by way of the ongoing activities of the habitus process that we develop perceptions about what foods are normal or strange, preferences for the foods we deem good, eating practices that reflect social status and values, products in terms of certain kinds of food-related packaging and waste, pollution, and infrastructure, to name only a few examples. In living in a particular way — maintaining and/or adjusting our ways of perceiving, thinking, doing, and classifying — we continually participate in the ongoing creation and recreation of habitus via reinforcement, change, or as is more often the case, both.

Putting It to Work

Suggesting the possibility of a foundational theory is a radical move but, in the realm of contemporary sociological theory, it is not nearly as radical as providing guidelines for using it. Below I provide a series of questions and prompts (see Figure 2) that are generalizable to attempts to better understand social phenomena and to study it empirically. Before proceeding, some caveats are in order. First, the steps outlined below are extremely general; adapting them effectively to a specific topic requires prolonged and careful thought. And each one is a significant undertaking in itself. Second, together the questions represent a wide array of levels of analysis—from large-scale trends over long periods of time to the minute details of today — and are not necessarily to be pursued by any one researcher, certainly not within any one project. One or more of them is likely to be of greater interest and relevance to a given researcher, but a sense of the range of basic questions can help show how one's particular research questions are connected to other questions at different levels of analysis. And, indicating the different kinds of expertise needed for exploring the topic in different ways, it facilitates the sort of collaboration increasingly recognized as valuable and necessary.

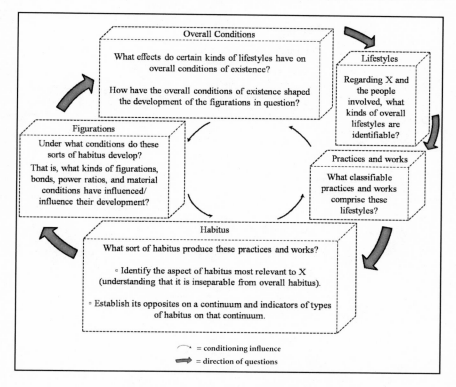

Figure 2. Guide to Using Relational Process Theory

For Example...

My environmental sociology research strives to better understand "environmental behavior": why people do what they do and *what* the environmental consequences of it are. In the effort to explore this topic using concepts more adequate to the task than conventional ones, I introduced the notion of ecological habitus (see Kasper 2009). Below, I provide a brief glimpse of what relational process theory, applied to the study of the ecologically relevant aspects of habitus, might look like. Posing the sequence of questions (see Figure 3) in the specific terms of this topic demonstrates the capacity of this framework to guide empirical research.

Each step represents a significant project in its own right, contains a number of more specific theories and hypotheses, and highlights a variety of methodological possibilities. Some require more time to explore than others; some more explicitly demand collaboration across disciplines. Whichever questions one decides to pursue, the point is that, in the context of a foundational sociological theory, we know where those questions fit in the big picture. In short, we can make better sociological sense of a topic from any angle.

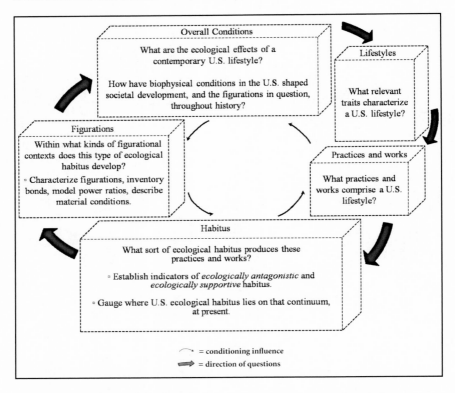

Figure 3. Example of Guide Applied to Environmental Sociology

Conclusion

To be sure, this theoretical framework demands an historical perspective and a wider view of a topic than is normally expected in sociological research. In Bourdieu's words, it demands the "combination of broad ambition and long patience that is needed to produce a work of science" discouraged by the current system that rewards a "safe thesis and a flash in the pan" (Bourdieu 1984, 512). Relative to existing sociological theory, this framework has a number of advantages: (1) in it individuals are never isolated from the necessarily social conditions of their existence and development; (2) it provides clear guidance for engaging in research, while allowing flexibility in terms of point of entry, data and methods, and time scale of interest; (3) it implies an understanding of human person as organism, highlighting the commensurability between sociological concepts and scientific knowledge; and (4) requiring a longer-term view, it encourages the kind of detachment that can provide a clearer—as in less ideological and personally invested—understanding of social processes.

Given the generations of warnings about and sober assessments of the state of sociology, it seems well beyond time to take genuine steps toward finally establishing a coherent, and thus sustainable, sociology. The theory presented here is intended to contribute to that end. It is a product of generations of efforts to seek a clearer understanding of sociology's task and provide the tools to more effectively carry it out. Contemporary social life and the many serious problems we confront are begging for deeper sociological understanding. Business as usual in the form of overly specialized sociology grounded in neither a reliable theory nor in a scientifically-informed understanding of the world and people is not going to get us there. For students who want to participate in bringing the necessary changes about, I offer the following recommendations:

• Become familiar with the problems of subject/object dualism and its implications for our understanding of human social life.[7]
• Understand the basics of human biology and neurology, especially the highlights of evolution and brain development and function, to deepen your understanding of the inherent sociality of being human.[8]
• Make figuration and habitus a part of your conceptual and verbal vocabulary. Strive to better understand these concepts and how to use them.[9]
• Use the relational process model to guide your thinking about, planning, and carrying out sociological research.

It was said that Elias' research program "contains a sweeping radicalism that has far-reaching implications ... [and] embraces scientific attitudes and obligations which, taken to their furthest conclusions, represent considerable challenges for sociologists" (Kilminster 2007, ix). It is conceivable that the theoretical framework proposed here represents such a "furthest conclusion." While it may involve some challenge, as transitions in thinking always do, I suggest that the changes it implies actually minimize the difficulties of teaching, learning, and doing sociology — and render all of these activities far more rewarding. At the very least, the changes proposed would introduce a greater degree of consistency and verifiability, both of which are necessary for a sociology that is — and is perceived to be — more coherent, legitimate, and genuinely useful.

Notes

1. This is a reference to *The Disobedient Generation: Social Theorists in the Sixties*, edited by Alan Sica and Stephen Turner (2005).
2. Half of these are well-established standards (i.e., "best-selling," "successful") and the other half are marketed as innovative alternatives (i.e., "unique" or explicit deviations from the norm). All have been published within the past five years.
3. Though Elias preferred the name "process sociology" for his work, the term "figurational sociology" caught on. Bourdieu's approach has no *one* consistent label. For the sake of convenience I will assign a referent here; and for maximum clarity, I call it "relational process theory."

4. "Functional interdependence" in this context refers to the real, dynamic, and multiperspectival purposes people (as individuals and groups) serve for each other, as opposed to the imagined needs of some collective entity.

5. For an elaboration, see *What is Sociology?* (1978, 122–57).

6. Once the concepts have become familiar, a simplified version of the model (e.g., one with components simply labeled figurations, habitus, classifiable practices and works, lifestyle, and overall conditions of existence) may be a more effective means of conveying and using relational process theory.

7. There are countless options for readings that elaborate on this problem. Particularly concise summaries can be found in Elias' *The Society of Individuals*, Parts I and II.

8. Basic biology and neuroscience texts are a great place to start. Recent discoveries (some of which are cited in this paper) are also important for better understanding brain functioning as it relates to social and other contexts. Examples of sociological works that integrate this knowledge include Elias 1978, 104–122; 1987a, 3–41; 1987b; 1991b, 17–64; Lenski 2005, 33–51; Massey 2005, 1–99.

9. Regarding figuration, see especially *What is Sociology?* (1978, 122–57). For the meaning of habitus, see Bourdieu's *Outline of a Theory of Practice* (1977, 72–95), *Invitation to a Reflexive Sociology* (1992, 126–39) and Elias' *The Society of Individuals* (1991a, 155–237). For examples of habitus studies, see Bourdieu's *Distinction* (1984, 168–225) and Elias' "Technization and Civilization" (1995), *The Civilizing Process* (2000), and *The Germans* (1996).

References

Alexander, Jeffrey C., and Kenneth Thompson. 2008. *A Contemporary Introduction to Sociology: Culture and Society in Transition.* Boulder: Paradigm.

Babchuk, Nicholas, and Bruce Keith. 1995. Introducing the Discipline: The Scholarly Content of Introductory Texts. *Teaching Sociology* 23 (3): 215–25.

Ballantine, Jeanne H., and Keith A. Roberts. 2009. *Our Social World: Introduction to Sociology.* Los Angeles: Pine Forge Press.

Becker, Howard S., and William C. Rau. 1992. Sociology in the 1990s. *Society* 30 (November/December): 70–4.

Bengston, William F., and John W. Hazzard. 1990. The Assimilation of Sociology into Common Sense: Some Implications for Teaching. *Teaching Sociology* 18 (1): 39–45.

Bourdieu, Pierre. 1977. *Outline of a Theory of Practice.* Cambridge: Cambridge University Press.

_____. 1984. *Distinction: A Social Critique of the Judgment of Taste.* Cambridge: Harvard University Press.

_____. 1988. Vive la Crise!: For Heterodoxy in Social Science. *Theory and Society* 17 (5): 773–87.

_____. 1990. *The Logic of Practice.* Stanford: Stanford University Press.

Bourdieu, Pierre, and Loïc J. D. Wacquant. 1992. *An Invitation to Reflexive Sociology.* Chicago: University of Chicago Press.

Calhoun, Craig, Joseph Gerteis, James Moody, Steven Pfaff, and Indermohan Virk, eds. 2007. *Contemporary Sociological Theory.* Malden, MA: Blackwell Publishing.

Colapinto, John. 2009. Brain Games: The Marco Polo of Neuroscience. *The New Yorker* May 11.

Cole, Stephen. 1994. Why Sociology Doesn't Make Progress Like the Natural Sciences. *Sociological Forum* 9 (1): 133–54.

Crossley, Nick. 2001. The Phenomenological Habitus and Its Construction. *Theory and Society* 30 (1): 81–120.

Dandaneau, Steven P. 2009. Sisyphus Had it Easy: Reflections of Two Decades of Teaching the Sociological Imagination. *Teaching Sociology* 37 (1): 8–19.

Davis, James A. 1994. What's Wrong with Sociology? *Sociological Forum* 9 (2): 179–97.

DeCesare, Michael. 2005. 95 Years of Teaching High School Sociology. Paper presented at

the annual meeting for the American Sociological Association, Philadelphia. http://www.
allacademic.com/meta/p18602_index.html.
_____. 2007. AP or Not AP? That is the Question. *Footnotes* December.
Deflem, Mathieu. 1999. Teaching Theory for Sociology Students: Junior Notes. *Perspectives*
21 (2): 7–8.
de Silva, E. T. 2003. Evaluating the Development of Sociological Perspective from Introduction
to Sociology: Problems with the Assessment Instrument. Paper presented at the annual
meeting for the American Sociological Association, Atlanta, GA. Online http://www.alla
cademic.com/meta/p106640_index.html.
Doidge, Norman. 2007. *The Brain That Changes Itself: Stories of Personal Triumph from the
Frontiers of Brain Science.* New York: Viking.
Eckstein, Rick, Rebecca Schoenike, and Kevin Delaney. 1995. The Voice of Sociology: Obstacles
to Teaching and Learning the Sociological Imagination. *Teaching Sociology* 23 (3): 353–
63.
Elias, Norbert. 1978. *What is Sociology?* New York: Columbia University Press.
_____. 1987a. *Involvement and Detachment.* Oxford: Blackwell.
_____. 1987b. On Human Beings and Their Emotions: A Process-Sociological Essay. *Theory,
Culture and Society* 4 (2–3): 339–61.
_____. 1991a. *The Society of Individuals.* Oxford: Blackwell.
_____. 1991b. *The Symbol Theory.* London: Sage Publications.
_____. 1995. Technization and Civilization. *Theory, Culture and Society* 12 (3): 7–42.
_____. 2000. *The Civilizing Process: Sociogenetic and Psychogenetic Investigations.* Oxford:
Blackwell.
Elliott, Anthony. 1999. *The Blackwell Reader in Contemporary Social Theory.* Malden, MA:
Blackwell.
Elliott, Anthony, and Larry J. Ray. 2003. *Key Contemporary Social Theorists.* Malden, MA:
Blackwell.
Emirbayer, Mustafa. 1997. Manifesto for a Relational Sociology. *American Journal of Sociology*
103 (2): 281–317.
Giddens, Anthony. 1979. *Central Problems in Social Theory.* Berkeley: University of California
Press.
_____. 1984. *The Constitution of Society: Outline of the Theory of Structuration.* Berkeley: Uni-
versity of California Press.
Grauerholz, Liz, and Sharon Bouma-Holtrop. 2003. Exploring Critical Sociological Thinking.
Teaching Sociology 31 (4): 485–96.
Henslin, James M. 2009. *Essentials of Sociology: A Down-to-Earth Approach.* Boston: Pear-
son/Allyn and Bacon.
Huber, Joan. 1995. Institutional Perspectives on Sociology. *The American Journal of Sociology*
101 (1): 194–216.
Kalberg, Stephen. 2007. A Cross-National Consensus on a Unified Sociological Theory? Some
Inter-Cultural Obstacles. *European Journal of Social Theory* 10 (2): 206–19.
Kasper, Debbie V.S. 2009. Ecological Habitus: Toward a Better Understanding of Socioeco-
logical Relations. *Organization and Environment* 22 (3): 311–26.
Kaspersen, Lars B., and Norman Gabriel. 2008. The Importance of Survival Units for Norbert
Elias's Figurational Perspective. *The Sociological Review* 56 (3): 370–87.
Keith, Bruce. 2000. Taking Stock of the Discipline: Some Reflections on the State of American
Sociology. *The American Sociologist* 31 (1): 5–14.
Keith, Bruce, and Morten G. Ender. 2004. The Sociological Core: Conceptual Patterns and
Idiosyncrasies in the Structure and Content of Introductory Sociology Textbooks, 1940–
2000. *Teaching Sociology* 32 (1): 19–36.
Kilminster, Richard. 2007. *Norbert Elias: Post-Philosophical Sociology.* New York: Routledge.
King, Anthony. 2000. Thinking with Bourdieu against Bourdieu: A "Practical" Critique of
the Habitus. *Sociological Theory* 18 (3): 417–33.
Lemert, Charles C. 1995. *Sociology after the Crisis.* Boulder: Westview Press.
Leming, Michael R. 1990. Prioritizing Sociological Perspective over Concepts. *Teaching Soci-
ology* 18: 533–35.

Lenski, Gerhard E. 2005. *Ecological-Evolutionary Theory: Principles and Applications*. Boulder: Paradigm.

Lopreato, Joseph, and Timothy A. Crippen. 1999. *Crisis in Sociology: The Need for Darwin*. New Brunswick, NJ: Transaction Publishers.

Macionis, John. 2007. *Sociology*. Upper Saddle River, NJ: Prentice Hall.

Massey, Douglas S. 2005. *Strangers in a Strange Land: Humans in an Urbanizing World*. New York: W.W. Norton.

Mouzelis, Nicos P. 1995. *Sociological Theory: What Went Wrong? Diagnosis and Remedies*. London: Routledge.

Nehm, Ross H., Therese M. Poole, Mark E. Lyford, Sally G. Hoskins, Laura Carruth, Brent E. Ewers, and Patricia J.S. Colberg. 2008. Does the Segregation of Evolution in Biology Textbooks and Introductory Courses Reinforce Students' Faulty Mental Models of Biology and Evolution? *Evolution: Education and Outreach* http://www.springerlink.com/content/vnt5075254900957/.

Phillips, Bernard. 1999. Confronting Our Tower of Babel. *Perspectives* 21(4): 2–6.

_____. 2001. *Beyond Sociology's Tower of Babel: Reconstructing the Scientific Method*. New York: Aldine de Gruyter.

Pinker, Steven. 2002. *The Blank Slate: The Modern Denial of Human Nature*. New York: Penguin Books.

Ramachandran, V.S. 2000. Mirror Neurons and Imitation Learning as the Driving Force Behind "the Great Leap Forward" in Human Evolution. http://www.edge.org/3rd_culture/ramachandran/ramachandran_p1.html.

_____. 2004. *A Brief Tour of Human Consciousness*. New York: Pi Press.

Ritzer, George, and Douglas J. Goodman. 2008. *Sociological Theory*. Boston: McGraw-Hill.

Rule, James B. 1994. Dilemmas of Theoretical Progress. *Sociological Forum* 9 (2): 241–57.

Seidman, Steven. 1991. The End of Sociological Theory: The Postmodern Hope. *Sociological Theory* 9 (Fall): 131–46.

Sewell, William H., Jr. 1992. A Theory of Structure: Duality, Agency, and Transformation. *American Journal of Sociology* 98 (1): 1–29.

Sica, Alan, ed. 1998. *What is Social Theory? The Philosophical Debates*. Oxford: Blackwell.

Stinchcombe, Arthur L. 1994. Disintegrated Disciplines and the Future of Sociology. *Sociological Forum* 9 (2): 279–91.

Thio, Alex. 2005. *Sociology: A Brief Introduction*. Boston: Pearson/Allyn and Bacon.

Tooby, John, and Leda Cosmides. 1992. The Psychological Foundations of Culture. In *The Adapted Mind: Evolutionary Psychology and the Generation of Culture*, ed. Jerome H. Barkow, Leda Cosmides, and John Tooby, 19–136. New York: Oxford University Press.

Turner, Jonathan. 2004. Is Grand Theory Dead and Should Sociology Care? A Reply to Lamont. *Perspectives* 27 (2): 2–12.

Turner, Stephen P., and Jonathan H. Turner. 1990. *The Impossible Science: An Institutional Analysis of American Sociology*. Newbury Park, CA: Sage Publications.

Zald, Mayer N. 1991. Sociology as a Discipline: Quasi-Science and Quasi-Humanities. *The American Sociologist* 22 (3–4): 165–87.

PART II: METHODOLOGY

8. "SHUT UP IN MEASURELESS CONTENT"
Confronting the Measurement Problem in Sociology

Michael DeCesare

> *Measurement problems constitute the key to the advancement of any science.*
> — Blalock 1968, 6

More than 30 years ago, Hubert Blalock devoted his Presidential Address to the American Sociological Association (ASA) to the topics of measurement and conceptualization. "I believe," he wrote, "that the most serious and important problems that require our immediate and concerted attention are those of conceptualization and measurement, which have far too long been neglected" (Blalock 1979, 882). He continued: "[C]onceptualization and measurement problems ... are so complex, and their implications for analysis so serious, that I believe that a really coordinated effort in this direction is absolutely essential." The urgency of Blalock's tone was most unusual among ASA Presidential Addresses.

Had he lived to see the year 2011, Blalock would have been disappointed to observe that the effort he so urgently called for has not been undertaken; for he, perhaps more than any other twentieth-century sociologist, understood the difficulties inherent in measurement and conceptualization — and warned about the dangers of ignoring them (1979, 893–94):

> If we do not make this concerted effort [toward solving conceptualization and measurement problems], I fear that sociology in the year 2000 will be no more advanced than it is today, though perhaps it will contain far more specializations, theoretical schools, methodological cults, and interest groups than, even today, we can readily imagine.

Many — perhaps most — sociologists would agree that Blalock's predictions have come to pass.

Indeed, conceptualization and measurement problems not only persist in sociology, but characterize nearly all of the field's empirical research. It is the thesis of this chapter that until sociologists confront the measurement problem, in particular, it will remain the biggest obstacle to theory development and methodological advancement that we face. This is not a novel argument. But it is one that is worth repeating, for sociologists continue to design and carry out research as if all of our concepts are perfectly operationalized, as if all of our variables are perfectly measured, as if we have no doubt that we are measuring exactly what we intend to measure in the most valid, reliable, precise, and accurate way of measuring it — as if, in other words, measurement error simply does not exist or, at least, is not worth talking about.

In an effort to highlight the ongoing measurement problem in sociology, I begin by defining social measurement. I then discuss the past and current states of measurement in sociology; in the process, I explain why measurement is a crucial component of sociological methodology. The second half of the chapter assesses the extent and consequences of the measurement problem in sociology, primarily by way of a case study of the ill-fated *Teachers for a New Era* (*TNE*) project. In conclusion, I suggest some ways in which sociologists can improve their measurement by answering the general question of why we measure.

What Is Social Measurement?

This chapter is, at heart, about clearly defining and measuring concepts, so it seems appropriate to begin by defining what exactly is meant by the term *measurement*. In the social sciences, measurement has traditionally been described as the process of systematically assigning symbols, usually numerals, to observations according to some prior rule(s) (cf., Chang and Cartwright 2008, 367; Cicourel 1964, 10–1; Kaplan 1964, 177; Stevens 1946, 677; Wallace 1971, 37). Wartofsky (1968, 172) points out that the use of measurement in any science "is to serve theory, in its two contexts of discovery and justification"; more specifically, measurement is used to confirm, falsify, and test scientific predictions, as well as to discover new scientific laws (cf., 172–80). Regardless of the purpose(s) measurement serves to a particular researcher in the context of a particular study, the measurability of social and physical phenomena is always both *practically limited* and *theoretically limited* (196). I am concerned in this chapter solely with *practically limited measurability*; that is, with "the limits of the instrument and the techniques of calibration beyond a certain degree of precision."[1]

Nominalism: Defining a Subjective Social World

Following Wartofsky (1968), philosophers of science have provided a general way of approaching measurement by staking out two positions. One, which may be called *nominalism*, assumes that the methods of measuring a concept actually define the concept itself (Chang and Cartwright 2008). Perhaps the most popular form of nominalism is *operationalism*. Credit has historically been given to the American physicist Percy W. Bridgman for the notion of an operational definition. In one of his earliest and best-known books, *The Logic of Modern Physics* (1927, 5), Bridgman applied operational thinking to the concept of length:

> To find the length of an object, we have to perform certain physical operations. The concept of length is therefore fixed when the operations by which length is measured are fixed; that is, the concept of length involves as much as and nothing more than the set of operations by which length is determined. In general, we mean by any concept nothing more than a set of operations; *the concept is synonymous with the corresponding set of operations.*[2]

The concept of length, then, according to the operationalist, is nothing more than or less than the physical act of putting a ruler or a yardstick (or any other standard measure of length) to an object. The instrument one uses, of course, determines how one conceptualizes length: as a cubit, as a yard, as a foot, or as something else altogether.

One need only think about standard versus metric units of measurement; whether dealing with length, weight, velocity, volume, or what have you, there can be no doubt that the application of either standard or metric units results in a very different conceptualization. One person who thinks and speaks in terms of inches adheres to a concept of length that is very different from that used by the person who thinks and speaks in terms of centimeters. The same holds true for the distinctions between pounds and kilograms, miles per hour and kilometers per hour, and gallons and liters. *The conceptualizations of weight, velocity, and volume change depending upon how they are measured.*

To take another example: From an operationalist's perspective, the concept of intelligence simply *"is* what an IQ test measures" (Blalock 1968, 8). One is only as "intelligent" (or "unintelligent," as the case may be) as his/her IQ test results indicate. But if I were to propose a different and empirically sound way of measuring intelligence — say by counting the lines on one's forehead rather than the points one scores on a test — the operationalist would have to accept it as just as valid as an IQ test. But this would lead to two very different conceptualizations of what it means to be "intelligent." For you, it depends on your test score; for me, it depends on the lines on your brow.

Conventionalism, a less extreme version of nominalism, is the notion that "we are free to choose by agreement the correct measurement method for a concept" (Chang and Cartwright 2008, 368). Rather than defining a concept in terms of measurement operations, conventionalists attempt to arrive at an agreed-upon measurement operation to regulate the use of a concept. And, "[b]ecause nature does not dictate the correct method of measurement, we are left with convention as the highest epistemic authority" (ibid). In terms of measuring the concept of gender, for instance, there has been general agreement for quite some time about using just two attributes: male and female. Whether this measure of gender is good or bad is quite irrelevant; what matters to conventionalists is that it has, in fact, become the convention.

Realism: Measuring an Objective Social World

The second broad philosophical position, what we may call *realism*, treats measurements as "methods of finding out about objective quantities that we can identify independently of measurement" (Chang and Cartwright 2008, 367). Realists do not treat measurements as definitive of concepts; rather, measurement is undertaken to discover "the true value of a specified quantity that exists independently of how we measure it" (368–69). In other words, an objective, observable reality exists, and accurate observations of it can only be accomplished through measurement.

S. S. Stevens (1946) long ago became one of the best-known of realists. Stevens famously delineated four types of measurement scale: nominal, ordinal, interval, and ratio. A *nominal* scale uses numerals—though words or letters or any other symbols would work just as well — simply as labels. Even this "primitive form" of a scale, Stevens (1946, 679) points out, "is an example of the 'assignment of numerals according to a rule.' The rule is: Do not assign the same numeral to different classes or different numerals to the same class. Beyond that, anything goes with the nominal scale." An *ordinal* scale is more complicated, though still not "quantitative" in the way sociologists use that term. It is based on data that have been rank-ordered: best to worst, highest to lowest, most to least, etc. *Interval* scales, by contrast, have a conventional or convenient, as opposed to a "true," zero point. Finally, a *ratio* scale both allows for the transformation of its numerical values and implies an absolute zero. Stevens' (1946) classification of the four scales of measurement is summarized, usually under the heading "Levels of Measurement," in every social research methods textbook and in every social statistics text; for better or worse, it has been the model of social measurement for 65 years.[3]

Measurement in Sociology: Past and Present

Sociologists' almost willful ignorance of measurement problems has a long history. Very little attention was paid to social measurement during the first few decades of sociology's existence in the U.S. It was not until the late 1930s that sociologists began to think and to write about operationalization and measurement in a systematic way. The earliest and most ardent champion of applying Bridgman's (1927) operational analysis in sociology was George Lundberg, who declared that "the only way of defining anything objectively is in terms of the operations involved" (Lundberg 1939, 58).

Lundberg was reacting to the current state of affairs in sociology: "The same sociologist frequently uses the same term in various senses in the same article" (Lundberg 1939, 58). The solution to this problem, Lundberg believed, was to try to understand concepts by way of the operations that were performed on them. I consider Lundberg's assertion in detail below (see "How Pervasive is the Measurement Problem in Sociology?"), but a quick contemporary example is in order here: Howard Becker (2008, 412) recently pointed out that Thomas Kuhn — the most important philosopher of science of the latter half of the twentieth century and, in Becker's esteemed opinion, "as careful and skilled a writer as the social sciences ever produced"— used his key term "paradigm" in about 20 different ways in his classic book *The Structure of Scientific Revolutions.*

Operationalists like Lundberg and Harry Alpert (1938) made little headway with their colleagues, and most sociological methodologists moved on to other interests related to measurement. Between the late 1940s and the early 1970s, sociologists' interest in measurement "seems to have been episodic rather than continuous," according to Blalock (1974, 1):

> During the late 1940s and early 1950s there was considerable interest in attitude measurement and procedures such as factor analysis, Guttman scaling, and latent-structure analysis, but a period of relative stagnation set in during the later 1950s and early 1960s that seemed to portend a declining interest.... Carefully conceived scales were replaced by rather simple two- or three-item indices in the belief that the latter were almost as good as the former. Since 1965, however, a kind of revival of interest in the measurement field has been apparent in sociology.

The revival during the late 1960s and early 1970s did not last long, though, prompting Blalock's (1979) ASA Address which urged sociologists to pay more attention to problems of measurement and conceptualization. Despite Blalock's warning, the problems and complexities inherent in measurement have been largely ignored by sociologists over the past three decades. Since the late 1970s, we have again kept ourselves, like Shakespeare's King Duncan, "shut up in measureless content."

Sociologists' "measureless content" can be attributed, at least in part, to two trends that have accelerated over the past 30 years: instructors' reliance on research methods textbooks and researchers' utilization of advanced statistical techniques. It is difficult to distinguish cause from effect here. Did we grow content with our measurements because of textbook authors' confident treatment of the topic, or is measurement treated so succinctly by textbook authors because sociologists are believed to have mastered the art? Do researchers pretend measurement error does not exist because of our blind devotion to statistical analysis, or do we utilize complex statistical techniques partly because we believe that we have solved our measurement problems? I do not claim to know the answer to either question. What I do know is that each appears to represent an inverse relationship; that is, as we have come to rely *more* heavily on textbooks, we have become *less* cognizant of serious measurement problems, and as we have developed and used *more* advanced statistical techniques, we have paid *less* attention to how we measure the variables in our models.

To be sure, every methods text in sociology devotes some space to measurement. The overwhelming majority of texts devote a chapter to measurement in the first half of the book (e.g., Adler and Clark 2011; Gray et al. 2007; Frankfort-Nachmias and Nachmias 2008; Neuman 2006). Interestingly, the most popular textbook on the market gives measurement the shortest shrift by incorporating it into a longer chapter on operationalization and conceptualization rather than devoting a separate chapter to it (cf., Babbie 2010). Regardless of where it is placed in the organization of the text, measurement is almost always presented in the same way: As a summary of S. S. Stevens' (1946) four "levels of measurement" (see above), followed by a brief discussion of reliability and validity (and sometimes precision and accuracy), and a concluding obligatory note about the importance of "triangulating" methods to overcoming measurement problems. No methods or statistics textbook that I am aware of cites Otis Duncan, Hubert Blalock, or any of the other sociologists who devoted most of their careers to thinking about, writing about, and improving the quality of social measurement.

The inadequate consideration given to measurement by sociologists is also evident in the articles that appear in sociological journals. With the exception of a handful of journals that specialize in so-called "qualitative" methods, there has been a clear shift in scholarly journals in sociology toward publishing more articles that rely on statistical analysis and modeling. This, in and of itself, is not necessarily problematic. What is problematic is that none of the analyses or types of modeling that have been appearing with greater frequency do anything to solve the measurement problem. In fact, they only compound it by assuming, usually implicitly, that every variable in the model is precisely and adequately measured. But as Duncan (1984, 231) reminded us a quarter-century ago: "[T]he measurement problem must be solved *before* the 'synthetic' index is computed."

It was precisely this state of affairs to which Duncan (1984, 226) was referring when he accused sociologists of *statisticism*: a "syndrome," he called it, that was based on

> the notion that computing is synonymous with doing research, the naïve faith
> that statistics is a complete or sufficient basis of scientific methodology, the
> superstition that statistical formulas exist for evaluating such things as the relative merits of different substantive theories or the "importance" of the causes of
> a "dependent variable"; and the delusion that decomposing the covariations of
> some arbitrary and haphazardly assembled collection of variables can somehow
> justify not only a "causal model" but also, praise the mark, a "measurement
> model."

Duncan regretted that there was no "clearly identifiable sector" of sociological research "wherein such fallacies were clearly recognized and emphatically out of bounds." Instead, he observed, "articles of exemplary quality are published cheek-by-jowl with transparent exercises in statistical numerology" (226).

The trend continues. Perhaps more troubling, though, is that even those sociologists who claim to be sensitive to the dangers of statisticism fall victim to it anyway. A recent exchange in the *American Sociological Review*, the ASA's flagship journal, is a case in point. In 2005, Ben Jann published a statistical critique of Xiaogang Wu and Yu Xie's (2003) article "Does the Market Pay Off? Earnings Returns to Education in Urban China." Xie and Wu (2005, 865) wrote a rejoinder that began with a description of what Duncan meant by the term *statisticism*, and proceeded to openly accuse their critic of practicing it:

> In the final analysis, our disagreement with Jann is not about the technical correctness of statistical methods, but about *how* statistical methods should be used in sociological research. We are strong believers in the viewpoint that statistical methodology should not be separated from substantive concerns in guiding research. Jann's "methodological" critique of our work is misdirected precisely because it is narrowly methodological, lacking an understanding of both the substantive research question and the underlying social processes.

The authors go on to note the statisticism epidemic among sociologists, as well as the tendency among "quantitative" researchers to privilege statistical tests over substantive knowledge (866):

> To be fair, Jann should not be singled out for falling into the trap of "statisticism" because such practice is so widespread in current sociology that it often makes quantitative research unappealing. Jann's comment illustrates a common temptation among quantitative sociologists: reliance on canned statistical tests rather than substantive knowledge. Thus, we take this opportunity to draw a general lesson for all of us: only when combined with a substantive understanding of the social processes involved can statistical methods result in fruitful research.

There are two ironies in this story. The first is that Xie and Wu's (2005) rejoinder is characterized by an even higher degree of statisticism than Jann's (2005) critique. In less than five pages of text, they managed to cram two equations, a flowchart, a scatterplot, and a propensity score analysis; Jann had only one equation and two tables in his five-page piece. The second, and more important, irony is Xie and Wu's (2005) juxtaposition of statistical methodology/tests and substantive concerns/knowledge/understanding. Potential measurement problems were completely ignored by everyone in the debate.[4]

And so, ironically enough, even among the statisticists we find a proclivity for criticizing statisticism. The trend toward what Duncan referred to as "statistical numerology" in sociological research has only accelerated since the early 1980s, while our work on improving measurement has significantly decelerated.

Blalock (1979, 883) made the same point in his ASA Presidential Address more than 30 years ago:

> We have recently made considerable progress with respect to data analysis but relatively little with respect to date collection, and in particular our ability to observe, categorize, and measure behaviors. Even if one does not accept this assertion, I assume there is consensus on the need to improve our measurement of behaviors.

Put plainly, our statistical analyses continue their rapid progress while our measurements remain prehistoric.[5]

How Pervasive Is the Measurement Problem in Sociology?

"That sociologists exhibit only slight agreement even in the use of the most common terms is a matter of common knowledge." George Lundberg (1939, 58) wrote these words more than 70 years ago. But they could have been written yesterday. In fact, the single example of the term *race*, a fundamental sociological concept, serves to illustrate the pervasiveness of measurement problems in sociology.

Consider the ways in which race has been measured in the General Social Survey (GSS) and by the U.S. Census Bureau, which are two of the most common sources of data for sociologists. The GSS has been conducted annually or bi-annually since 1972; it is one of the most widely relied upon national surveys in existence. The Census has been conducted regularly since 1790; its importance needs no explanation.[6] The race item in the GSS has asked of each respondent since 1972: "What race do you consider yourself?" There are three substantive response categories: White, Black, and Other. By contrast, the 2010 Census asked "What is Person #'s race?" There are 14 substantive response categories, plus a "Some other race" category.

Adhering to the operationalist position, we are forced to the absurd conclusion that the concept of race is correctly and fully defined by the measurement operations (i.e., the GSS and Census items) themselves. Race, quite simply, is what these questionnaire items about race measure — they just happen to be very different items with very different response categories. One obvious problem with this line of reasoning, in this example, is that three categories almost certainly do not capture the complexities of the concept of race, while 14 categories may very well paint *too* detailed of a picture. Second, one could fairly easily write a few dozen questionnaire items, different from these two, which purport to measure race. This realization leaves us with a number of troubling questions: Does each of these dozens of items really represent a different definition of race? If so, with all of these different definitions, how can sociologists ever hope to theorize about race? How can we possibly understand or analyze it? And, ultimately, which of these definitions is best — which is most precise, most accurate, most valid, most reliable? Which one gets us closest to the essence of the concept of race?

Taking a purely realist position does not take us any further. There is a serious argument to be made against the assumptions that (1) race is an objective quantity and that (2) we can identify the categories of race independently of measurement. Many, if not most, sociologists would take the stance that race is both a cultural and a social construction; at various points in history, members of many societies around the world, for various and not particularly pleasant reasons, concocted the idea of racial categories and proceeded to behave as if they were objectively real and meaningful rather than arbitrary and contextual. Further, one cannot identify racial categories without measuring some physical attribute(s) — skin color, facial features, etc. Each of us measures race, on a personal level, every time we see another person, just as we measure gender, age, sexuality, social class, and other variables every time we see another person. We *must* measure something if we hope to construct categories that group different people or phenomena.

Race is just one of many examples of basic sociological concepts that have been and continue to be poorly measured — and that neither the operationalist nor the realist position brings us significantly closer to measuring in a better way. It is important to point out that race is not a selective example; I could just as easily have used social class, socioeconomic status, social disorganization, or any other of dozens of fundamental sociological concepts to make the same points. But why does it matter — and to whom does it matter — whether race is measured using 3 or 14 categories, or how social class or social disorganization are measured? What happens, in other words, when we ignore measurement problems and proceed directly to data collection and analysis?

The Consequences of Ignoring Measurement Problems: A Case Study of Teachers For a New Era (TNE)

This penultimate section offers a case study of the *Teachers for a New Era* project, which illustrates the conceptual, methodological, and practical dangers of ignoring measurement problems. In 2001, the Carnegie Corporation of New York announced an initiative to restructure teacher-training programs at colleges and universities "so as to set a national standard for excellence" ("Institutions" 2010). The project, called *Teachers for a New Era* (*TNE*), was described as "a landmark initiative designed to strengthen K-12 teaching by developing state-of-the-art programs at schools of education" ("Home" 2010). Indeed, it is difficult to think of a more pressing problem in the U.S. than the state of schooling. Liberals and conservatives alike constantly bemoan the poor performance of American schoolchildren; comparatively low standardized test scores and unfavorable comparisons to students in other countries support their complaints. The *TNE* initiative was undoubtedly a timely project aimed at one of this country's most persistent problems.

The funding for the project — $5 million to each of five institutions over five years — was to come from Carnegie, the Annenberg Foundation, and the Ford Foundation. As it turned out, only four, not five, institutions were chosen for the initial round of funding: Bank Street College of Education (New York), California State University–Northridge (CSUN), Michigan State University, and the University of Virginia. Each school began receiving funding in 2002. Seven additional institutions began receiving the same amount of funding in 2003: Boston College, Florida A & M University, Stanford University, and the Universities of Connecticut, Texas–El Paso, Washington, and Wisconsin–Milwaukee. Soon, the *TNE* initiative was expanded beyond the U.S. ("Scottish Teachers for a New Era" 2010).

The *TNE* project had three design principles: decisions based on evidence, engagement with the arts and sciences, and teaching as a clinical practice profession ("About TNE" 2010):

> First, a teacher education program should be guided by a respect for evidence, including attention to pupil learning gains accomplished under the tutelage of teachers who are graduates of the program. Second, faculty in the disciplines of the arts and sciences must be fully engaged in the education of prospective teachers, especially in the areas of subject matter understanding and general and liberal education. Finally, education should be understood as an academically taught clinical practice profession, requiring: close cooperation between colleges of education and actual practicing schools; master teachers as clinical faculty in the college of education; and residencies for beginning teachers during a two year period of induction.[7]

The design principles made *TNE* unique. Rarely before had there been such an overt emphasis on empirical, as opposed to anecdotal, evidence in the study of teacher training. Even more unique was the explicit mandate to include faculty in the arts and sciences in a teacher training program; such programs almost always fell under the purview of education researchers and faculty in schools of education. The most unusual principle, however, was the treatment of teaching as a "clinical practice," akin to the practice of medicine and, to a lesser extent, law.

Not surprisingly, the 11 funded institutions began their work diligently. On each campus, and across the campuses, faculty and administrators were teamed, research was conducted, papers were written, workshops were organized, and conferences were held. Between September 2006 and February 2009, *TNE* sponsored regular forums, conferences, and workshops, often in conjunction with a professional association's annual meeting, at the national level ("Home" 2010).

But almost as quickly as it blossomed, *TNE* wilted — on each of the 11 campuses. In-fighting and confusion began to set in. The purpose and direction of the project became unclear. The most recent news article on the *TNE* website is from May 2007. According to the same website, *TNE* has not sponsored any national events or produced a single publication since February 2009 ("Home" 2010). It is no longer a secret that the overly-ambitious *TNE* initiative fizzled out just about five years after it began, as had so many similar previous projects.

The question, naturally, is why. How could such an important undertaking, as well-funded by as many distinguished sources as *TNE* was, fail so quickly? Many reasons contribute to the failure of a large-scale initiative, and *TNE* is no exception: the project seemed doomed from the beginning by being administratively top-heavy, unwieldy in size, too broad in scope, and ambiguous in its ultimate purpose and direction. In my view, however, a much more important reason for the project's failure had to do with the measurements— or lack thereof— of its key concepts.

I was one of the original six *TNE* Faculty Fellows at CSUN, which was one of the first four grantee institutions.[8] Between 2004 and 2007, I split my research, teaching, and service duties equally between *TNE* and the Department of Sociology. In addition to my role as a Faculty Fellow, I was a member of the project's Evidence Team. Composed of sociologists and education researchers, the group worked toward the first *TNE* Design Principle of "Decisions Based on Evidence."

We struggled from the outset. Our primary question, which we labored over for several months, was whether to gather quantitative or qualitative data. We eventually decided to collect both types. Then the true difficulties set in. Our job was deceptively simple: to map the relationship between teacher training and student learning outcomes. But how to define *teacher training*? As if that were not difficult enough to answer, a much thornier question arose: How should we define *student learning outcomes*?

Our theoretical model of the relationship between teacher training and student learning ultimately included no fewer than 11 concepts: teacher characteristics, teacher preparation, the credential program structure, teacher abilities and skills, teacher school/class assignment, teaching performance, teaching environment, teacher retention, student learning, community context, and student background. And we easily came up with several measures of each of these 11 concepts. The entire process became so frustrating and convoluted, that we ultimately decided, for the purposes of our pilot study, to measure student learning outcomes simply with standardized test scores. The pilot flopped, we went back to struggling to measure our fundamental concepts, and we floundered.

So why did *TNE* fail? In part for the same reason that all education reform efforts have failed in this country: because no one has figured out how best to measure basic concepts like *student learning* and *teacher training*. Indeed, we cannot reach an agreement about how to measure whether a person is a "qualified" teacher (Ingersoll 1999) or even whether someone is a "good" teacher! And if we were to come up with a list of attributes—good teachers are funny and caring and knowledgeable and approachable and so on—how should we measure each? In what concrete way(s) do we best measure how funny a person is, or how caring, or knowledgeable, or approachable? The answer is that, presently, we cannot. And the only reason is that we have not devoted nearly enough of a collective effort to trying.

How Can Sociologists Measure Better or Why Do We Measure at All?

Otis Duncan (1984, 233) once suggested the following: "It could happen that some of the answers to questions about how to measure better will be found in a search for answers to the question of why we measure." It stands to reason that if we have a clear idea about why we are interested in measuring a particular concept, then we will work toward measuring it in the best way(s) that we can. Why do we measure race, for instance? Is it solely to look for differences among whites, blacks, and "others"? Often it is, which is why the GSS measure of race has stood for nearly 40 years. But sometimes it is not, which is why social scientists have developed alternative ways of measuring the concept. Following up on Duncan's idea, it seems worthwhile in conclusion to consider not only why we measure but, by extension, how we can measure better.

First, why do we measure? The answer, to my mind, is straightforward: to make statements that are as precise as possible about the social world generally, and about the relationships between social variables specifically. We measure so we can understand social life; the better our measurements, the fuller our understanding. If we cannot measure the concept of race in consistently valid, reliable, precise, accurate ways, we cannot hope to understand it in and of itself as a concept—let alone as a concept that structures relationships, perpetuates inequality, and fosters everything from unspoken fear to outright violence. Perhaps it is no surprise, then, that American sociologists have struggled so long with the question of race, or that the so-called "race problem" in this country persists.

But my answer to the question of why we measure is not the only one. For each of us, as social scientists, measures social phenomena for different reasons: to make (or refute) a political or ideological point, to gather evidence for (or against) a particular position, or merely to satisfy intellectual curiosity. Our measures always depend on the purpose(s) of our research, regardless of what they are. And that is why the question of why we measure is so difficult to answer; there are as many answers to it as there are sociologists who ask it. Though it is difficult to answer, it is not unanswerable. Adhering to different reasons for measuring certainly does not preclude us, as methodologists, from having a wide-ranging, intelligent, open dialogue. We have only acted as if it does, which leads inevitably to the kind of "measureless content" we have experienced for so long.

Let us assume, in conclusion, that sociologists do have sound reasons for measuring social phenomena, and that we agree on what they are. Now how can we measure better? "Better" here means some combination of the following: more precisely, more accurately, more validly, and more reliably. Whether we want to understand the social world or we seek to change it, our measurements of social variables had better be as precise, accurate, valid, and reliable as possible. Measuring race with three categories of white, black, and other is certainly not precise; it also is not accurate, valid, or reliable. Thus, it is unlikely that we will be able to say anything meaningful about race as long as we rely on this particular measurement of the concept.

What we need, if we sincerely hope to measure better, is the concerted effort that Blalock (1979) called for more than 30 years ago. Rather than racing each other to develop and use the fanciest statistical modeling, we should be talking to each other about the best ways to measure our most fundamental concepts. Instead of rehashing the argument over quantitative versus qualitative methods, we should emphasize the importance to each approach of precise measurement. Rather than mass-producing research methods textbooks and churning out statistics-based journal articles, we should devote serious and conscious thought to the ways in which we measure social phenomena.

Nearly 85 years ago, Percy Bridgman (1927, 34) wrote in *The Logic of Modern Physics*: "It is a general consequence of the approximate character of all measurement that no empirical science can ever make exact statements." Physics as an empirical science is, of course, able to make more exact statements than sociology, but Bridgman's point remains. I do not intend for this chapter to imply that sociology is capable of making precise statements about the nature of the social world; I only wish to argue that sociology is capable of making *much more* precise statements than it has and does. But realizing that capability requires a renewed and collective commitment to solving problems of measurement.

Acknowledgments

Preliminary work on this chapter was presented at the 2010 annual meeting of the Eastern Sociological Society. I wish to thank Peter Moskos, Jason Rodriquez, and Kevin Stainback for their feedback at that small and informal yet stimulating session. I also thank John Dalphin, Afshan Jafar, and Ieva Zake for their very helpful comments on a previous draft. My work on this chapter was funded in part by a 2010 Faculty Development Grant from Merrimack College.

Notes

1. A full treatment of *theoretically limited measurability*—the notion that the instrument itself disturbs what it is attempting to measure — would take us into a realm of the philosophy of science that is far afield of the narrow terrain of this chapter.

2. It is worth mentioning that although Bridgman later expressed "distaste" for the terms *operationalism* and *operationism*, he remained committed to the idea that the most useful approach to studying the physical world was "operational analysis" (Bridgman 1938, 114).

3. Duncan's (1984, 222–23) warning about the presumed "special authority" of Stevens' statements is important to note here. Writing more than 25 years ago, Duncan claimed that at least some of the authors of statistics textbooks felt "irresistible pressure from their publisher[s] to include a summary of the Stevens discussion because of reader demand" (Duncan 1984, 222). This, despite the fact that Stevens himself was not a statistician, and was averse to using formal statistical models in his own field of psychology or in his own research (222–23).

4. Perhaps a third irony in this story is that the namesake of Xie's current position was primarily concerned with measurement: Xie, at the time of this writing, is the Otis Dudley Duncan Distinguished University Professor of Sociology at the University of Michigan.

5. One sometimes wonders whether our statistical techniques have, in fact, progressed, for even the old debate about the value of significance testing persists— and not only in sociology (cf., Cohen 1994; Morrison and Henkel 1970).

6. It is worth mentioning here that Peter Marsden and Michael Hout, the Co-Principal Investigators of the GSS, are sociologists, as is the Director of the Census Bureau, Robert Groves.

7. For a more detailed explanation of the three design principles, see the TNE prospectus at http://www.teachersforanewera.org/index.cfm?fuseaction=home.prospectus.

8. Of the original six *TNE* Faculty Fellows at CSUN, only two remain at the University, as of this writing. The four others of us left CSUN to take positions at other institutions in 2007 or 2008. I would argue that this pattern is yet another indication of the failure of *TNE*— at least at CSUN.

References

Adler, Emily S., and Roger Clark. 2011. *An Invitation to Social Research: How It's Done.* Belmont, CA: Wadsworth.

Adler, Franz. 1947. Operational Definitions in Sociology. *American Journal of Sociology* 52 (5): 438–44.

Alpert, Harry. 1938. Operational Definitions in Sociology. *American Sociological Review* 3: 855–61.

Babbie, Earl. 2010. *The Practice of Social Research.* Belmont, CA: Wadsworth.

Becker, Howard S. 2008. Above All, Write with Clarity and Precision. *Sociological Inquiry* 78 (3): 412–16.

Blalock, Hubert M. 1968. The Measurement Problem: A Gap Between the Languages of Theory and Research. In *Methodology in Social Research*, ed. Hubert M. Blalock and Ann Blalock, 5–27. New York: McGraw-Hill.

_____. 1974. Introduction. In *Measurement in the Social Sciences: Theories and Strategies*, ed. Hubert M. Blalock, 1–7. Chicago: Aldine.

_____. 1979. Measurement and Conceptualization Problems: The Major Obstacle to Integrating Theory and Research. *American Sociological Review* 44: 881–94.

_____. 1982. *Conceptualization and Measurement in the Social Sciences.* Beverly Hills: Sage Publications.

Bridgman, P. W. 1927. *The Logic of Modern Physics.* New York: Macmillan.

_____. 1938. Operational Analysis. *Philosophy of Science* 5: 114–31.

Chang, Hasok, and Nancy Cartwright. 2008. Measurement. In *The Routledge Companion to Philosophy of Science*, ed. Stathis Psillos and Martin Curd, 367–75. London: Routledge.

Cicourel, Aaron V. 1964. *Method and Measurement in Sociology.* New York: Free Press.

Cohen, Jacob. 1994. The Earth is Round (*p* < .05). *American Psychologist* 49 (December): 997–1003.

Duncan, Otis D. 1984. *Notes on Social Measurement: Historical and Critical.* New York: Russell Sage.

Frankfort-Nachmias, Chava, and David Nachmias. 2008. *Research Methods in the Social Sciences.* New York: Worth.

Gray, Paul S., John B. Williamson, David A. Karp, and John R. Dalphin. 2007. *The Research Imagination: An Introduction to Qualitative and Quantitative Methods.* New York: Cambridge University Press.

Ingersoll, Richard M. 1995. The Problem of Underqualified Teachers in American Secondary Schools. *Education Researcher* 28 (2): 26–37.

Jann, Ben. 2005. Earnings Returns to Education in Urban China: A Note on Testing Difference among Groups. *American Sociological Review* 70 (October): 860–64.

Kaplan, Arthur. 1964. *The Conduct of Inquiry: Methodology for Behavioral Science.* San Francisco: Chandler.

Lundberg, George A. 1939. *Foundations of Sociology.* New York: Macmillan.

Morrison, Denton E., and Ramon E. Henkel. 1970. *The Significance Test Controversy: A Reader.* Chicago: Aldine.

Neuman, W. Lawrence. 2006. *Social Research Methods: Qualitative and Quantitative Approaches.* Boston: Allyn and Bacon.

Scottish Teachers for a New Era. 2010. http://www.abdn.ac.uk/stne/index.php?id=1.

Stevens, S. S. 1946. On the Theory of Scales of Measurement. *Science* 103 (2684): 677–80.

Teachers for a New Era. 2010. *About TNE.* http://www.teachersforanewera.org/index.cfm?fuseaction=home.aboutTNE.

_____. 2010. *Home.* http://www.teachersforanewera.org/index.cfm?fuseaction=home.home.

_____. 2010. *Institutions.* http://www.teachersforanewera.org/index.cfm?fuseaction=home.institutions.

_____. 2010. *TNE Prospectus.* http://www.teachersforanewera.org/index.cfm?fuseaction=home.prospectus.

Wallace, Walter L. 1971. *The Logic of Science in Sociology.* Chicago: Aldine.

Wartofsky, Marx W. 1968. *Conceptual Foundations of Scientific Thought: An Introduction to the Philosophy of Science.* New York: Macmillan.

Wu, Xiaogang, and Yu Xie. 2003. Does the Market Pay Off? Earnings Returns to Education in Urban China. *American Sociological Review* 68 (June): 425–42.

Xie, Yu, and Xiaogang Wu. 2005. Reply to Jann: Market Premium, Social Process, and Statisticism. *American Sociological Review* 70 (October): 865–70.

9. IN DEFENSE OF DOING NOTHING
The Methodological Utility of Introversion

Peter Moskos

One could be forgiven for thinking that everything has already been written about qualitative methods. There are articles, chapters, and books on research design, internal review boards, access, symbolic interactionism, grounded theory, the dramaturgical perspective, ethnography as work, paradigm development, entry, online research, semiotics, professionalization, ethnomethodology, autoethnography, interviewing, thick description, ethics, phenomenology, immersion, going native, exiting, analyzing field notes, writing field notes, *ad infinitum* and perhaps, dare I say, *ad nauseam.*[1]

Still with me? Good. I will leave well enough alone (and a thorough review of the literature to future graduate students). My goal is much more modest: to introduce a psychological concept — introversion — into the sociological world. A greater awareness and understanding of introversion could help current and future ethnographers appreciate and exploit natural skills beneficial to qualitative fieldwork, particularly the difficult and overlooked early stage of participant-observation research.

Introversion as a Methodological Tool

Carl Jung (1921) defined introversion and extroversion in terms of "psychic energy." Extroverts have an outward flow of energy, Jung believed, and introverts have an inward flow. While this language is dated in contemporary psychology, Jung's basic concept still provides a useful framework for a sociological understanding of social interaction. Unfortunately, perhaps because of its psychological roots and application to the individual, introversion has been ignored by sociologists and qualitative methodologists. Merriam-Webster's dictionary defines introversion as "the state of or tendency toward being wholly or predominantly concerned with and interested in one's own mental life." But this dictionary definition does not explain the social and methodological concept of introversion, nor does it explain how the researcher can exploit introverted traits as fieldwork tools.

To understand introversion it may first be helpful to understand what introversion is not. For starters, introversion is not shyness. Even though there can be and often is overlap between introversion and shyness, they are not synonymous. Some introverts are shy, but many are not. Some introverts have terrible stage fright; others are excellent public speakers. Some introverts are asocial; others may have elegant social graces. Put another way, introversion is simply the opposite of being an extrovert. And it may be easier to grasp the qualities of extroverts: people who are talkative, the life of the party, and comfortable with social situations and strangers. Extroverts are energized by crowds and mingling, while introverts become tired at the mere thought and need to be alone to gain energy.[2] Alone, extroverts become bored.

Introversion and extroversion are not dichotomous variables but rather divergent ends of a wide spectrum of personality types. Neither is good or bad or better than the other. Introversion is not a problem to be overcome (which may contrast with general shyness and anxiety, for which your doctor will be happy to write a prescription). And it should be noted that many introverts have traits associated with creativity, concentration, and success in school. That said, American culture generally favors extroverts in business and social situations. Perhaps, as some have claimed, introverts make up about a third of the general population and over half of the gifted population. Who knows? Whatever the real figures may be, it is no stretch of the imagination to observe that the halls of academia are filled with a disproportionately large share of socially awkward, bookish, and introverted personalities.

Here, I wish to present introversion as a simple way of understanding individual traits in fieldwork situations. Marti Olsen Laney (2002) provides an excellent quick test of introversion.[3] A person who agrees with fourteen or fifteen of the following questions has a personality evenly split between introversion and extroversion. The more statements you agree with, the more introverted you are; the fewer you agree with, the more extroverted you are. More than half these questions (which I have put in bold) directly relate to qualitative fieldwork.

1. When I work on projects, I like to have larger uninterrupted time periods rather than smaller chunks.

2. I sometimes rehearse things before speaking, occasionally writing notes for myself.

3. In general, I like to listen more than I like to talk.

4. People sometimes think I'm quiet, mysterious, aloof or calm.

5. I like to share special occasions with just one person or a few close friends, rather than have big celebrations.

6. I usually need to think before I respond or speak.

7. I tend to notice details many people don't see.

8. **If two people have just had a fight, I feel the tension in the air.**

9. **If I say I will do something, I almost always do it.**

10. **I feel anxious if I have a deadline or pressure to finish a project.**

11. I can "zone out" if too much is going on.

12. **I like to watch an activity for a while before I decide to join in.**

13. **I form lasting relationships.**

14. **I don't like to interrupt others; I don't like to be interrupted.**

15. When I take in lots of information, it takes me a while to sort it out.

16. I don't like over-stimulating environments. I can't imagine why folks want to go to horror movies or go on roller coasters.

17. I sometimes have strong reactions to smells, tastes, foods, weather, noises, etc.

18. **I am creative and/or imaginative.**

19. I feel drained after social situations, even when I enjoy myself.

20. **I prefer to be introduced rather than to introduce others.**

21. I can become grouchy if I'm around people or activities too long.

22. **I often feel uncomfortable in new surroundings.**

23. I like people to come to my home, but I don't like them to stay too long.

24. I often dread returning phone calls.

25. I find my mind sometimes goes blank when I meet people or when I am asked to speak unexpectedly.

26. I talk slowly or have gaps in my words, especially if I am tired or if I am trying to speak and think at once.

27. I don't think of casual acquaintances as friends.

28. I feel as if I can't show other people my work or ideas until they are fully formulated.

29. **Other people may surprise me by thinking I am smarter than I think I am.**[4]

Undoubtedly participant-observation fieldwork involves a lot of boredom and standing around. In any fieldwork there will be periods of downtime. After all, the purpose of participant-observation is to observe unedited reality. When observing a work environment, not only does the researcher have to overcome any natural boredom inherent in that work, but the researcher needs to justify his or her presence — and probably an unpaid presence at that — to those who are paid to be there and still wish they were elsewhere.

Ethnographers needn't and indeed shouldn't be too eager for things to happen. The researcher is not filming an episode of *Cops* or a foreign documentary. You, as the researcher, are there to observe people in their normal setting. And when those you observe have nothing to do, they may not want to talk to you. Don't take it personally. You may see their break as prime time to ask down-and-dirty questions. But they, at least the introverts among them, may simply want to be left alone.

There is no need to go out and be the life of the party. In a new research situation, it's good to stay on the reserved side, to be (or at least act like) the introvert. I like to advise researchers to bring something to pass the time, something to read (this, of course, is good advice for life in general). Catching up on homework is fine. And there's no shame in reading magazines or pulp fiction. The point here isn't to make an impression or impress people with your varied or edgy selection of reading material (or the simple fact that you read at all) but rather to survive the drudgery of fieldwork. Luckily, introverts are less easily bored than extroverts and are happier to spend time alone in their thoughts. Fieldwork is not a sprint. Reading allows you to settle in for the long haul. There may be months or even years ahead. And days or even weeks of unproductive fieldwork are par for the course.

Unlike those you are observing, who actually have something to do, the participant observer lacks a clear function. Most of my research in Baltimore, which culminated in my book *Cop in the Hood*, was conducted while I was employed as a police officer. This helped me and my research tremendously, but other participant-observers may not have that luxury. Without a clear function in a social setting, the introvert's natural reaction is to withdraw and become silent. While this may be a problem at the annual Christmas party, it can come in handy for the researcher.

The actual purpose of participant-observation research is to observe. And one attribute associated with introversion is the ability to notice details lost on others (see #7 above). I doubt the ability to notice details is the unique province of introverts, but inasmuch as this is a characteristic of introverts, it gives introverts a tremendous advantage in observational research. If you're an extrovert, it can even help to act like an introvert. An extroverted ethnographer once told me, "I'm an extrovert by nature. But when I do my fieldwork I become an introvert." The fact that he can overcome his natural extroversion to conduct excellent fieldwork is as much a testament to his research ability as it is a demonstration of how much easier social scientific fieldwork might be for a natural introvert. While some extroverts can act introverted, it's certainly easier if you don't have to consciously make the effort.

In conversation, introverts have a natural desire not to impose themselves on others (see #3 above). This, more than any other introvert personality trait, may keep potentially excellent participant-observers from conducting research. Introverts don't like starting conversation with strangers. Luckily, you don't have to. There are numerous advantages to keeping your mouth shut. I'm not talking about cloister-order silence (there's something to be said for good social graces and the ability to make polite small talk) but natural conversational reticence certainly benefits the researcher. Having the right question at hand is less important than the ability to listen. And if you talk too much you may say the wrong thing (#2 above) or, quite frankly, people may not like you. While in life it may or may not be better to be loved by some and disliked by others, for the ethnographer it is much more important to be tolerated by all. Better to lose the Miss Congeniality Contest than turn off half the group you wish to study.

If you're quiet and accessible, people will approach you (see #20 above). Although being approached has certain methodological hazards — dealing with non-random selection, conversing with people with a grudge to settle, having to listen to crazy people — it is also a great research opportunity. People who approach you want to get to know you. And for the introvert, who usually feels better talking one-on-one than in groups, an exchange of personal information through conversation functions as a ritual exchange of gifts (Mauss 2000). The more you tell, the greater the subject's debt to you.

The first person to approach you may be a loudmouth or a bully of the group who wants to test you. Or perhaps it's somebody who's just curious or bored. The problem on "Day One" is that you, the researcher, don't know this particular society's Who's Who. If you buddy it up with Mr. Blowhard, you may alienate other people present. This is much more likely in a work environment, where people may have little control over their associations. In a social setting, however, the alpha dog's acceptance of you may be absolutely essential to the continuation of your research.

Since there is a risk every time you open your mouth, researchers should play it safe in the beginning. You may think you're charming and a joy to be around. Indeed, you may be. But things are different in the field. People who interrupt routines — especially researchers perceived as eggheads who probably know less about the matter than the people being studied — should not expect to be greeted with open arms and a loving embrace. The researcher isn't there to tell those being observed what to do or how to do it. Extroverted researchers should remind themselves that they may not be as charming or smart as they think they are. A bad joke or witty aside can come back to haunt you. You can always build access over time, but it can be impossible to recover from a bad first impression. Extroverts have to watch what they say. The introvert is naturally disinclined to do so. This was actually put to me very bluntly in the police academy: "If in doubt, shut your mouth and look sharp."

Long-term immersion and participant-observation researchers — especially if the researcher is actually participating — will inevitably see life's usual squabbles and feuds and friendships. Leaving aside issues of objectivity, the simple fact is that when you pick friends, you pick sides. And while it's almost impossible to imagine good data coming from a long-term ethnography that does not involve friendship, the researcher should resist seeking friendship too early. Before you join a team, it's good to know the sides, or at least what game is being played. Here again the natural reservations of introverts come in handy, as introverts are less likely than extroverts to develop quick friendships.

My police research started in 1997, in Amsterdam. I generally conducted my observations in the evening through the early hours of the morning. During periods late at night when nothing much was happening, cops would down cup after cup of lousy coffee to stay awake. Sometimes I would be asked, "Why don't you go home?" I explained that I wasn't there to see "action" but rather to understand police officers. And the late shift was better because bosses weren't around and cops were more natural and relaxed (plus, I'm naturally a night owl). This answer worked for two reasons. One, it was honest. Two, and though I barely knew it at the time, it showed a moderately advanced understanding of police culture (see #29 above). Then, if there were no more questions, I'd go back to reading my book. But I also realized that I wasn't going to win any award for staying to the bitter end of the midnight shift. I am no martyr. And sometimes sticking around just made me look like a fool. I could leave. So sometimes I did. If you can't think of an answer as to why you're there, perhaps you *should* go home

Introversion in the Field

For the doctoral student, it's only after completing the initial scholastic and logistical hassles—finishing course work, selecting an advisor, writing a dissertation proposal, winning the internal review board's approval, gaining access, and perhaps moving to a new and foreign city or country—that the fieldwork starts. The fun is supposed to begin. But when you arrive at the research site, *what are you actually supposed to do?* It's a shockingly basic question that is all but absent from the literature on methodology. Introverts should not fear because, as a T-shirt should say, "introverts do it better in the field."

Day One is probably the most awkward and difficult day for the researcher. There is no how-to-section for Day One ethnography. While some may relish the opportunity to jump headfirst into a new environment filled with people they don't know, introverts most certainly do not. And the anxiety of anticipating the unknown may be matched only by the fear of what to actually do when there.

Some, the more extroverted, may feel a need to simply "do something." And this isn't always a bad idea. Generally, soon after I start research, I like to hand out a questionnaire. Qualitative and quantitative researches complement each other very well (an idea too often lost on both sides of the great methodological divide). Questionnaire data serve nicely to supplement qualitative intuition. And questionnaires have an added benefit for the introverted researcher in serving as a calling card and form of introduction. It explains the researcher's presence. It makes it look like the researcher is actually doing something productive. If that works for you, great. But it's not essential.

In 1999, I entered the Baltimore City Police Academy, in uniform but unpaid, for what I thought would be twelve months of research on the socialization of police officers. Surrounded by strangers and immersed in a new and foreign social environment, it seemed to me as if I had dropped in on one of the world's worst cocktail parties— only without the cocktails. As a researcher, you will likely have a similar experience. It's not easy. Everybody else already has a role defined by contract, custom, tradition, or need. You're a clueless college boy or girl coming to observe. Some people may briefly introduce themselves before returning to whatever they were doing. Others may sign a consent form that serves (contrary to its only stated purpose) to protect the researcher far more than it informs or protects the too clinically named "research subjects."[5]

At the beginning of the fieldwork, the researcher should expect to be viewed with some suspicion (if not downright bafflement). The obvious question you will be asked is, "What are you doing?" You need an answer, and you should probably hold off on delving into Marxist theories of class oppression. A simple answer is usually best. I've found that the entire field of sociology remains a foreign concept to most police officers and is often confused with psychology or social work. Ethnography? Forget about it. Something like "writing a book" or "doing a school research project" is usually more than adequate. But if questioned further, I tried to explain my research goals as clearly as possible (a task made difficult by the fact that I really had no clear research goals). And to ease suspicion that comes natural to police officers, I would truthfully add that I was writing a book about policing in general and not police officers in particular.

On the first day of the academy, each member of my class was asked why he or she wanted to be a police officer. I had to explain to this class of police officer recruits (educational requirements: high-school diploma or G.E.D.) that I was a Harvard University graduate student doing research. It was not an easy speech to give. At the time, I didn't even know I was going to be a police officer, much less why I wanted to be one. Despite my academy uniform, I labeled myself as an outsider in a room full of people hoping desperately to become insiders. In hindsight — and though the introvert in me would not have been so quick to make this proclamation — it turned out for the best. Being overt, which was an internal review board requirement, made research much easier. And I hate to think I might have put myself in a position, months later, of having to explain my apparent deception to those who had since become my friends. During that first day, as the fates would have it, my research status changed drastically. My project had been rather quickly and unexpectedly disapproved by the acting commissioner. He gave me the rather stark choice of trying to join the department as a bona fide police officer or returning to graduate school with my tail between my legs and no obvious doctoral dissertation plan in sight. Even at this point, introversion, as I later identified it, came in handy. To some extent, I did not control my destiny. There were larger bureaucratic and institutional factors at work in both the Baltimore City Police Department and Harvard's sociology department. Rather than overreacting and attempting to "do something," I simply rolled with the waves and drifted where the prevailing winds pushed me. Six months later, I was given a badge, a gun, and went to police the rough streets of the Eastern District. This was an opportunity, more than any other, that helped and defined my academic life.

So what should you do on Day One? The short answer is simple: nothing! Of course that over-simplifies. You actually do a lot. Sort of. But you don't have to *do* anything. Say hello. Observe. Acclimate. The only essential thing is that you write everything up when you go home. And the more you write the better. Especially in the first few days. After the first day of research you may not even know what you saw. But the important thing is to write. I'm not necessarily talking about Geertzian "thick description," but write about what you saw, your thoughts, your feelings, your fears, your expectations. Write letters to friends (and save a copy for yourself). Do whatever allows you to write. The more you write, the better. And even if these early words do not become part of your finished dissertation or book, at the end, when you feel like you understand everything too well (or not at all), these will be great pages to read. So whatever you do, write!

But writing is hard work, so let's get back to the introverted benefits of doing nothing. When I began my Amsterdam research, I met a supportive station chief and was given a brief tour of the building and introduced to the men and women working the shift. Then I was left to my own devices. I had no clue what to do. I was nervous and anxious. So I did what comes naturally to any introvert in a crowded room full of strangers. I did nothing. I stood around. Other times I sat. And so, slowly and steadily, my research began. Paul Rock (2007, 23) offers excellent advice, or, at least for me, ex post facto justification:

> It is best to look and see what can be seen, to try to get some sense of the regularities of what is before one. It would be foolish to plunge in too soon with naïve questions. Such a step might only expose the sociologist's lack of understanding, and exhaust whatever limited goodwill there may be. Busy people will not consent to be interviewed repeatedly by the manifestly inept.
>
> It is better to remain on the margins at first, available, just about visible, but not too demanding. Show interest. See who the others about one are. Observe those whom they deal with. Be available. Observe and chart everyday routines. Listen to others: being prepared to listen is a rare enough asset in social life and it will be rewarded (La Rouchefoucauld once defined a bore as someone who talks about himself when you want to talk about *your* self).

If you're an introvert, all this should come naturally. Gradually I slipped into a routine. Before too long, as I would hang out, I noticed more and started to see greater order in the chaos. When things were happening, I would follow. This didn't always work. At least not at first. More than once a police officer seemed hell-bent on an urgent mission. I jumped up and followed him or her ... right up to the bathroom door. This left me in the not-so-suave position of covering my faux pas by pretending to be really interested in the notices posted in the hallway. Luckily, my cluelessness and blasé-fronted anxiety were often mistaken for confidence and professionalism. Gradually officers invited me along to things they felt would interest me. Without me being pushy, police officers opened up to me. This is generally typical of ethnographic work. And perhaps somewhat surprising to the uninitiated.

After my presence became expected, I began interviewing police officers one-on-one. This was not a complicated process (it helped that I had previously been granted carte blanche by the station's chief). I started by asking officers I felt more comfortable with if they would be willing to be interviewed. Nobody declined. People generally like to tell their story. Plus some had questions for me. Once I had done a few interviews, word spread through the grapevine. A few officers even volunteered to be interviewed.[6]

Conclusion

The interpersonal nature of qualitative research and the perceived "action" of participant-observation research may perpetuate a belief that extroversion is a good quality for ethnographers. In fact, nothing is further from the truth. Ethnographer Mitchell Duneier told me that too often students come to him saying, "I'm not outgoing enough to do fieldwork." But one does not need to be extroverted to be successful in fieldwork. Indeed, it may be more useful for ethnographers *not* to be extroverted. Certainly there is no single "correct" way to conduct qualitative fieldwork. But the qualities associated with introversion are, if not essential, at the very least incredibly helpful for successful long-term ethnographic research. And the kinds of social skills needed for ethnography may go against popular convention as to what it means to have "good social skills."

If you've ever seen a group of ethnographers party, you may be struck by a general sense that we may not have been the most popular kids in high school. Despite what is often a very lively style of writing, ethnographers can be soft-spoken and introverted. Now don't get me wrong: As a group, we ethnographers are hardly the dorkiest in school (a few other academic disciplines spring to mind, but for politics' sake I'll refrain.). Certainly qualitative researchers must have basic social skills, but let's be honest, no prom king or queen ever went on to write an ethnography As a group, almost by definition, academics are nerds. We like the library. We don't mind being alone. We walk down the street reading. We thrive in small groups and intellectual conversations. And yet mingling and making small talk with strangers is tiresome at best or frightening at worst.

Is all of this sociology of the obvious? I hope not. Is it simple? Perhaps, but I hope not simplistic. What is an "informal interview" other than a twenty-five-cent word for talking to people? What is "grounded theory" but a fancy way of saying you don't have a theory? Just because the concept of introversion is relatively simple does not limit its potential application. To rise above the "sociology of the obvious" one needs to see the significance of the mundane and make connections and theories where others might just see business as usual. "Sociology will be satisfying, in the long run," wrote Peter Berger (1963, 24), "only to those who can think of nothing more entrancing than to watch [people] and to understand things human." And this is where introverts thrive.

All too often, sociological writing ends with call for further research. And I will to. But unlike some, I really mean it. It is my hope that qualitative researchers in general and ethnographers in particular begin to examine the role that introversion plays in qualitative methodology. By habit and professional pride, sociologists are disinclined to focus on individual traits. Introversion, though popularized by Jung, could just as easily have come from the mind of Durkheim. Does not the inward or outward flow of individual "psychic energy" greatly affect organic solidarity? It is but a small sociological step from introversion to group dynamics, which places the concept of introversion firmly in the realm of sociology tradition.

With a greater understanding of introversion, I hope sociologists can take advantage of psychological traits that come naturally to many already in the field. Students considering qualitative research should see introversion as an asset rather than a hindrance. I hope I have shown, or at least opened the possibility, that introverts have unique skills that benefit ethnography, participant observation, and qualitative fieldwork. And if a simple awareness of introversion encourages more researchers to enter the field, then I have succeeded. At the very least, I hope to ease the qualitative researcher's dread about that one simple question on Day One: *Now that I'm here and surrounded by strangers, what do I do?* Don't despair. Do nothing!

Notes

1. The above concepts can be found, respectively, in the works of LeCompte 1999; Miller and Bell 2002; Blumer 1969; Glaser and Strauss 1967; Glaser 1978; Goffman 1959; Willin and Fine 2007; Willis 2007; Fetterman 2010; Kozinets 2010; Lee 1999; Janowitz 1972; Katz 1988; Reed-Danahay 1997; Kvale and Brinkmann 2009; Rubin and Rubin 2005; Geertz 1977; Mauthner et al. 2002; Moustakas 1994; Madden 2010; O'Reilly 2009; Van Maanen 1988; Emerson et al. 1995 and Becker 1998. Of course this is not an exhaustive list.

2. In the interests of full disclosure, I am not shy and have no fear of public speaking, yet I positively dislike mingling with strangers at parties and usually find extroverts extremely tiring. My rather recent personal understanding of introversion led to the formulation of the concepts in this chapter. I also wish to thank all the presenters and audience members who failed to attend one of the last scheduled sessions at the Eastern Sociology Society's 2010 annual meeting in Boston. The result, five people talking informally in an empty room, proved to be the most interesting and productive conference session I have ever attended!

3. Myers-Briggs Type Indicator (Myers et al. 1998) provides another more well-known personality test that includes an introversion/extroversion scale. But Laney's test is perfectly suited for the scope of this chapter.

4. Copyright Marti Olsen Laney. Reprinted here with permission. For a full explanation

see Laney (2002, 30–5). I scored 21 out of 29 on her test, which would make me a moderate introvert.

5. I strongly urge researchers to gain internal review board approval without requiring a signed consent form. It is possible, and, in reality, much more possible than having groups of people sign consent forms in fluid situations. Though it might facilitate approval to state that all research subjects will sign consent forms and confidentiality would never be violated, it is not honest. The former, at least in the police world, denies the reality of participant-observation research, and the latter, potentially, your ethical obligations as a human being.

6. In the police world, I find formal interviews to be less productive than casual conversations (aka "informal interviews"). Honest opinions, casual quips, and common-sense observations can be held against police in our legalistic and politically correct culture. Police officers generally, and often with good reason, clam up when being recorded. When a tape recorder is running, police begin to sound like cops on the TV show *Cops*. I rather quickly abandoned formal recorded interviews in the field and gathered all conversational data through normal (if focused) conversation. Along with saving me the hassle of transcription, non-recorded interviews give the interviewees plausible deniability should they ever need to cover themselves. For instance, just today I had dinner with a friend and ranking police officer who offered a lively quote that would never be captured in a recorded interview: "Russians in Brighton Beach do nothing but steal cars! Then they go to sleep and dream about stealing more cars."

References

Becker, Howard S. 1998. *Tricks of the Trade: How to Think about Your Research While You're Doing It.* Chicago: University of Chicago Press.

Berger, Peter L. 1963. *Invitation to Sociology: A Humanistic Perspective.* New York: Anchor Books.

Blumer, Herbert. 1969. *Symbolic Interactionism: Perspective and Method.* Englewood Cliffs, NJ: Prentice-Hall.

Emerson, Robert M., Rachel I. Fretz, and Linda L. Shaw. 1995. *Writing Ethnographic Fieldnotes.* Chicago: University of Chicago.

Feterman, David M. 2010. *Ethnography: Step-by-Step.* Thousand Oaks, CA: Sage Publications.

Geertz, Clifford. 1977. *The Interpretation of Cultures.* New York: Basic Books.

Glaser, Barney G. 1978. *Theoretical Sensitivity.* Mill Valley, CA: The Sociology Press.

Glaser, Barney G., and Anselm Strauss. 1967. *The Discovery of Grounded Theory: Strategies for Qualitative Research.* Chicago: Aldine Transaction.

Goffman, Erving. 1959. *The Presentation of Self in Everyday Life.* New York: Doubleday.

Janowitz, Morris. 1972. Professionalization in Sociology. In *Varieties of Political Expression in Sociology*, ed. Robert K. Merton, 105–35. Chicago: University of Chicago Press.

Jung, Carl G. 1921. *Psychological Types.* Zurich: Rascher Verlag.

Katz, Jack. 1988. *Seductions of Crime: The Moral and Sensual Attractions in Doing Evil.* New York: Basic Books.

Kozinets, Robert V. 2010. *Netnography: Doing Ethnographic Research Online.* Thousand Oaks, CA: Sage.

Kvale, Steinar, and Svend Brinkmann. 2009. *InterViews: Learning the Craft of Qualitative Research Interviewing.* Thousand Oaks, CA: Sage Publications.

Laney, Marti O. 2002. *The Introvert Advantage: How to Thrive in an Extrovert World.* New York: Workman.

LeCompte, Margaret D. 1999. *Designing and Conducting Ethnographic Research.* Walnut Creek, CA: AltaMira Press.

Lee, Benjamin. 1997. *Talking Heads: Language, Metalanguage, and the Semiotics of Subjectivity.* Durham: Duke University Press.

Madden, Raymond. 2010. *Being Ethnographic: A Guide to the Theory and Practice of Ethnography.* Thousand Oaks, CA: Sage Publications.

Manning, Peter K. 2007. Semiotics, Semantics, and Ethnography. In *Handbook of Ethnography*, ed. Paul Atkinson, Amanda Coffey, Sara Delamont, John Lofland, and Lyn Lofland, 145–59. Thousand Oaks, CA: Sage Publications.

Mauss, Marcel. 2000. *The Gift: The Form and Reason for Exchange in Archaic Societies.* New York: W.W. Norton.

Mauthner, Melanie, Maxine Birch, Julie Jessop, and Tina Miller, eds. 2002. *Ethics in Qualitative Research.* Thousand Oaks, CA: Sage Publications.

Miller, Tina, and Linda Bell. 2002. Consenting to What? Issues of Access, Gate-keeping, and "Informed" Consent. In *Ethics in Qualitative Research,* ed. Melanie Mauthner, Maxine Birch, Julie Jessop, and Tina Miller, 53–69. Thousand Oaks, CA: Sage Publications.

Moustakas, Clark. 1994. *Phenomenological Research Methods.* Thousand Oaks, CA: Sage Publications.

Myers, Isabel Briggs, Mary H. McCaulley, Naomi L. Quenk and Allen L. Hammer. 1998. *MBTI Manual.* Palo Alto, CA: Consulting Psychologists Press.

O'Reilly, Karen. 2004. *Ethnographic Methods.* New York: Routledge.

_____. 2009. *Key Concepts in Ethnography.* Thousand Oaks, CA: Sage Publications.

Reed-Danahay, Deborah, ed. 1997. *Auto/Ethnography: Rewriting the Self and the Social.* Oxford: Berg.

Rock, Paul. 2007. Symbolic Interactionism and Ethnography. In *Handbook of Ethnography*, ed. Paul Atkinson, Amanda Coffey, Sara Delamont, John Lofland, and Lyn Lofland, 26–38. Thousand Oaks, CA: Sage Publications.

Rubin, Herbert J., and Irene S. Rubin. 2005. *Qualitative Interviewing: The Art of Hearing Data.* Thousand Oaks, CA: Sage Publications.

Saldaña, Johnny. 2009. *The Coding Manual for Qualitative Researchers.* Thousand Oaks, CA: Sage Publications.

Van Maanen, John. 1988. *Tales of the Field: On Writing Ethnography.* Chicago: University of Chicago Press.

Willis, Jerry W. 2007. *Foundations of Qualitative Research: Interpretive and Critical Approaches.* Thousand Oaks, CA: Sage Publications.

Wellin, Christopher, and Gary A. Fine. Ethnography as Work: Career Socialization, Settings and Problems. In *Handbook of Ethnography*, ed. Paul Atkinson, Amanda Coffey, Sara Delamont, John Lofland, and Lyn Lofland, 323–38. Thousand Oaks, CA: Sage Publications.

10. THE NEGLECTED VIRTUES OF COMPARATIVE-HISTORICAL METHODS

Mikaila Mariel Lemonik Arthur

To so many social researchers, the words "comparative-historical methods" conjure images of dusty, musty manuscripts recounting details of long-ago social change that seems disconnected from issues of current concern. Traditional research methods textbooks may be partly responsible for this state of affairs: Of seven general social science research methods texts (Adler and Clark 2008; Babbie 1995; Cargan 2007; Chambliss and Schutt 2006; Gray, Williamson, Karp, and Dalphin 2007; Leedy and Ormord 2005; Neuman 2003) on my bookshelf, only two offer a chapter focusing on comparative-historical methods that is not primarily about content analysis or the analysis of existing statistical data (while all offer chapters on experiments, much less utilized as a sociological research technique). But comparative-historical methods are perhaps the most fundamental to our discipline. The classical theoretical texts of Weber and Durkheim relied on comparative-historical methods to draw their conclusions about society. Indeed, of the top 30 books on the International Sociological Association list of Books of the Century (International Sociology Association 1998), 10 rely on comparative-historical methods (most of the remainder are theoretical texts). Comparative-historical methods can moreover serve as a useful corrective to some of the assumptions made by other methodological perspectives. They emphasize process, path dependency, necessity, and sufficiency rather than probabilistic causation, for instance. They offer an eclectic array of tools that can be combined and recombined to allow for novel understandings of the foundations of social life.

This chapter provides an introduction to the assumptions behind comparative-historical methodology and will outline several key approaches to comparative-historical research, including historiography, large-N comparative scholarship, negative case methods, and formal methods. It will then review critiques of comparative-historical approaches that come from both positivist and interpretivist researchers before turning to the new directions in which comparative-historical methods can be employed, such as exploring the recent past and incorporating new technology into comparative-historical research.

Comparative-historical research is not a tool only suited to the dreary questions of yesterday's scholars, but rather a tool that can provide new windows into our social organizations, our culture, and indeed our future.

What Makes the Comparative-Historical Approach Different?

Comparative-historical methodology transcends the qualitative-quantitative division. It is neither qualitative nor quantitative in its approach to data collection and analysis but instead has its own approach that is distinguished by five key characteristics (Ragin 2008, 5):

• Comparative-historical research looks for consistent connections. Instead of aiming to demonstrate the strength of an association between two variables, comparative-historical research aims to show that particular factors interact in a consistent fashion. For instance, perhaps a researcher wants to explore the hypothesis that writing a business plan is essential to the success of a new business venture. To a comparative-historical researcher, the important question is whether those businesses that do not write business plans consistently fail, rather than how strong the connection is between writing a business plan and business success. Why? There could be other reasons for failure besides not having a business plan, and these would reduce the strength of the association between business plans and business success. They wouldn't matter to a consideration of consistent connections, though.

• Comparative-historical research relies on the accumulated knowledge of specific cases. It is not sufficient, in comparative-historical research, to draw on a few disparate bits of information in putting together an analysis; nor are cases considered interchangeable. Rather, comparative-historical methods require that cases be selected for inclusion in the analysis and that the researcher develops an understanding of the particularities of each case.

• Comparative-historical research sees utility in selecting on the dependent variable. Most qualitative and quantitative researchers argue that cases should never be selected on the dependent variable. In other words, researchers should not choose the cases they will include in their analysis on the basis of the outcome they are interested in studying. The reason typically given for this prohibition is that selecting on the dependent variable results in selection bias that prevents the researcher from studying the full variation in potential causal pathways and thus biases the results towards particular explanations without the ability to determine if other explanations might be better. However, in some circumstances, selecting on the dependent variable is entirely appropriate — particularly when there are few cases and little knowledge about them and when researchers are interested in uncovering those factors that are necessary precursors to an event (see Dion 2003). For example, if researchers want to know why wars start in some countries and not others, they would need to consider both countries that have had wars and those that have not; but if what they want to know is which particular events MUST happen in order for a war to start, then they need only include countries that have had wars.

• Comparative-historical methods look for configurations of factors that interact to create outcomes (see Mahoney and Rueschemeyer 2003). In much sociological research, researchers consider the various independent variables as unique elements that each account for a particular percentage of the variation in the outcome. Statistical techniques do allow for modeling interactions between the independent variables, but these methods are cumbersome and have their own limitations. In contrast, comparative-historical methods are founded upon the notion that the various factors that are important to an outcome interact with one another. For example, a researcher working to explain what sorts of legal challenges are most likely to result in the Supreme Court overturning past precedent might determine that having a new legal theory that has not been tried before will result in overturning past precedent only where the configuration of political power has changed substantially since the prior case; where the configuration of political power remains the same, new legal theories might not have any effect at all.

• Comparative-historical methodology considers counterfactuals. Counterfactuals are questions that ask "what if something else had happened?" Rather than staying wedded to the data that we already have, comparative-historical methods leave room to consider alternative paths that did not occur and therefore to build stronger theoretical models. For instance, let's say a researcher has determined that where faculty members push assertively for curricular change on a campus with an open and flexible administration, the administration adopts those changes. In all of the cases the researcher has studied, student involvement in the curricular change effort is minimal. But this does not tell us that minimal student involvement is a necessary condition for curricular change — instead, we must engage in counterfactual thinking to consider what the impact of student involvement on the outcome might be.

Comparative-historical methodology incorporates these five characteristics into a framework that emphasizes comparison and the importance of history.

The fact that comparative-historical research is comparative means that it always seeks to consider the things that make each case distinct. Comparison involves determining the similarities and differences between cases and between contexts (Mahoney and Rueschemeyer 2003). It is true that some comparative-historical research draws only on a single case — but even in such circumstances, the research remains comparative by drawing comparisons to other published research or by relying on within-case comparisons. Within-case comparisons can involve comparing an individual case across different points of time or comparing sub-parts of a given case. In other situations, comparative-historical research involves large-scale comparisons— those across eras or continents. In such instances, researchers may struggle with language and other kinds of translation difficulties as they seek to employ concepts across contexts.

The fact that comparative-historical research is historical means that it considers events that have occurred in the past. In some sense, most sociological research is historical. Large-scale social surveys that collect longitudinal or cross-sectional data on individuals' educational trajectories are collecting historical data. In-depth interviews that ask about individuals' sexual behavior are collecting historical data. But whereas interviews and surveys can also ask individuals questions about what they are thinking or feeling right now, and ethnographies and experiments observe actions happening right in front of the researcher, comparative-historical research always considers the past. But the "past" need not mean some time distant to our memory and experience; it only means time that has already elapsed. And in order to draw on the strengths of comparative-historical methodological strategies, preferably time that has elapsed long enough ago to leave some sort of record.

There are of course difficulties in researching the past. Records are often incomplete, for a variety of reasons. They may never have been recorded in the first place. They may have been lost over time. Sometimes records are purposely discarded, either because someone does not want the information in them to be retained, because the place where they are stored has limited space, or because the record-keeper does not see them as valuable. The meanings of records change over time, so what was recorded in the past may not be fully understandable today. And when historical data is gathered by speaking to people who remember those times, researchers must face the unreliability of human memory.

There are limitations to all research methods— in return for struggling with the limitations and difficulties imposed by the focus on comparison and history, comparative-historical researchers have the opportunity to rely upon varied data sources and useful analytical techniques in order to explore contexts and research questions that often would not be accessible to other sorts of methodologies.

Sources of Data in Comparative-Historical Analysis

Comparative-historical research draws on four main types of data: primary sources, often located in archives; secondary sources; running records; and recollections. Let us consider each of these in turn.

Primary sources are original texts created by those who have direct personal knowledge of the context, event, or situation being described in the source. Primary sources may include diaries, letters, meeting minutes, photographs, or any number of other documents and texts; what they all have in common is a close connection to the actual historical events that has not been filtered through a commentator. While primary sources can be located in a variety of places, comparative-historical researchers most commonly find them in *archives*, or depositories that collect historical records. There are many types of archives; most are located in libraries, museums, or other bodies specifically charged with the preservation of material for scholarly study. There is no master list of archives, and researchers must search to locate the individual archives that hold materials necessary for a particular research project (Hill 1993).

Archives are not organized like other types of libraries. Most do not use a standardized system such as the Library of Congress classifications for organizing their materials, instead aiming to preserve documents in their original order. Visitors to the archives therefore locate the materials they are interested in with the help of an archivist and a document called a *finding aid* that outlines the contents of particular archival collections. Many archives have special rules governing access to the documents. These rules may restrict the types of researchers that can view documents, the degree to which documents can be quoted, and how documents can be handled. For this reason, researchers who plan to work in archives should contact the archivist ahead of time to discuss the research project and any rules governing access to the archives and to the specific documents of interest.

The use of archives enables the researcher to get as close as possible to the historical events of interest, but it is not without its problems (Platt 1981). Archival documents may contain (intentional or unintentional) errors, some documents may have been lost, the original arrangement of documents may have been changed (resulting in misinterpretations of the contexts in which documents were produced), and most importantly researchers generally have no idea of the extent of loss or error that their research must confront. Researchers use various strategies in response to these limitations, including triangulating between data sources (such as the use of recollections, discussed below, when there are living people who remember the events of interest) and carefully exploring documents and archives for hints of omission and error.

Secondary sources are analyses that draw on primary sources. Most typically, these are published books and articles that comment on historical periods, events, and individuals. Many comparative-historical researchers in sociology, for instance, draw on published works of historical scholarship that may do an excellent job of recording the details of events and situations but which do not provide a sociological perspective on these occurrences. While there is much significant comparative-historical scholarship published that draws only on secondary sources, researchers using secondary sources must still be cautious. One important reason why is that secondary sources have particular perspectives on the events they discuss and may have left something out in their own analysis.

As Lustick (1996) says, the choice of secondary sources to use in a research project may itself result in a kind of selection bias. Lustick argues that comparative-historical researchers who rely on secondary sources should use four strategies to ensure that their work is done in a methodologically sound way that accounts for the inconsistencies among and between secondary sources. First, researchers should choose a particular set of secondary sources that have a convincing approach to the subject and indicate what is distinct about this approach (or school). Second, researchers should aim to explain the sources of variation between explanations they locate in the secondary literature. Third, researchers should triangulate between the sources and schools that they have access to. Finally, researchers should be clear in the course of their publications about the choices they made between secondary sources and why they made such choices.

Running records are ongoing series of statistical or other sorts of data that can be compared across time. These records are typically maintained by government or other official agencies, and include data such as historical Census records, registries of passengers or freight on ships, tombstones, property ownership and tax records, and other similar documents. Running records allow comparative-historical researchers to track larger-scale social changes that would not be able to be understood through a focus on individuals or specific case studies. For instance, using old tombstones might allow a researcher to uncover data about life expectancy or the spread of epidemics in historical eras; ships' registries and historical Census records allow researchers to track international migration patterns; and property ownership records can help researchers untangle inheritance practices and socioeconomic distributions in villages of several hundred years ago.

Finally, *recollections* are systematically collected data on the memories that people have of events and occurrences in the past. While these are sometimes recorded in texts after the fact (as in autobiographical documents), the most common source of recollections is oral history interviewing (Hoopes 1979). According to the Oral History Association (2010), oral history is "a method of gathering, preserving, and interpreting the voices and memories of people, communities, and participants in past events." Typically, oral histories are collected by interviewers who spend a long time with participants facilitating the participants' telling of their own stories; these stories are then recorded and transcribed before being used as data sources by comparative-historical researchers and being archived for future use.

Methodological Strategies in Comparative-Historical Analysis

While there is a vast array of methodological strategies used by comparative-historical researchers, most of these strategies can be categorized into three broad types: macro-comparative scholarship, or scholarship that makes comparisons across large social units; case methods and historiography, or research that relies on detailed analysis of specific cases; and formal methods, or specific sets of formalized procedures for conducting comparative-historical analysis. Let's consider each of these in turn.

Macro-Comparative Scholarship

Macro-comparative scholarship refers to comparative-historical analysis drawing on large-scale comparisons across societies or nations. This sort of research can involve a small or a large number of cases, but the core commonality across macro-comparative studies is the use of national cases to develop or test theoretical propositions. Researchers interested in conducting macro-comparative studies choose whether to employ case-study techniques or quantitative and statistical methodology based on the number of "causal determinants" (independent variables) and the number of cases to be studied. When the number of causal determinants is much larger than the number of cases — and where the number of cases is sufficiently large — statistical methodology is often employed (Valenzuela 1998), though Quantitative Comparative Analysis, especially in its more recent formulations (Ragin 2008), may be used as well (this will be discussed in greater detail below). Macro-comparative scholarship, regardless of whether it is grounded in case-study or quantitative methods, relies on the comparisons of cases with similar outcomes and those with different outcomes. Comparing cases with similar outcomes enables the researcher to determine whether one or multiple explanations are responsible for producing the same outcome, while comparing cases with different outcomes enables the researcher to confirm that different outcomes are created by different factors (Valenzuela 1998).

Like other methodological strategies, macro-comparative scholarship suffers from limitations. Most importantly, concepts, terms, and ideas are not always easily able to be translated across cultures, contexts, and languages. One simple example of this translation problem involves a term in the Yiddish language which is transliterated as *machatunim*. There is no English equivalent for this term, which refers to the relationship you have with the parents of your child's spouse. Such translation problems can make cultural differences clear, but they can also limit the utility and accuracy of cross-national comparisons, particularly where large-scale datasets that are based on more superficial knowledge of nations and cultures are used. For instance, different countries use very different definitions for particular types of crime and have different conceptions of what crime is in the first place (United Nations Office on Drugs and Crime 2010), both of which significantly limit the utility of cross-national comparisons of crime rates.

Case Methods and Historiography

Many comparative-historical researchers develop their analyses through in-depth focus on one or a few carefully-selected cases. Case methods are often criticized for being limited in scope and applicability, but they can be particularly useful in theory development and in assessing the applicability of theoretical models (Rueschemeyer 2003). Case methodologists have developed strategies for utilizing cases in ways that enable them to have the greatest analytical strength (Amenta 1991) in light of the criticisms that are made of these methods. First, the proper use of case methods must be theoretically grounded; it is particularly useful in this context to rely on ideal types (Weber 1949). Ideal types are analytical constructs that bring together all the theorized elements of a particular phenomenon, without the expectation that any real example of the phenomenon would exhibit all of the elements that are part of the ideal type. They are useful in comparative-historical research because they provide a basic framework for comparison that enables the researcher to show how particular cases do (or do not) deviate from the expectations of the ideal type. Theoretical framing can also be used to illuminate the ways in which a particular case deviates from the predictions that might be expected from a theoretical model. Second, the case can be subdivided into different elements, periods, or themes that can be internally compared; alternatively, researchers may make comparisons between the particular case being studied and other cases about which researchers have previously published (Gerring 2007). Third, when researchers use a small number of individual cases, they can be chosen to be as similar as possible across explanatory factors while being *different* in the key outcome(s) to be explained, which thus increases the explanatory power of the analysis. This choice illustrates the utility of negative case methods.

The development of negative case methods stems from the desirability of including variation in the selection of cases. Researchers who use multiple cases can easily include variation by including multiple disparate cases, but researchers who are focused on one or a small number of in-depth case studies must instead rely on deviations from a theoretical construct (Emigh 1997); in other words, on instances in which a case deviates from theoretical predictions. Some research projects must rely on more than one negative case — or even more than one *type* of negative case — in order to illuminate multiple parts of the theory being considered. For instance, Jeff Goodwin's work on post–World War II revolutionary movements in Latin America and Asia considers revolutions that successfully changed their societies, attempts at revolution that were not successful in creating large-scale social change, and a nation similar to the others under consideration but where no revolutionary movement ever developed (Goodwin 2001).

When conducting case studies, comparative-historical researchers rely on the practice of *historiography*, or writing detailed historical narrative. Historiographic accounts may rely on any of the four main types of comparative-historical data; what they have in common is the goal of presenting a narrative that will allow readers to judge for themselves whether the researcher's claims are supported. In this regard, historiography has much in common with the ethnographic practice of "thick description" (cf., Geertz 1973). Researchers have, however, many choices about how to proceed in the writing of historiography. They may provide a more general overview of the case in question, asking the reader to trust that the evidence is sound; they may mimic the historian's practice of detailed footnotes that come close to completely representing the original data sources; they may choose to present a series of strategically selected illustrations that represent the fullness of the original data; or they may select some combination of these strategies (Platt 1981).

Formal Methods

One of the most important critiques of comparative-historical methodology has been its lack of rigor. For instance, case studies are often accused of providing "nothing more" than hypotheses, rather than rigorous explanations for phenomena (Almond, Appleby, and Sivan 2003); similarly, they may be considered "nonrigorous" because the researcher has flexibility in developing the structure of the narrative and specifying its component parts (Griffin 1993). These criticisms have led some comparative-historical methodologists to develop more formal approaches to comparative-historical scholarship that rely on careful specification and a mathematically-based logic.

Perhaps the first example of formal methods of comparative-historical analysis are Mill's Methods (Mill 1843). In developing his Methods, John Stuart Mill aimed to formalize the process of comparing instances of a particular phenomenon so as to make clear when similar explanations are responsible for similar outcomes and when they are not. Mill's Methods, on the basic level, have two component parts: the Method of Agreement and the Method of Difference (Skocpol 1984). The Method of Agreement is used to determine conditions that are *necessary* for producing a particular outcome. In performing the Method of Agreement, the researcher examines a set of cases with a similar outcome and looks for characteristics that they all have in common. The Method of Difference is used to determine conditions that are *sufficient* for producing a particular outcome. In performing the Method of Difference, the researcher examines a set of cases with different outcomes and looks for characteristics that differ in concert with these different outcomes. In the Joint Method, the approaches of the Method of Agreement and the Method of Difference are combined, in order to determine *both* the necessary *and* the sufficient factors.

Mill did articulate two more advanced variations on his Methods—the Method of Concomitant Variation and the Method of Residues (Mill 1843). In the Method of Concomitant Variation, analysts consider whether the properties and extent of various causal factors vary in concert with the extent of particular effects. For instance, a researcher interested in the factors that lead to changes in the dominant political party in a democratic state might find that economic crises are related to shifts in party power. Using the Method of Concomitant Variation, the researcher would look to see if deeper economic crises are related to larger shifts in party power. Finally, the Method of Residues enables the researcher to isolate those causal factors which are already known and understood in order to determine the extent of the contribution of a remaining factor.

Mill's various Methods provided a useful corrective for the practices of historical reasoning that came before him, but they remain limited as analytical tools. Each Method makes particular assumptions about the nature of causal factors that rely on advance knowledge of the various potential antecedents of a given outcome, and furthermore do not leave room for interactions between the various causal factors in producing outcomes. Finally, Mill's Methods, despite being used as the foundation for much comparative-historical scholarship, do not provide for the possibility of analyzing temporal variation, which many comparative-historical researchers see as a fundamental characteristic of comparative-historical analysis (Mahoney and Rueschemeyer 2003). Yet for many years, Mill's Methods were the only technique available to comparative-historical researchers who wanted to use formal methods to ensure analytical rigor in their research.

Of course, research can certainly be methodologically rigorous without the use of formal methods. Researchers who conduct case study analysis can ensure that their work is rigorous by carefully structuring their data collection, relying on triangulation to cross-check methods and data sources, and providing the reader with access to the original data. But critics of case study research argue that while such techniques improve comparative-historical research, they still fall short in pursuit of the ultimate goal of rigorous hypothesis testing (King, Keohane, and Verba 1994). While Mill's Methods do allow for hypothesis testing, the criticisms noted above limit the analytical power of these methodological techniques. Because of these limitations, various methodologists in the contemporary period have proposed more advanced systems of formal comparative-historical analysis.

Qualitative Comparative Analysis

Qualitative Comparative Analysis (QCA) is a formal method of analysis that relies at its foundation on the logic of necessity and sufficiency developed in Mill's Methods, as discussed above (Ragin 1994). While conventional statistical models of association do not differentiate between necessity and sufficiency in their explorations of the strength of association between variables, QCA techniques allow researchers to differentiate between those conditions that are necessary and those that are sufficient, as well as determining which conditions are both necessary and sufficient. In particular, QCA is useful in situations in which multiple constellations of factors may lead to interesting outcomes by allowing researchers to see the full complexity of their data. In brief, QCA relies on the logic of sets and Boolean algebra to determine which factors or groups of factors are necessary and which factors or groups of factors are sufficient for each important outcome. Boolean algebra is the mathematical expression of logical relationships based in the principles of syllogism — deductive reasoning based on a series of premises (Boole 1848). Sets simply represent groups of similar objects that are classified together.

Fuzzy-Set Qualitative Comparative Analysis, or fsQCA (Ragin 2000; 2008), expands on traditional QCA by allowing researchers to specify cases as having degrees of membership within a set, making QCA techniques available to researchers who wish to use data that cannot be easily coded into binary categories. This advance incorporates the concept of fuzzy sets. A fuzzy set is "a class of objects with a continuum of grades of membership (characteristics) ... [and that] assigns to each object a grade of membership between zero and one" (Zadeh 1965, 338). The point of fuzzy sets is that many concepts in the real world cannot be easily, usefully, or realistically operationalized as a binary opposition (in other words, presence or absence).

Hypothesis-testing in QCA/fsQCA requires separate tests of both necessary and sufficient conditions. In necessity testing, which aims to demonstrate which conditions are necessary precursors to an outcome, individual causal factors are evaluated. In sufficiency testing, which aims to demonstrate what conditions or sets of conditions will be sufficient to lead to an outcome at least some of the time, all theoretically possible sets of conditions are evaluated. Necessity and sufficiency can both be evaluated using a veristic test (which allows no counter-indications) or a probabilistic test (using statistical significance to assess the likelihood that a result did not surpass a benchmark proportion by chance). While it is possible in datasets with a small number of cases and a small number of factors being considered for necessity and sufficiency to conduct the analysis by hand using a truth table, or a table that lays out all of the logical possibilities of combinations of factors, more complex QCA/fsQCA models rely on a software package that simplifies the coding and analysis process (Ragin 2009). In its current version, the fsQCA software is able to handle large and sophisticated datasets (Ragin 2008). While QCA and fsQCA have served as a key corrective to concerns about the lack of rigor in comparative-historical methodology, they are not useful in all circumstances. Many comparative-historical projects continue to utilize case studies; even where datasets are large enough for formal analysis, QCA and fsQCA lack the ability to account for timing and sequence and thus cannot be applied to studies in which these are essential analytical factors.

Critiques of Comparative-Historical Methodology

Positivist researchers often complain that comparative-historical methods are lacking in rigor (King, Keohane, and Verba 1994) and thus are unable to provide social scientists with the tools to move forward in the production of new knowledge. On the other side, interpretivists argue that comparative-historical scholarship suffers from an overemphasis on causation at the expense of context, culture, and meaning (Skocpol 2003). Such critiques cause many young scholars to neglect or reject comparative-historical methods, perceiving them on the one hand as analytically limited and on the other as "boring," lacking in both the power of statistics and the intrigue of ethnography or in-depth interviewing. However, an alternative perspective suggests that comparative-historical research can provide the middle ground that mediates between the "paradigm debates" of social science: a middle ground between "grandiose theory" and narrow statistical hypothesis testing, a middle ground in which both causal arguments and an understanding of subjectivity are retained (Mahoney and Rueschemeyer 2003, 25).

The Positivist Critique

Positivism is a philosophy of knowledge in which reality is understood as something ultimately knowable through carefully designed, deductive, generalizable research. While some comparative-historical research can attain some of the standards of positivism, there are many constraints on positivist approaches to comparative-historical research.

Positivist research logic typically requires that the individual cases be independent of one another in order to test the association between independent and dependent variables. Because of the nesting of cases in historical context that is a hallmark of comparative-historical research, comparative-historical researchers typically cannot guarantee this sort of independence — individual cases and elements of cases are quite likely to have influenced one another (Haydu 1998). Furthermore, positivists argue that case study research and comparisons of small numbers of cases do not offer sufficient power to develop causal arguments. To address these limitations, positivists advocate that case study researchers expand the number of cases and observations to as great an extent as possible and that they draw on random selection to avoid the possibility of bias (King, Keohane and Verba 1994).

The Interpretivist Critique

Interpretivism is a philosophy of knowledge that articulates the belief that what we know about the world is derived from our own experience — in other words, there is no "knowable" reality apart from individuals' own interpretations of it. Interpretivism draws on postmodernist theory in developing critiques of positivist social science research. Interpretivists often emphasize research concerned with meanings, experiences, identities, and similar concepts, rather than engaging in causal analysis (Mahoney and Rueschemeyer 2003). One of the fundamental beliefs of interpretivist researchers is that sociology is not an experimental science but rather a tool of cultural analysis. Therefore, interpretivists argue that comparative-historical researchers devote too much attention to causal arguments and too little attention to meaning and context. They also argue that comparative-historical researchers ask questions that are too focused on "what happened" rather than on what actors believed to be happening or on giving voice to marginalized people. Finally, interpretivists argue that the comparative-historical analyst's focus on large-scale causal factors overlooks the importance of individual actions in specific contexts (Adcock 2006). These critiques do not mean that interpretivists are opposed to research that considers history and takes on the task of comparison; rather, interpretivists argue for a shift in the focus of comparative-historical questions and techniques.

New Directions in the Use of Comparative-Historical Methods

When students are introduced to comparative-historical methods, they often first encounter classic works of scholarship such as Theda Skocpol's *States and Social Revolutions* (1979) or Barrington Moore's *The Social Origins of Dictatorship and Democracy* (1966) that make causal arguments about large-scale political events a century or more in the past by drawing on a set of national case studies. These sorts of analyses are important, and they continue to be central in comparative-historical scholarship (see, for instance, Goodwin 2001). But this is not the only type of comparative-historical research being done today. Researchers draw on the techniques of case study based comparative-historical analysis to research a wide variety of other question and topics, such as punishment (Meithe and Lu 2005), military weapons (Goldstein 2006), primary and secondary school curricula (Benavot and Braslavsky 2007), poverty (Eldersveld 2007), and environmental issues (Ndubisi 2002). Beyond expanding the range of topics about which comparative-historical scholarship has been pursued, however, comparative-historical methodologies can be expanded in a number of promising directions: exploring the recent past, incorporating geographical information, using network analysis, and relying on the increasing availability of online archival materials.

Exploring the Recent Past

Comparative-historical research need not be limited to explorations of the distant past. It can be used to expand our understanding of more recent times as well. Many researchers who wish to study the recent past choose *not* to rely on comparative-historical methodologies. Instead, they choose to interview individuals who were involved in the events under study and ask them about their recollections, then analyze the data using a conventional approach to qualitative analysis. This approach can be very useful — not everything is recorded in documents, and qualitative analysis techniques do have much to offer. But it is not the only approach. Even very recent events can be explored through comparative-historical techniques.

To provide an example of how comparative-historical research might be conducted concerning the recent past, consider a study of curricular change at colleges and universities in the United States (Arthur 2011). In this study, six colleges and universities—varying in terms of public or private status, geographical location, size, selectivity, and religious affiliation — were studied to understand how new academic curricula in women's studies, Asian American studies, and LGBT/queer studies developed. The project involved archival data collection at each site, examining documents such as student newspapers, course catalogues, faculty meeting minutes, and records of student organizations. Those individuals identified as participants in the process of curricular change were then contacted for interviews about their recollections. The project concluded that, at least for non-vocational fields of study such as those it considered, curricular change is likely to occur when faculty and students work together in social movement-like organizations that adapt their strategic choices to the organizational context of a particular college or university.

The oldest events considered in this project occurred around 1970; the most recent occurred within weeks of data collection. So why use archival data to study such recent events? There are two particularly important reasons. First of all, when contentious events occur, individuals involved are not always willing to tell the story. Indeed, faculty members in women's studies at one of the institutions in the study discussed here were unwilling to talk about the genesis of their program for fear it would jeopardize its chance of winning approval for a new major. Archival documents, therefore, made it possible to tell a story that would otherwise go untold, as well as to locate and interview former members of the department who had no such concerns. Secondly, sometimes documents tell different stories than participants do. Even after just a few months, individuals' memories of the trajectory of particular events, and their own roles in them, often become reshaped — consider, for instance, the stories people tell themselves about why their relationships break up. Given a slightly longer time period — a decade, say — individuals may not remember the events in question at all. Archival research can therefore provide a useful form of triangulation that allows the researcher to double-check and expand on findings gained from other sources. There are many potential projects that concern the recent past and would benefit from a comparative-historical approach, starting right on campus with the stories of curricular change and other issues at colleges and universities. But beyond campus, researchers might look to political changes, decision-making processes at not-for-profit organizations, the handling of court cases, or other phenomena that leave behind many written records.

Geographical Information Systems and Historical Mapmaking

Comparative-historical methodology can also benefit from the utilization of advanced computer technologies such as Geographical Information Systems (Schwartz 2010) or other forms of mapmaking as well as network analysis (Gould 2003). Geographical Information Systems (GIS) refers to a series of computer technologies that enable the development and analysis of data through the use of electronic mapping. GIS maps can contain both spatial elements, such as the location and size of places, and non-spatial elements, such as comparative rankings of population size or levels of pollution. These maps can be made for an individual point of historical or contemporary time, or they can be developed in series across time to develop an understanding of change. For instance, Robert Schwartz used historical GIS to examine the impact of railroad development on the restructuring of agriculture in France and England during the Industrial Revolution (Schwartz 2010).

Historical GIS has become popular in history and geography (Gregory and Ell 2007; Knowles 2002; Knowles 2008), and thus a wide variety of resources are now available for researchers who want to utilize this technology. For instance, researchers can download GIS-compatible U.S. Census data from 1790–2000 in order to study migration, demography, and other social changes over time (Minnesota Population Center 2010). Similar resources are now available for many other countries. However, GIS — particularly its historical applications — are still underutilized within sociological research. The August 2009 special issue of the *Social Science Computer Review* provides some highlights in recent social science historical GIS research: a paper on historical changes in sex ratios on the American frontier, the development of telecommunication technologies in London, environmental change in Texas, and tourism in central Pennsylvania are just a few examples. Future historical GIS research might consider issues such as changes in drug markets or the effects of natural disasters on urban environments.

Network Analysis

Over the past few decades, network analysis has grown significantly in popularity as a tool for social science research (Borgatti et al. 2009); it is slowly picking up in use among comparative-historical researchers as well (Gould 2003). Network analysis refers to a set of methodological practices that are designed to study the relationships, interactions, connections between actors (whether individuals or organizations). Early studies drawing on network analysis were limited to the production of hand-drawn diagrams (sociograms) that depicted the connections between individuals or organizations; in these diagrams, individual actors are referred to as *nodes*, while the links between the nodes are called *edges*. Today, network analysts can draw on sophisticated computer software packages that allow the creation and mathematical analysis of large-scale networks (Bruggeman 2008). These software packages include, but are not limited to, GUESS and R. Analytical questions that network analysis can answer include both those that explain the overall shapes and dynamics of the network as well as those concerning the effects of network connections on individual members of the network. Network analysis thus allows for the study of a variety of types of phenomena, such as the connections between members of a network, the presence and configuration of subgroups, the effects of networks on members' behavior and activities, and the process of network generation over time (Burt 1987; Emirbayer and Goodwin 1994).

Network analysis methods offer comparative-historical researchers several advantages. First and most fundamentally, there are research questions, which can be answered with network analysis and not as well with other techniques. In addition, scholarly debates can be more easily resolved when analysts agree on a methodological technique and use it to address a common question and a common set of data (Gould 2003). Comparative-historical network analysis techniques have been applied recently to a number of worthwhile questions, such as terrorism (Sageman 2004), international trade (Mahutga 2006), and the development of new forms of music (Crossley 2009). Future researchers might consider questions such as the ways that network ties between organizations change over time, or how connections between legislators shape legislation.

Comparative-Historical Analysis Online

The Internet itself can now become a site for comparative-historical analysis by drawing on resources such as the Internet Archive (Internet Archive 2009), and newly digitized archives have democratized comparative-historical research so that travel funding is no longer an obstacle to individuals with research questions that archival materials can answer. Researchers who are interested in conducting comparative-historical research have always been faced with obstacles in locating their data, particularly when they are searching for primary source documents. The documents a researcher wants are rarely archived in a convenient location, and thus comparative-historical researchers must make trips elsewhere — trips that can become expensive in terms of both time and money. This is a particular obstacle to researchers who do not have access to institutional or grant funding or who those who are trying to combine research with other life responsibilities; in addition, inexperienced researchers sometimes face barriers in gaining permission to enter certain restricted archives. In the past, the most common way for comparative-historical researchers to avoid these difficulties was to conduct research relying on secondary sources, but not all questions can be answered using secondary sources. Secondary sources tend to cover more macro-scale questions, for instance, making them less useful for researchers interested in family life, labor, or other similar topics.

Online resources offer a new way out of this dilemma, providing researchers access to archived digital materials that can be accessed from anywhere in the world. Some archives have digitized portions of or even complete collections. These digitized archives range in content and scope, from those on specialized topics (see, for instance, Griswold 2006) to those on individual institutions (see, for instance, Mount Holyoke College Archives and Special Collections 2010), from government records (see, for instance, New York City Department of Finance 2010) to much more general collections (see, for instance, New York Public Library 2010).

Beyond digitized documents and images, online resources make possible new sorts of comparative-historical analysis. For instance, each Wikipedia page provides an archive of its own history (Wikipedia 2010). Wikipedia was initiated in 2001, so pages may now offer up to ten years of editing history. This resource has not yet been explored by many scholars, but it offers significant research potential. For instance, researchers could look at the ways in which pages created during the course of a particular event, like Hurricane Katrina, differ as time passes after the event.

An even more promising resource is the Internet Archive, a site founded in 1996 that contains (as of this writing) two petabytes of archived web pages, along with images, films, and texts (Internet Archive 2010). While the Internet Archive does not currently offer a full-text search function, the site does plan to make one available in the future. In the mean time, researchers can look at the history of specific pages, and some have begun to develop projects that draw on its capabilities (Howell 2006), though more within the legal research field than within sociology. Because full-text searching is not available, projects using the Internet Archive need to be based in specific pages or domains, but there are many interesting projects that could be developed within these limits. For instance, researchers could look at headlines over time on news websites; another worthwhile project would be a consideration of issue framing on the sites of political parties or social movement organizations.

As we have seen, comparative-historical methodology offers many tools and opportunities for sociological researchers. It draws on a variety of data sources and analytical techniques, and there are many unanswered research questions — some drawing on promising new tools and data sources — for researchers to explore. Yet comparative-historical research remains less frequently utilized by sociological researchers than qualitative interviewing and ethnography or quantitative survey research techniques. In part, this is due to the lack of training that students receive and the lack of coverage textbooks provide in these methodological strategies, as discussed at the beginning of this chapter.

But perhaps one of the other reasons why comparative-historical methodology has been so often ignored by texts that introduce students of sociology to the "methodological toolbox" of the discipline is that comparative-historical sociologists are often less clear about their own methodological strategies. For instance, *States and Social Revolutions* (1979), Theda Skocpol's groundbreaking work on the dynamics leading to revolutions in the modern world and a work that exemplified comparative-historical scholarship to a generation of researchers, provides readers with little sense of her research process. Similarly, many recent articles employing comparative-historical methods that are published in sociological journals do not provide a methodology section as qualitative or quantitative articles would (see, for instance, Goodwin 2007; Kaufman 2008). This absence makes it harder for new sociologists—and any sociologist who is not a practitioner of comparative-historical research — to see and understand the research process employed by comparative-historical analysts. This is unfortunate, for comparative-historical research is not a tool only suited to the dreary questions of yesterday's scholars, but rather a tool that can provide new windows into our social organizations, our culture, and indeed our future.

References

Abbot, Andrew. 1995. Sequence Analysis: New Methods for Old Ideas. *Annual Review of Sociology* 21: 93–113.

_____. 1997. Optimal Matching. http://home.uchicago.edu/~aabbott/om.html.

Adcock, Robert. 2006. Generalization in Comparative and Historical Social Science: The Difference that Interpretivism Makes. In *Interpretation and Method: Empirical Research Methods and the Interpretive Turn*, ed. Dvora Yanow and Peregrine Schwartz-Shea, 50–66. Armonk, NY: M.E. Sharpe.

Adler, Emily S., and Roger Clark. 2008. *How It's Done: An Invitation to Social Research*. Belmont, CA: Wadsworth.

Almond, Gabriel A., R. S. Appleby, and Emmanuel Sivan. 2003. *Strong Religion: The Rise of Fundamentalisms around the World*. Chicago: University of Chicago Press.

Amenta, Edwin. 1991. Making the Most of a Case Study: Theories of the Welfare State and the American Experience. *International Journal of Comparative Sociology* 32 (March): 172–94.

Arthur, Mikaila M. L. 2011. *Student Activism and Curricular Change in Higher Education*. Surrey, UK: Ashgate.

Babbie, Earl. 1995. *The Practice of Social Research*. Belmont, CA: Wadsworth.

Benavot, Aaron, and Cecilia Braslavsky. 2007. *School Knowledge in Comparative and Historical Perspective: Changing Curricula in Primary and Secondary Education*. Dordrecht: Springer.

Boole, George. 1848. The Calculus of Logic. *Cambridge and Dublin Mathematical Journal* III: 183–98.

Borgatti, Stephen P., Ajay Mehra, Daniel J. Brass, and Giuseppe Labianca. 2009. Network Analysis in the Social Sciences. *Science* 323 (5916): 982–95.

Bruggeman, Jeroen. 2008. *Social Networks: An Introduction*. London: Routledge.

Burt, Ronald. 1987. Social Contagion and Innovation: Cohesion versus Structural Equivalence. *American Journal of Sociology* 92(6): 1287–1335.

Caren, Neal, and Aaron Panofsky. 2005. TQCA: A Method for Adding Temporality to Qualitative Comparative Analysis. *Sociological Methods and Research* 34(2): 147–72.

Cargan, Leonard. 2007. *Doing Social Research*. Lanham, MD: Rowman and Littlefield.

Chambliss, Daniel F., and Russell K. Schutt. 2006. *Making Sense of the Social World: Methods of Investigation*. Thousand Oaks, CA: Pine Forge Press.

Crossley, Nick. 2009. The Man Whose Web Expanded: Network Dynamics in Manchester's Post/Punk Music Scene, 1976–1980. *Poetics* 37(1): 24–49.

Dion, Douglas. 2003. Evidence and Inference in the Comparative Case Study. In *Necessary Conditions: Theory, Methodology, and Applications*, ed. Gary Goertz and Harvey Starr, 95–112. Lanham, MD: Rowman & Littlefield.

Eldersveld, Samuel James. 2007. *Poor America: A Comparative Historical Study of Poverty in the United States and Western Europe*. Berkeley: University of California Press.

Emigh, Rebecca Jean. 1997. The Power of Negative Thinking: The Use of Negative Case Methodology in the Development of Sociological Theory. *Theory and Society* 26(5): 649–84.

Emirbayer, Mustafa, and Jeff Goodwin. 1994. Network Analysis, Culture, and the Problem of Agency. *American Journal of Sociology* 99(6): 1411–54.

Geertz, Clifford. 1973. *The Interpretation of Cultures*. New York: Basic Books.

Gerring, John. 2007. *Case Study Research: Principles and Practices*. Cambridge, UK: Cambridge University Press.

Goldstein, Lyle J. 2006. *Preventive Attack and Weapons of Mass Destruction: A Comparative Historical Analysis*. Stanford, CA: Stanford University Press.

Goodwin, Jeff. 2001. *No Other Way Out: States and Revolutionary Movements, 1945–1991*. Cambridge, UK: Cambridge University Press.

_____. 2007. "The Struggle Made Me a Nonracialist": Why There Was So Little Terrorism in the Antiapartheid Struggle. *Mobilization* 12(2): 193–203.

Gould, Roger V. 2003. Use of Network Tools in Comparative Historical Research. In *Comparative Historical Analysis*, ed. James Mahoney and Dietrich Rueschemeyer, 241–69. Cambridge, UK: Cambridge University Press.

Gray, Paul S., John B. Williamson, David A. Karp, and John R. Dalphin. 2007. *The Research Imagination: An Introduction to Qualitative and Quantitative Methods*. Cambridge, UK: Cambridge University Press.

Gregory, Ian, and Paul Ell. 2007. *Historical GIS: Technologies, Methodologies, and Scholarship*. Cambridge, UK: Cambridge University Press.

Griffin, Larry J. 1993. Narrative, Event-Structure Analysis, and Causal Interpretation in Historical Sociology. *American Journal of Sociology* 98(5): 1094–1133.

Griswold, Ralph E. 2008. On-Line Digital Archive of Documents on Weaving and Related Topics. http://www.cs.arizona.edu/patterns/weaving/index.html.

Haydu, Jeffrey. 1998. Making Use of the Past: Time Periods as Cases to Compare and as Sequences of Problem Solving. *American Journal of Sociology* 104(2): 339–71.

Heise, David. 2007. The ESA Site. http://www.indiana.edu/~socpsy/ESA/.

Hill, Michael R. 1993. *Archival Strategies and Techniques*. Thousand Oaks, CA: Sage Publications.

Hoopes, James. 1979. *Oral History: An Introduction for Students*. Chapel Hill, NC: University of North Carolina Press.

Howell, Beryl A. 2006. Proving Web History: How to Use the Internet Archive. *Journal of Internet Law* 9(8): 3–9.

International Sociology Association. 1997. Books of the Century. http://www.isa-sociology.org/books/vt/bkv_000.htm.

Internet Archive. 2010. Internet Archive. http://www.archive.org.

Kaufman, Jason. 2008. Corporate Law and the Sovereignty of States. *American Sociological Review* 73(3): 402–25.

King, Gary, Robert O. Keohane, and Sidney Verba. 1994. *Designing Social Inquiry*. Princeton, NJ: Princeton University Press.

Knowles, Anne Kelly. 2002. *Past Time, Past Place: GIS for History*. Redlands, CA: ESRI.

_____. 2008. *Placing History: How Maps, Spatial Data, and GIS Are Changing Historical Scholarship*. Redlands, CA: ESRI.

Leedy, Paul D., and Jeanne Ellis Ormord. 2005. *Practical Research: Planning and Design*. Upper Saddle River, NJ: Pearson.

Lustick, Ian S. 1996. History, Historiography, and Political Science: Multiple Historical Records and the Problem of Selection Bias. *American Political Science Review* 90(3): 605–18.

Mahoney, James, and Dietrich Rueschemeyer, eds. 2003. *Comparative Historical Analysis in the Social Sciences*. Cambridge, UK: Cambridge University Press.

Mahoney, James, and Dietrich Rueschemeyer. 2003. Comparative-Historical Analysis: Achievements and Agendas. In *Comparative Historical Analysis*, ed. James Mahoney and Dietrich Rueschemeyer, 3–40. Cambridge, UK: Cambridge University Press.

Mahutga, Matthew C. 2006. The Persistence of Structural Inequality? A Network Analysis of International Trade, 1965–2000. *Social Forces* 84(4): 1863–89.

Meithe, Terance D., and Hong Lu. 2005. *Punishment: A Comparative-Historical Perspective*. Cambridge, UK: Cambridge University Press.

Mill, John Stuart. 1843. *A System of Logic*. London: Harrison and Co.

Minnesota Population Center. 2010. National Historical Geographic Information System (NHGIS). http://www.nhgis.org/.

Moore, Barrington, Jr. 1966. *Social Origins of Dictatorship and Democracy*. Boston: Beacon Press.

Mount Holyoke College Archives and Special Collections. 2009. Digital Resources. http://www.mtholyoke.edu/archives/15024.shtml.

Ndubisi, Forster. 2002. *Ecological Planning: A Historical and Comparative Synthesis*. Baltimore: Johns Hopkins University Press.

Neuman, W. Lawrence. 2003. *Social Research Methods: Qualitative and Quantitative Approaches*. Boston: Allyn and Bacon.

New York City Department of Finance. 2009. Automated City Register Information System. http://www.nyc.gov/html/dof/html/jump/acris.shtml.

New York Public Library. 2010. Digital Gallery. http://digitalgallery.nypl.org/nypldigital/index.cfm.

Oral History Association. 2010. Oral History. http://www.oralhistory.org/do-oral-history/.

Platt, Jennifer. 1981. Evidence and Proof in Documentary Research, Parts 1 and 2. *Sociological Review* 29(1): 31–66.

Ragin, Charles C. 1994. *Constructing Social Research: The Unity and Diversity of Method*. Thousand Oaks, CA: Pine Forge Press.

_____. 2000. *Fuzzy-Set Social Science*. Chicago: University of Chicago Press.

_____. 2008. *Redesigning Social Inquiry: Fuzzy Sets and Beyond*. Chicago: University of Chicago Press.

_____. 2009. Fuzzy set/Qualitative Comparative Analysis Software. http://www.u.arizona.edu/~cragin/fsQCA/software.shtml.

Rueschemeyer, Dietrich. 2003. Can One or a Few Cases Yield Empirical Gains? In *Comparative Historical Analysis*, ed. James Mahoney and Dietrich Rueschemeyer, 305–36. Cambridge, UK: Cambridge University Press.

Sageman, Marc. 2004. *Understanding Terror Networks*. Philadelphia: Pennsylvania State University Press.

Schwartz, Robert M. 2010. Rail Transport, Agrarian Crisis, and the Restructuring of Agriculture: France and Great Britain Confront Globalization, 1860–1900. *Social Science History* 34(2): 229–55.

Skocpol, Theda. 1979. *States and Social Revolutions: A Comparative Analysis of France, Russia, and China*. Cambridge, UK: Cambridge University Press.

_____. 1984. Emerging Agendas and Recurrent Strategies in Historical Sociology. In *Vision and Method in Historical Sociology*, ed. Theda Skocpol, 356–91. Cambridge, UK: Cambridge University Press.

_____. 2003. Doubly Engaged Social Science: The Promise of Comparative Historical Analysis.

In *Comparative Historical Analysis*, ed. James Mahoney and Dietrich Rueschemeyer, 407–28. Cambridge, UK: Cambridge University Press.

United Nations Office on Drugs and Crime. 2010. Compiling and Comparing International Crime Statistics. http://www.unodc.org/unodc/en/data-and-analysis/Compiling-and-comparing-International-Crime-Statistics.html.

Valenzuela, J. Samuel. 1998. Macro Comparisons without the Pitfalls: A Protocol for Comparative Research. In *Politics, Society, and Democracy: Latin America*, ed. Scott Mainwaring and Arturo Valenzuela, 237–66. Boulder: Westview Press.

Weber, Max. 1949. "Objectivity" in Social Science and Social Policy. In *The Methodology of the Social Sciences*, ed. Edward A. Shils and Henry A. Finch, 49–112. New York: Free Press.

Wikipedia. 2010. Help: Page History. http://en.wikipedia.org/wiki/Edit_history.

Zadeh, Lofti A. 1965. Fuzzy Sets. *Journal of Information and Control* 8(3): 338–53.

11. AUTOETHNOGRAPHY
The Sociological Through the Personal
Natalia Ruiz-Junco *and* Salvador Vidal-Ortiz

Autoethnography is recognized in academia as a first-person narrative (Ellis 1995), as poetic writing (Clough 2000), as performance (Spry 2001), or as co-constructed conversations (Ellis and Bochner 1992), all of which destabilize conventional voices representing knowledge in the human and social sciences. It is now practiced in several disciplines. Autoethnographies are published within and from the perspectives of sociology, anthropology, communications, psychology, and queer studies among others. Our goal in this chapter is to situate the multiple meanings of autoethnography within the sociological literature.

In recent years sociologists have proposed new conceptions of ethnography: institutional ethnography (Smith 2005), the extended case method (Burawoy 1991; 1998), and global ethnography (Burawoy et al. 2000; see also Gille and Riain 2002). These forms of ethnography give ethnography a political role or purpose, although in different ways. Whereas institutional ethnography critiques the relations of ruling within social institutions, the extended case method and global ethnography provide critiques of power based on the analysis of structural forces upon groups. We argue in this chapter that autoethnography shares elements with these ethnographic genres.

We begin with an exposition of the interpretive origins of autoethnography. In particular, Ellis and Denzin are two foundational figures of autoethnography that developed the method in productive tension with the interpretive framework. These autoethnographers pushed interpretive narratives to an extreme, to the point of leaving the ethnographic method, focusing less on the notions of ethnography as analytical text (Anderson 2006), and more on the centrality of the "I" either for political or "therapeutic" (Ellis 2004) purposes.

Succinctly, we understand autoethnography to be a way of doing research that uses the personal to investigate the social. Autoethnography can "be defined as a self-narrative that critiques the situatedness of self with others in social contexts" (Spry 2001, 710). To take an example, Vidal-Ortiz (2004) uses personal vignettes to narrate larger social and historical racialization processes that link his narrative to other Puerto Ricans in their experiential and political relation to the U.S. Autoethnographies, however, do not necessarily have to be restricted to the narrative form. In fact, as one author puts it, "[a]utoethnographers vary in their emphasis on *auto-* (self), *-ethno-* (the sociocultural connection), and *-graphy* (the application of the research process)" (Wall 2008, 39).

One of our arguments is that there are several conceptions of autoethnography. Some of these took place before the early 1990s, when the dominant autoethnographic form emerged within sociology. Mainstream autoethnographic texts developed the depth of reflexive work insisted upon in sociological and anthropological writings in the early 1990s, and renovated the interpretive framework of ethnography considered to be traditional at the time. Autoethnographic writing was infused by the desire of engaging one's subjectivity in the field and in the world, just at the time when ethnographers were interrogating the practice of ethnography. It is important for us to stress that at the same time that Burawoy's (1991) critique of most ethnographic practice as merely focused on understanding (and not achieving explanation), there was a reformulation of interpretive paradigms, benefiting from the critiques developed by feminist, poststructuralist, and postmodern scholars.

As noted in our opening paragraph, there are many forms of presenting autoethnography linked to recent epistemological debates in the humanities and social sciences: stage performance, poetry, whole essays written in the first person, or simulated conversations — to name but a few. Within these texts, common strategies include video diaries (Holliday 2004), drawing on "the visual" of pictures to explore "the verbal" in autoethnography (Watson 2009), or the use of vignettes as illustrations that blend and rupture the theoretical text (Vidal-Ortiz 2004), or layered accounts (Lather and Smithies 1997) that break linear readings of the text.

Autoethnographies are often used to disrupt scientistic narrative thinking and writing. Drastic or dramatic description, insider/outsider debates, and a critique of realism and representation are all part of what makes autoethnography distinct in social scientific circles (Clough 2000; Reed-Danahay 1997). Indeed, autoethnography is only one among many of the manifestations of these fertile debates about the validity of scientific representation as well as the values involved in doing research in connection with larger social issues. Not always influenced by post-structural frameworks, but when so, autoethnography is considered a text based on the self-as-social. Due to the impact of several disciplines that influence autoethnographic writing/performing in various ways, some scholars, depending on their field and theoretical alliances, argue that a clean, well written text makes a good autoethnography (Spry 2001). Others privilege the emotional aspects of writing that make the self central to the story — for example, in stories that reflect on trauma (see Clough 2000; Mitchell 2005). One's experiences, including difficult reflections about emotions, and the interpretations of these experiences as they speak to bodily phenomena, are some of the aspects that guide recent autoethnographies (Gannon 2006; Spry 2001; Vidal-Ortiz 2004).

Whether autoethnographers place their emphasis on self-reflexivity, sociocultural explanation, or the power of textual strategies to represent the link between the self and the social, our examination of their work reveals that autoethnographers use emotions as part of the rational analysis of the social, inviting readers to a form of knowledge that does not exclude their own feelings. We start this chapter with the history of autoethnography to show the projects of autoethnography from the perspective of sociology. We then focus on significant sociological contributors to autoethnography, and later discuss the benefits and critiques of autoethnography. We conclude with several considerations of the future of the autoethnographic method and with suggestions for further work.

Origins and Influences of Autoethnography

The terms "auto-ethnography" and "autoethnography" have been in circulation for decades and are frequently used interchangeably. Hayano is often credited with the first use of "auto-ethnography" (Hayano 1979).[1] However, it was Heider (1975) who first used the term. These two contributions have been recognized as important to the foundation of contemporary autoethnography (Ellis 2004).[2]

Karl Heider's (1975) auto-ethnography is an account of a group —*ethno*— by the members of that group —*auto*. In his 1975 article on the Dani, "What Do People Do? Dani Auto-Ethnography," he introduces two meanings of the prefix *auto*: firstly, *autochthonous* because it represents "the Dani's own account"; and secondly *automatic*, in the sense that "it is the simplest routine-eliciting technique imaginable" (Heider 1975, 3). Heider reduces the notion of auto-ethnography to the link between *ethno* and *graphy* that we referred to above. The emphasis on the self or the auto-positioning of the researcher, however, is not present in this early statement of auto-ethnography. In Heider's view, auto-ethnography is still self-distancing from the researched "natives."

The next conceptualization of auto-ethnography comes from David Hayano (1979). For him, auto-ethnography is an account of the anthropologist as insider —*auto*— writing about the group to which she or he belongs—*ethno*. Departing from Heider's definition, Hayano (1979, 103) stresses the situatedness of the researcher:

> The foremost prospects and possibilities of auto-ethnography in anthropology at this time lie in the following: (1) the substantive and heuristic values of its diverse concepts and theories; (2) the ethical and moral issues it perpetually confronts with respect to the use of human subjects as sources of data; (3) the voices from within — the internal political affirmation of cultural diversity and

autonomy for sometimes neglected populations and peoples; and (4) its potential advisory capabilities in programs of change or development.

Thus, Hayano's contributions to this debate are: complicating Heider's (1975) rigid epistemological distinction — for Hayano, it is problematic to make someone "subject" to research without recognizing the researcher as part of the knowledge-making relation; activating marginalized and minoritized groups by enunciating that these "voices from within" must articulate themselves on their own terms and not on the outsider's terms; and finally, defining auto-ethnography's politics as moving beyond the self. Hayano's auto-ethnography stops short of contemporary notions of autoethnography.[3]

Nowadays, anthropologists (Hemmingson 2009; Reed-Danahay 1997), sociologists (Ellis 1995), education scholars (Chang 2008), and scholars in other fields (Gannon 2006) are concerned with the legitimation of autoethnography within the larger ethnographic tradition. Some autoethnographers conceive their work as a critique of power and scientistic discourse. Perhaps Laurel Richardson (2000) has offered the best analysis of the rhetorical properties of social scientific writing, exposing the researcher to the complexities of the construction of knowledge. She defines autoethnography as "highly personalized, revealing texts in which authors tell stories about their own lived experiences, relating the personal to the cultural. The power of these narratives depends upon their rhetorical staging as 'true stories,' stories about events that really happened to the writers" (Richardson 2000, 512). This definition signals autoethnography's impact as "a radical reaction to realist agendas in ethnography and sociology" (Spry 2001; see also Clough 1998).

Autoethnography in Sociology

In thinking about the placement of autoethnography within sociology, we start by asking: What does the field of ethnography look like from the perspective of autoethnography? The main figures in autoethnography found a landscape of definitions of ethnography and crafted an understanding of autoethnography in opposition to traditional forms of doing ethnography. Definitions of ethnography abound. In sociology, the term ethnography is often used interchangeably with participant observation. For example, in his early statement of the extended case method, Michael Burawoy (1991) makes no distinction between participant observation and ethnography. He defines the method as "the study of people in their own time and space, in their own everyday lives" (Burawoy 1991, 2). Simultaneously, William Shaffir and Robert Stebbins (1991, 5) reinforce this idea while explaining that "[f]ieldwork is carried out by immersing oneself in a collective way of life for the purpose of gaining firsthand knowledge about a major facet of it." They add to this that ethnographers "share with other scientists the goal of collecting valid, impartial data about some natural phenomenon" (Shaffir and Stebbins 1991, 4). At the same moment that some ethnographers defined the field of what ethnography is, some directed a reflexive gaze toward ethnography as it is constituted as text. Characteristically, John Van Maanen (1988, 1) defines ethnography as "written representation of a culture (or selected aspects of a culture)." Van Maanen charges that ethnographers must address in their writing the following points: "the assumed relationship between culture and behavior (the observed)"; "the experiences of the fieldworker (the observer)"; "the representational style selected to join the observer and the observed (the tale)"; and "the role of the reader engaged in the active reconstruction of the tale (the audience)" (Van Maanen 1988, xi). These famous methodological prescriptions—that call researchers to interrogate their practice as text—are symptomatic of a reflexive movement within ethnography, which autoethnographers inherit. Note, however, that autoethnography does not fit neatly into any of the main representations of ethnographic knowledge or "tales" discussed by Van Mannen (1988), namely: *realist, confessional, impressionist, critical* and *formal.*

Like ethnography, autoethnography produces a representation of the social, and in many of its applications, it shares with ethnography the goal of illustrating the social; unlike ethnography, in autoethnography the analysis of one person's life, the evocation of emotions, and even the person's potential connection to members of particular social groups all take center stage. Autoethnography may or may not represent specific aspects of culture, although in doing so, autoethnographers risk representation of such experiences as "universal" and bring up the question of whether they consider themselves members of the same group as the people they talk about in their autoethnographies.

Main Figures of Sociological Autoethnography

Carolyn Ellis and Norman Denzin are two sociologists whose influence in shaping the field of autoethnography is beyond dispute. The two share a commitment to autoethnography and have common origins in the interpretive paradigm, more specifically in symbolic interactionism. The interactionist perspective can be characterized by the study of society with a focus on self, society and symbolic interaction (Cooley [1902] 1998; Mead [1934] 1992; Blumer 1969). For Denzin, this perspective focuses on self, identities, culture, and structural constraints on people's interactions, and seeks to "speak always to those persons who occupy powerless positions in contemporary society" (Denzin 1995, 57); however, Denzin notes, since its inception, the perspective has been significantly enriched and transformed by cultural studies, poststructuralist ideas and feminism. Similarly, Ellis has been influenced by and has in turn influenced interactionism in critical directions. For example, in her early work she attacked the neglect of emotions in the common interactionist theorization of self. In a well-known piece that pays tribute to Cooley's ideas, she proposes introspection as a method to "generate interpretive materials from self and others useful for understanding the lived experience of emotions" (Ellis 1991, 26).

CAROLYN ELLIS

Carolyn Ellis is one of the major proponents of autoethnography in the human and social sciences. Many others join her in the autoethnographic project she initiated in the early 1990s, including Gene Weinstein, Art Bochner, Norman Denzin, Laurel Richardson and several of her students.

Ellis's autoethnographies explore a number of topics that have become recurrent in her writing: emotions, romantic and family relationships, death and dying and care work (see e.g. Ellis 1993; 1995; 2001). Her latest proposal is meta-autoethnography, a subgenre that she coins in her last book, *Revision: Autoethnographic Reflections on Life and Work* (2009). This recent volume is a collection of autoethnographic pieces she has published along the years and includes several meta-autoethnographic exercises on them, where she reflects, reconstructs, and in some ways rewrites the past experiences expressed in her published autoethnographies.[4]

Ellis and Bochner (2003, 209) define the autoethnographic method as follows: "Autoethnography is an autobiographical genre of writing and research that displays multiple layers of consciousness, connecting the personal to the cultural." The definition of autoethnography has gone through a series of reformulations in the hands of Ellis (and collaborators) since the 1990's. At this early moment, Ellis's second book, *Final Negotiations: A Story of Love, Loss, and Chronic Illness* (1995) characteristically intended to validate the autoethnographic method; in fact, she wrote it with the purpose in mind that sociologists would judge it and authorize it as "legitimate sociology" (Ellis 2009, 95). *Final Negotiations* is a brilliant example of autoethnography that offers a moving analysis of her relationship with Gene, her partner, first husband, and co-author, and of the changes that their relationship undergoes through Gene's illness and subsequent death (for a critique see Clough 1997).

Frontally opposed to realism, Ellis argues for autoethnography to "evoke" instead of simply describe or explain the social, and the use of alternative writing techniques to upset the traditional scientific narrative to position the "I" as a haunting presence to the former (see Ellis 2004). When Ellis writes autoethnographically, she is aware of her feelings and deep and conflicting thoughts, and does not seem to feel unqualified or unprepared to speak about them, even if she often admits to emotional ambivalence. Has the story evoked an emotional reaction in the readers? Do the readers have an in-depth understanding of a social issue through their exposure to autoethnographic material? These are some questions that she poses in order to evaluate the autoethnographic.

NORMAN DENZIN

Norman Denzin's work spans sociology, anthropology, and communications. Among his contributions are an international qualitative conference, and the founding of a journal, *Qualitative Inquiry*. Denzin is often seen as too critical of a sociologist, and his work is often dismissed (Seale 1999) because of how far from empiricism he has taken the discipline — as he is often associated with cultural studies, postmodernism, anti-empiricism, or post-scientific proposals for understanding everyday life interaction among people. Autoethnography has been one of the ways in which Denzin has reacted radically to the realism of ethnography in particular, and sociology in general.

He discusses the epistemological and politico-historical trajectories of qualitative research; in particular, he explores the place of the "crisis of representation" (for instance, about modernism and data collection as an impossible match), clashes between epistemological ways of thinking, and co-constructions of methods through interdisciplinarity. These all pose challenges to a certain traditional view of the social sciences. This work is often utilized to mark the study (even the "mapping") of qualitative research.[5] In his individual work, he has also extended symbolic interactionism to discussions of its relationship toward racial subjects; he has examined racialization and cultural performance that contribute to the analysis of race, and provided studies of inequalities in general, and on Native Americans in particular. Denzin's (2001; 2003) substantive interests in the study of race position him as a key player within autoethnography.

For Denzin, autoethnography falls within the "biographical method," which includes autobiography, ethnography, autoethnography, biography, ethnographic story, oral history, case history, case study, life history, life story, self story, and personal experience story (Reed-Danahay 1997). Denzin (1989, 34) defines the method in this way: "An *auto-ethnography* is an ethnographic statement which writes the ethnographer into the text, in an autobiographical manner.... A fully grounded biographical study would be auto-ethnographic and contain elements of the writer's own biography and personal history.... Such an auto-ethnography would be descriptive and interpretive." In Denzin's view, autoethnography is thus neither fully ethnographic nor biographical, but something new that has elements of both. The undoing of ethnographic realism heavily influences the destabilization of the narrative, where the author is simultaneously representing his/her narrative in more direct ways than the traditional, fragmented ethnography, while at the same time destabilizing the positivism foundational in contemporary social thought.

Both Denzin and Ellis have substantially shaped the field of autoethnography. Ellis validated topics through autoethnography that had been neglected and conveniently placed under the rug, such as personal feelings and emotional ambivalences. Similarly, Denzin's influence-through editorial advice, mentoring, and intellectual statements— is notable in the field of autoethnography. For instance, his efforts to make performance autoethnography vibrant within the field are numerous.

Emerging Voices in Autoethnographic Writing

We focus in this section on the work of women feminists of color who wrote from the margins, accompanied by people from the Borderlands, because those works are representative of the 30-year-old critical work on oppression and domination in U.S. society made visible by them. Autoethnographic writings that follow an autobiographical model posed by Moraga, Anzaldúa, and other women of color, effectively connect with more recent autoethnographic writings.[6] These autobiographical writings "from the margins" (of both society and academia) are ways of writing the self that are meant to transcend rigid positionalities altogether (Guzmán 2006; see also Alarcón 1999).

Anzaldúa's, Moraga's, and other writing by women of color has certainly influenced autoethnography. Moraga's writing has done so through the use of her experience in relation to both sides she inhabits, making a complex illustration of her racial and racialized experiences. Similarly, Anzaldúa's notion of borderlands, occupying these liminal spaces that are constitutive of a series of marginalized experiences, makes the writing complex in terms of a web of social location categories rarely explored in traditional sociological writing — and sometimes even in mainstream autoethnographies. All in all, their autobiographical work is foundational to revealing the interconnection of one's personal experiences and larger social structures, foregrounding the work queer feminists and feminists of color achieved through autobiographies (Martin 1988). This is especially crucial when complicating identities and their negotiation (Malhotra and Pérez 2005), and could be a fundamental shift in thinking through the evocative and empathy orientation of some autoethnographers. Referring to Susan Stanford Friedman, Miller (1994, 3–4) notes how for the autobiographical work by women and minorities, "group consciousness, the sense of having one's individual identity inextricably bound to a community's identity, is essential to the formation and representation of an individual life story" and that "women writers tend to locate the self of their autobiographical project not only in relation to a singular, chosen other, but also — and simultaneously — to the *collective* experience of women as gendered subjects in a variety of social contexts." In this respect, autobiographies by women of color — like Moraga and Anzaldúa — represent early articulations of the sociological through the personal, or what we now call autoethnographies.

Moraga and others of her time (in the 1970s and 1980s) wrote both autobiographically and autoethnographically. They put forth accounts infused with feminist ideas, and revealing a methodological strategy: the subaltern's voice speaking in an authorized tone, a tone that challenges established tenets of qualitative inquiry and evidence (Mitchell 2005). It is a counterpoint to mainstream autoethnographic narratives in U.S. academia today (see Anderson 2006). This new genealogy revisits the notion that autoethnographies were founded in the 1990s. By reclaiming these new origins, the project of autoethnography is expanded and enriched.

Why Does Autoethnography Matter?

Many praise autoethnography as research that matters. In many quarters, autoethnography, to paraphrase the subtitle of Ruth Behar's (1996) classic, is research "that breaks your heart." In what follows, we discuss the advantages for sociologists of using this method. We also introduce a distinction between writing/reading and doing, which serves in clarifying the different dimensions on which autoethnography makes a contribution.

First, autoethnography presupposes an emotional interaction, not only with oneself, but with others in the audience. Ellis (1991, 26) spoke of introspection as a method to "generate interpretive materials from self and others useful for understanding the lived experience of emotions." With Ellis, we argue that autoethnography is a perfect methodological venue for exploring emotional dynamics when conventional sociological methods and categories do not do justice to theorize and examine emotions. Feelings or emotions are central to the method of autoethnography, both in terms of their discovery and their problematization. Moreover, this emotionally-directed conversation, when successful in evoking feelings in readers, engages others in the writer's life. Some autoethnographers in their reflexive writing suggest that this emotional interaction turns into a social bond, even a community of the ones who find identification, recognition or affective engagement with autoethnographic texts. To view this as such social bond, however, could be misleading since the affective responses that autoethnography provokes are never certain.

Second, autoethnography becomes useful when the conditions of knowledge production do not allow for experiences to be neatly contained in sociological categories or in social scientific frameworks. Standard social scientific narratives are useless to examine marginalized experiences of the social, as is the case when scholars try to formulate movements between identities or identity slippages. For example, the work of Cho (2008) explores collective memory through the figure of the *yanggongju*. Cho is able to reconstruct collective experiences that could not have been tapped otherwise. Another example is Vidal-Ortiz's (2004) autoethnography. He analyzes the identity shifts across national, pan-ethnic, and coalitional terms. This discussion points to the potential of autoethnography to bring to light marginal voices and to reclaim the visibility of marginalized groups. As we have highlighted, these voices do not have to be the voices of academics, even if people with academic credentials and in academia are legitimized to "speak for" others on the margins.

Third, autoethnography facilitates the comprehension of experiences based on performative acts that are bodily-focused and helps in the project of theorizing the body from the perspective of sociology. As is well-known, sociology has just started to officially theorize the body.[7] Tami Spry (2001) discusses how autoethnographies that are enacted through performance "turn[s] the internally *somatic* into the externally *semantic*" (2001, 721). We assume that the advantages of autoethnography for theorizing the body are multiple: from staging the body-as-self to evoking experiences that circulate somatically and semantically. In these autoethnographies, far from being excluded from the analysis at hand, the body can be a protagonist of the autoethnographic text or performance. The body can be the medium and the focus of the autoethnographic exploration through voice and singing, dance, etc. Simultaneously, it can be the focus of theorization, as a recent autoethnographic study on breastfeeding shows (Crossley 2009).

Autoethnography: Writing/Reading vs. Doing

We now introduce a distinction that helps clarify the theorization of autoethnography in the literature. We speak of two main dimensions that structure the work that autoethnographers do. The first dimension has to do with the writing/reading of autoethnography. For the most part, autoethnographies represent freedom from conventional scientistic narratives that privilege the impartial observer epitomized in the third person voice of writing. As sociologist Laurel Richardson (1990, 10) contends, "social scientific writing depends upon narrative structure and narrative devices, although that structure and those devices are frequently masked by a scientific frame, which is itself a meta-narrative." That is, autoethnography may signify a break from objectivistic models of knowledge and an experimental journey into literary forms of expression as an epistemological statement. The reading of autoethnography, in addition, calls into being the audience, which especially in the case of the confessional genre, is as important as the narrator of the self-narrative. This is why, for Spry, autoethnography can be of "transformative and efficacious potential for researcher, researched, and reader/audience [a]s a primary goal of effective autoethnography in print and performance" (2001, 712). Autoethnography has a complex manner of activating the audience, from participating in a therapeutic engagement for self-discovery to understanding the social world in novel ways (Ellis 1995; Spry 2001). As an example, Art Bochner (1996, 19) directs the following comment to Carolyn Ellis, "We worry about how our readers will interpret what we write, what they may think, and how they will feel." This illustrates that the audience is constitutive to autoethnographic writing. Indeed, it is for all of these reasons that, instead of thinking of writing as a separate activity from reading, we conceive of writing/reading conjoined.

Writing/reading refers to the constitution of the relationship between reader and writer. This relationship can be materialized in different contexts, with different impacts. For example, some sociologists use autoethnographic writings in the classroom as an effective teaching tool, because of its power to comprehend the social through personal cases. While doing so is generally effective, it is not without problems for teaching professionals. Carolyn Ellis in her

The Ethnographic I: A Methodological Novel about Autoethnography (2004, 78) discusses the responses that the students give to reading some of her autoethnographic writing. This is how she narrates what happened when she assigned her piece on abortion, in an undergraduate course:

> After reading it there, a student began to talk about an abortion she had some years ago, how she had not come to terms with it, but how reading my story made her feel better about what had happened. Suddenly, a second student began to condemn the first student and abortion in general. "It's a sin, and there is no coming to terms with it. You shouldn't feel better," she said. The woman telling her story immediately came silent and slumped in her chair, looking as though she hoped the chair would swallow her. Other students looked uncomfortable, but no one rose to her defense. I did the best I could to diffuse the situation and return to the topic of dealing with complexities in revealing emotional experiences. I suspect that the condemnation really was directed at me — at my experience and at my willingness to raise an "inappropriate" topic in an "inappropriate" way — but the condemning student couldn't quite bring herself to confront me directly.

There are pitfalls to assuming the reading-in-the-writing relation, often unknown to the autoethnographer, as the previous quote manifests. On the one hand, the evocative response of the first student to Ellis' abortion illustrates empathic feelings aroused by reading. In particular, the student sees her experience of abortion validated. After all, Ellis (2004, 78) reports that this was "the first time she [the student] had talked openly about this experience." On the other hand, this student was silenced and her act publicly repudiated as her personal experience disappeared back into shame.

Writing/reading and doing autoethnography are two interrelated processes. First, as we have just illustrated with Ellis' account, autoethnographers author a text that may have several purposes depending on the effects that the writing has either for autoethnographers or audiences. Writing may be focused on self-discovery and documentation of one's always partial subjectivity and emotions. Autoethnographers should be advised not to expect to have an intended affective response because this cannot be presumed in the audience. Rather, given the myriad meanings and interpretations, autoethnographic texts always exceed projected readings. This situation leads us to ask how the writing/reading of autoethnography relates to the ethnographic project at large. This speaks to what we call doing autoethnography.

We consider the doing of autoethnography a dimension that transcends the concrete manifestations of autoethnography in writing/reading. It is the perspective of autoethnography from the point of view of a project in the making. The view that considers autoethnography in its dimension of writing/reading is incomplete; it is necessary to go beyond this focus to explore the larger impact of autoethnography through the doing. This entails conceiving of autoethnography as a project that bridges social analysis (graphy) to articulations of the personal (auto) and the cultural (ethno) in the larger contexts of social transformation in which autoethnographers act. As an example of this, we argue that the writing of feminist women of color previously discussed can be understood under this dimension.

Critiques

As is well-known, autoethnography provokes thorny theoretical problems to those who defend and are invested in the conventional postulates of objectivity in the social sciences. These postulates, Denzin (quoted in Spry 2001, 710) notes, create a hierarchy between "the researcher over the subject, method over subject matter, and maintain commitments to outmoded versions of validity, truth, and generalizability." Here, we join Ellis (2009) in distinguishing critiques posed by scholars from outside and within autoethnography. Ellis (2009, 231) identifies three types of criticism of autoethnography by realist social scientists, poststructuralists, and literary critics, namely: "*Social science critics* complain that autoethnographic 'data' are suspect, not real data, and autoethnographers provide no real analysis"; "*poststructuralists* complain that autoethnographers tend to be too realist"; and "*Literary/aesthetic critics* often begin by demeaning the quality of autoethnographic writing." We concentrate here on the criticism received from what Ellis calls "the social science camp."[8]

A predictable reaction from the social science camp is to equate autoethnography with postmodernism. By association to postmodern ideas, autoethnography is automatically impregnated with the common charges against postmodernism. Fetterman (2010, 131), in a sufficiently biased account that is indicative of the former tendency, defines autoethnography as "a form of postmodern ethnography. In autoethnography, the researcher is the center of focus and inquiry. It uses many of the conventions of literary writing. Critics of the approach consider it postmodern excess and narcissism. However, advocates view it as a tool to connect the personal story with the cultural issues that surround them, with the intent to unearth bias and socialization influences. Autoethnography also often aims to provoke thought and reconsideration about the status quo."

While reluctance to embrace autoethnography is still evident in social scientific contexts, the move of many social scientists to using autoethnography as a tool to describe events that range from the mundane (for example, an injury or an exclusion from a group), to personal trauma (e.g. incest, rape, death, and for some, potential and actual deportation) has made autoethnography a common academic household phrase, even if controversial when judged with an empiricist gaze. Joined by testimonials (for example, the Latina Feminist Group 2001) and personal narratives (Berger and Quinney 2005), autoethnography is more often than not cited in qualitative methods networks and journals (Culyba, Heimer and Coleman Petty 2004), although its legitimacy continues to be contested (Plummer 2009).

Ken Plummer (2009, 267–68) reflects on the traits of autoethnography and associated "problems," which for him are: that autoethnography's focus on the individuality of the researcher is "self indulgent and can lead to awkwardness and embarrassment. Even shame" is charged with "bringing their discipline into ill repute" and provokes "all kinds of methodological questions linked to the truth of the story and the life that tells it." This is posed as he, as editor of a journal, publishes autoethnography in sexuality scholarship, perhaps situating the researcher outside of the frame of data-conversion-to-evidence.

The existence of these criticisms signals that autoethnography has generated enough enthusiasm and attention that it is giving rise to internal splits but also theoretical growth within the autoethnographic field and sociology. These are some indications of the possibilities for expansion of autoethnography.

Conclusion

This chapter has traced the origins of autoethnography and spoken of a diversity of autoethnographic forms.[9] Opening up a discussion on autoethnographic reading, writing, and doing to incorporate marginalized experiences and narratives into sociological inquiry, we suggest less of a "gatekeeping" of autoethnography, and more of a nurturing move forward. In what follows, we concentrate on the future or, better said, futures of autoethnography and its relationship to sociology.

One of the main expectations we have is that in the future autoethnography could be enriched through crosspollination with feminist scholarship. Our chapter advances this point by foregrounding the autoethnographic roots in the writings of feminists of color. We also contend that other feminist projects in sociology could benefit from the use of autoethnography beyond topics that focus on ethno-racial minorities. Although the work that incorporates race, class, and gender — a trilogy central to sociological analyses — remains important to feminist projects, we envision feminist analyses moving outside the purview of intersectionality.

In addition to feminist scholarship, autoethnography may be enriched through an open dialogue among sociologists about autoethnography, a debate that this chapter contributes to. Further dialogue could prove extremely useful in the future. In this dialogue sociologists should clearly discuss how we conceive of reflexivity in sociological inquiry. As it is well-known, sociologists continue to push for the incorporation of researcher reflexivity into sociological analysis — even emotions are becoming progressively integrated into field reflections (Kleinman and Copp 1993); however, the results outside the method of autoethnography have only started to touch the surface of the issue.

Autoethnography trumps other sociological methods by enlarging our understanding of reflexivity in the research process. No other sociological method has the potential to disclose the multiple reflexivities that are involved in our everyday research projects, which include not just the researcher's reflexivity — but also the reflexivities of the researchers' subjects. Nor can other methods uncover the multidimensionality of the researcher's positions, including her position within academia, in a more sophisticated and detailed manner. Some of the most powerful critiques of academia's scientistic rhetoric, assumptions and modus operandi come from autoethnographic accounts.

Although not existent right now, we foresee new ethnographies fully embracing the combination of autoethnography and more conventional ethnographic writing. In addition, we argue that a movement to mixed-method approaches in sociological research is growing and that autoethnography may have an important role to play in it (Creswell 2009). We anticipate, for example, that teams of ethnographers might write autoethnographically — and not just simply reflexive analytic memos— as they conduct research using a combination of methods, such as interviews, participant observation and document analysis among others.

So far we have noted the methodological contributions and impact that autoethnography may have in the future. What about theory? Can autoethnography contribute something more in this front? To date, autoethnography has been a method closely linked with interpretive and interactionist theory, and has enriched our theoretical critiques of sociological research, complicating the multiple interests and "truths" that may be articulated in the process. In the same manner that interpretive and interactionist researchers are inspired by different theoretical postulates in their conceptions of autoethnography (Anderson 2006; Ellis 2006), other researchers working from different theoretical traditions can fashion their use of the method according to their differing theoretical interests. For example, ethnographers following Michael Burawoy's and Dorothy Smith's theoretical approaches to ethnography may be in a position to interrogate their research programs and put to use new autoethnographic forms, making them compatible with their theoretical agendas. Autoethnography, however, should not be conceived as tied to any single theoretical perspective.

We would like to conclude with a call to expand the research agenda of autoethnography. From using autoethnography to clarify the multiple dimensions of analysis that link the person to the social, including its macro structures, to the mining of "old" and "new" topics of research, this future agenda is filled with challenges. Substantive areas in which autoethnography has made some initial contributions include the study of emotions and body and embodiment. Subsequent work should expand the untapped knowledge in these areas of study. Just as feminists of color enunciated intersectional approaches to experience, future autoethnographic work could include usually difficult areas to document through quantitative and traditional ethnographic methods. Some of those areas include: transnational and migratory experiences on or at the border, experiences with racism, sexism, homophobia, and notions of the body that extend to illness and disability. Nowadays, experiences with illnesses such as cancer and AIDS may articulate new realities, not only about death and dying, but also about current negotiations surrounding living with chronic or terminal illnesses, which were not fully explored in early autoethnographic statements related to these topics, such as Carolyn Ellis's (1995) *Final Negotiations*. Similarly, the combination of racialized and sexualized experiences, only tapped into in recent work (Vidal-Ortiz 2004), must be developed and extended to health and other sociological areas.

Regardless of the focus of research, we expect that this new scholarship will further articulate how the personal is linked to the social — or how individual narratives constitute and are in turn constituted by social ones— as other scholars have already sufficiently delineated innovative writing techniques and effected pertinent critiques of positivism. We contend that sociology faces the present autoethnographic moment with the pressing task of elaborating the role of cultural meanings and larger narratives, of the media and other institutions of social power and control, and of other structural factors in shaping this link.

A final contribution that autoethnography can make to the future of sociology revolves around the projects of interdisciplinarity. Autoethnography is not currently part of a full-fledged movement toward interdisciplinary methods in the social sciences. For this to happen, disciplinary boundaries would have to be renegotiated. However, we can conceive a future in which teams of researchers may negotiate their disciplinary attachments differently, working toward a more robust shared methodology. As a result, the autoethnographic method may become transformed in the direction of interdisciplinarity. If so, future scholars would not be talking about anthropological or sociological autoethnography, but the autoethnographic enterprise itself.

Notes

1. The hyphenated term "auto-ethnography" has not completely disappeared. In fact, a recent book, *Auto-ethnographies: The Anthropology of Academic Practices* (Meneley and Young 2005) maintains its use. However, "autoethnography" is now the dominant spelling.

2. In her novel on autoethnography, Ellis (2004) recognizes Heider as the creator of the term and Hayano as another precursor, but fails to note the use of auto-ethnography (with a hyphen) by these two anthropologists. This might be due to her intention to write retrospectively on the history of autoethnography; in other words, a-historicizing the term.

3. However, he discounted ethnographic analyses of "one's own life" because "these studies are not only auto-ethnographic, they are self-ethnographic, but it is not immediately shown how they are applicable to other cultural members" (Hayano 1979, 103). Hayano's absolute rejection of the possibilities of "self-ethnography" carries a certain short-sightedness. But,

we contend that it is precisely Hayano's auto-positioning of the researcher in the ethnographic text which opens the door to the discovery and inquiry into the social that characterizes contemporary forms of autoethnographic writing.

4. Meta-autoethnography is not a separate form of autoethnography. As we pointed out, Ellis is known for reformulating autoethnography through the use of many terms. She states: "When you think back to all the terms we have for this kind of writing, some of them designate particular types, such as *personal ethnography*, and *reflexive ethnography*, while other terms refer to methodological approaches, such as *systematic sociological introspection, narrative inquiry*, and *biographical method*" (Ellis 2004, 45).

5. The seven moments of qualitative inquiry are historically situated by Denzin and Lincoln (2003, 3) as: "the traditional (1900–1950); the modernist or golden age (1950–1970); blurred genres (1970–1986); the crisis of representation (1986–1990); the postmodern, a period of experimental and new ethnographies (1990–1995); postexperimental inquiry (1995–2000); and the future, which is now (2000–)" (see Holt 2003 for a discussion). Since then, they have added an 8th moment, starting in 2005 (Denzin and Lincoln 2005). In this chapter, we have noted the arbitrariness of this periodization by our inclusion of feminist women of color in the history of autoethnography, and believe that autoethnographies continue to play a role in successive moments outlined by Denzin and Lincoln.

6. Although Ellis notes that "[m]ore White women do autoethnography than any other group ... though more and more, members of other groups are joining in" (2004, 120), we claim that feminist women of color have been writing autoethnograhically for some time. To her credit, Ellis cites Richard Rodríguez's *Hunger for Memory* (2004, 377) as a classic of methodological work that bridges autobiography and autoethnography, and she also mentions Moraga and Anzaldúa (Ellis 2004, 121). But, as we contend, it is important to make the politics of invisibilizing feminists of color from this origin/genealogy of autoethnography known.

7. The American Sociological Association approved a new section called The Sociology of the Body and Embodiment in 2009. The International Sociological Association has also recently (2009) made the working group "The Body in the Social Sciences" into a research committee.

8. Due to space and topic limitations, we do not discuss analytical autoethnography (Anderson 2006), poststructural autoethnography (Clough 2000), and feminist autoethnography (Anzaldúa 1987; Anzaldúa and Moraga 1983) in detail; we also do not address the criticisms by the so-called literary critics.

9. While we propose movement forward in this conclusion, we wish to note that several elements of the past and history of autoethnography need further reflection: (1) a recovery of the history of autoethnography—from Heider and Hayano and through its social science roots—which will help sociologists understand the scope of autoethnographic projects today; (2) a more complete articulation of the links among writing, reading, and doing autoethnography; and (3) an elaboration of the interlocking relationships of biography, autobiography, ethnography and autoethnography, initially discussed by Denzin and Ellis. Part of this project is to link alternate versions of autoethnography that we have mentioned, in passing, in this chapter.

References

Alarcón, Norma. 1990. The Theoretical Subject(s) of This Bridge Called My Back and Anglo-American Feminism. In *Making Face, Making Soul — Haciendo Caras: Creative and Critical Perspectives by Feminists of Color*, ed. Gloria Anzaldúa, 356–69. San Francisco: Aunt Lute Foundation Books.

Anderson, Leon. 2006. Analytic Autoethnography. *Journal of Contemporary Ethnography* 35(4): 373–95.

Anzaldúa, Gloria. [1999] 1987. *Borderlands/La Frontera: The New Mestiza*. San Francisco: Aunt Lute Foundation Books.

Anzaldúa, Gloria, and Cherrie Moraga. 1983. *This Bridge Called My Back: Radical Writings by Women of Color.* New York: Kitchen Table Press.

Behar, Ruth. 1996. *The Vulnerable Observer: Anthropology that Breaks Your Heart.* Boston: Beacon Press.

Berger, Ronald J., and Richard Quinney. 2005. *Storytelling Sociology: Narrative as Social Inquiry.* London: Lynne Rienner.

Blumer, Herbert. 1969. *Symbolic Interactionism: Perspective and Method.* Englewood Cliffs, NJ: Prentice-Hall.

Burawoy, Michael. 1991. *Ethnography Unbound: Power and Resistance in the Modern Metropolis.* Berkeley: University of California Press.

_____. 1998. The Extended Case Method. *Sociological Theory* 16(1): 4–33.

Burawoy, Michael, Joseph A. Blum, Sheba George, Zsuzsa Gille, Teresa Gowan, Lynne Haney, Maren Klawiter, Steve H. Lopez, Seán Ó Riain, and Millie Thayer. 2000. *Global Ethnography: Forces, Connections, and Imaginations in a Postmodern World.* Berkeley: University of California Press.

Chang, Heewon. 2008. *Autoethnography as Method.* Walnut Creek, CA: Left Coast Press.

Cho, Grace M. 2008. *Haunting the Korean Diaspora: Shame, Secrecy, and the Forgotten War.* Minneapolis: University of Minnesota Press.

Clough, Patricia T. 1997. Autotelecommunication and Autoethnography: A Reading of Carolyn Ellis's Final Negotiations. *Sociological Quarterly* 38(1): 95–110.

_____. 1998. *The End(s) of Ethnography: From Realism to Social Criticism.* New York: Peter Lang.

_____. 2000. *Autoaffection: Unconscious Thought in the Age of Teletechnology.* Minneapolis: University of Minnesota Press.

Cooley, Charles Horton. [1902] 1998. *On Self and Social Organization.* Chicago: University of Chicago Press.

Creswell, John W. 2009. *Research Design: Qualitative, Quantitative, and Mixed Methods Approaches.* Thousand Oaks, CA: Sage Publications.

Crossley, Michele L. 2009. Breastfeeding as a Moral Imperative: An Autoethnographic Study. *Feminism & Psychology* 19(1): 71–87.

Culyba, Rebecca J., Carol A. Heimer, and JuLeigh C. Petty. 2004. The Ethnographic Turn: Fact, Fashion, or Fiction? *Qualitative Sociology* 27(4): 365–89.

Denzin, Norman K. 1989. *Interpretive Biography.* Newbury Park, CA: Sage Publications.

_____. 1995. Symbolic Interactionism. In *Rethinking Psychology,* ed. Jonathan A. Smith, Rom Harré, and Luk Van Langenhove, 43–58. Thousand Oaks, CA: Sage Publications.

_____. 2001. Symbolic Interactionism, Poststructuralism, and the Racial Subject. *Symbolic Interaction* 24(2): 243–49.

_____. 2003. The Call to Performance. *Symbolic Interaction* 26(1): 187–207.

Denzin, Norman, and Yvonna Lincoln. 2003. *The Landscape of Qualitative Research: Theories and Issues.* Thousand Oaks, CA: Sage Publications.

_____. 2005. *The Landscape of Qualitative Research: Theories and Issues.* Thousand Oaks, CA: Sage Publications.

Ellis, Carolyn. 1991. Sociological Introspection and Emotional Experience. *Symbolic Interaction* 14 (1): 23–50.

_____. 1993. "There Are Survivors": Telling a Story of Sudden Death. *Sociological Quarterly* 34(4): 711–30.

_____. 1995. *Final Negotiations.* Philadelphia: Temple University Press.

_____. 2001. With Mother/With Child: A True Story. *Qualitative Inquiry* 7(5): 598–616.

_____. 2004. *The Ethnographic I: A Methodological Novel about Autoethnography.* Walnut Creek, CA: Altamira Press.

_____. 2009. *Revision: Autoethnographic Reflections on Life and Work.* Walnut Creek, CA: Left Coast Press.

Ellis, Carolyn, and Arthur Bochner. 1992. Telling and Performing Personal Stories: The Constraints of Choice in Abortion. In *Investigating Subjectivity: Research on Lived Experience,* ed. Carolyn Ellis and Michael G. Flaherty, 79–101. Newbury Park, CA: Sage Publications.

_____. 1996. Talking Over Ethnography. In *Composing Ethnography: Alternative Forms of Qualitative Writing*, ed. Carolyn Ellis and Arthur Bochner, 13–45. Walnut Creek, CA: Altamira Press.

_____. 2003. Autoethnography, Personal Narrative, Reflexivity: Researcher as Subject. In *The Landscape of Qualitative Research: Theories and Issues*, ed. Norman Denzin and Yvonna Lincoln, 199–258. Thousand Oaks, CA: Sage Publications.

Fetterman, David M. 2010. *Ethnography: Step-by-Step*. Thousand Oaks, CA: Sage Publications.

Gannon, Sussanne. 2006. The (Im)possibilities of Writing the Self-writing: French Poststructural Theory and Autoethnography. *Cultural Studies <−>Critical Methodologies* 6(4): 474–95.

Gille, Zsuzsa, and Seán Ó Riain. 2002. Global Ethnography. *Annual Review of Sociology* 28: 271–95.

Guzmán, Manolo. 2006. *Gay Hegemony/Latino Homosexualities*. New York: Routledge.

Hayano, David. 1979. Auto-Ethnography: Paradigms, Problems, and Prospects. *Human Organization* 38(1): 99–104.

Heider, Karl G. 1975. What Do People Do? Dani Auto-Ethnography. *Journal of Anthropological Research* 31(1): 3–17.

Hemmingson, Michael. 2009. *Auto-ethnographies: Sex and Death and Symbolic Interaction in the Eighth Moment of Qualitative Inquiry*. San Bernardino, CA: The Borgo Press.

Holliday, Ruth. 2004. Filming "The Closet": The Role of Video Diaries in Researching Sexualities. *The American Behavioral Scientist* 47(12): 1597–1616.

Holt, Nicholas L. 2003. Representation, Legitimation, and Autoethnography: An Autoethnographic Writing Story. *International Journal of Qualitative Methods* 2(1): 1–22.

Kleinman, Sherryl, and Martha A. Copp. 1993. *Emotions and Fieldwork*. Newbury Park, CA: Sage Publications.

Lather, Patti, and Chris Smithies, eds. 1997. *Troubling the Angels: Women Living with HIV/AIDS*. Boulder: Westview Press.

The Latina Feminist Group. 2001. *Telling to Live: Latina Testimonials*. Durham: Duke University Press.

Malhotra, Sheena, and Kimberlee Pérez. 2005. Belonging, Bridged, and Bodies. *NWSA Journal* 17(2): 47–68.

Martin, Biddy. 1988. Lesbian Identity and Autobiographical Difference[s]. In *Life/Lines: Theorizing Women's Autobiography*, edited by Bella Brodzki and Celeste Schenck, 77–103. Ithaca: Cornell University Press.

Mead, George H. [1934] 1992. *Mind, Self, and Society*. Chicago: University of Chicago Press.

Meneley, Anne, and Donna J. Young, eds. 2005. *Auto-ethnographies: The Anthropology of Academic Practices*. Peterborough, Canada: Broadview Press.

Miller, Nancy K. 1994. Representing Others: Gender and the Subjects of Autobiography. *Differences: A Journal of Feminist Cultural Studies* 6(2): 1–27.

Mitchell, Grace. 2005. *Diasporic Visions: Transgenerational Haunting and the Figure of the Yanggongju*. PhD dissertation. CUNY Graduate Center.

Plummer, Ken. 2009. Introduction: Autoethnography of Sexualities. *Sexualities* 12(3): 267–69.

Reed-Danahay, Deborah, ed. 1997. *Auto/ethnography: Rewriting the Self and the Social*. New York: Oxford University Press.

Richardson, Laurel. 1990. *Writing Strategies: Reaching Diverse Audiences*. Newbury Park, CA: Sage Publications.

_____. 2000. Writing: A Method of Inquiry. In *Handbook of Qualitative Research*, ed. Norman Denzin and Yvonna Lincoln, 209–19. Thousand Oaks, CA: Sage Publications.

Seale, Clive. 1999. *The Quality of Qualitative Research*. London: Sage Publications.

Shaffir, William, and Robert Stebbins. 1991. Introduction. In *Experiencing Fieldwork: An Inside View of Qualitative Research*, ed. William Shaffir and Robert Stebbins, 1–24. Newbury Park, CA: Sage Publications.

Smith, Dorothy. 2005. *Institutional Ethnography. A Sociology for People*. Lanham, MD: Altamira Press.

Spry, Tami. 2001. Performing Autoethnography: An Embodied Methodological Praxis. *Qualitative Inquiry* 7(6): 706–732.

Van Maanen, John. 1988. *Tales of the Field: On Writing Ethnography*. Chicago: University of Chicago Press.

Vidal-Ortiz, Salvador. 2004. On Being a White Person of Color: Using Autoethnography to Understand Puerto Ricans' Racialization. *Qualitative Sociology* 27(2): 179–203.

Wall, Sarah. 2008. Easier Said Than Done: Writing an Autoethnography. *International Journal of Qualitative Methods* 7(1): 38–53.

Watson, Cate. 2009. Picturing Validity: Autoethnography and the Representation of Self? *Qualitative Inquiry* 15(3): 526–44.

12. FICTIONAL STORIES

A Method for Doing Sociology

Todd Schoepflin *and* Peter Kaufman

"Alas," said the mouse, "the world is growing smaller every day. At the beginning it was so big that I was afraid, I kept running and running, and I was glad when at last I saw walls far away to the right and left, but these long walls have narrowed so quickly that I am in the last chamber already, and there in the corner stands the trap that I must run into." "You only need to change your direction," said the cat, and ate it up.— Franz Kafka, A Little Fable

After studying sociology for many years it is inevitable that many of us start to feel like the mouse in Kafka's very short story. When we begin our studies the world does seem big and frightening. We learn so many new concepts and analytical frameworks— the sociological imagination, the social construction of reality, the intersections of race, class, gender — that our perception is radically altered. This is both exciting and overwhelming. So as we continue our studies we may find some solace in the conceptual and methodological walls that appear to guide our pursuit of knowledge. But soon, these walls narrow and force us into using discipline-specific (or even sub-discipline-specific) theories and methods. Instead of the blank palette with which we began, we now find ourselves following the conventional sociological protocol and painting by numbers (quite literally, actually, for those who are quantitatively inclined). If only we could heed the advice of the cat in Kafka's fable and simply change our direction.

Our goal in this chapter is to offer a change in direction by promoting the use of fictional stories as a method of doing sociology. Most of us are familiar with fiction as a form of pleasure reading. But we believe that fiction can be used sociologically in two discernable ways: as a method of the researcher to capture, analyze, and convey sociological insights; and as content to be mined and studied for its sociological insights. We distinguish these two forms as sociology *through* fiction and sociology *of* fiction. As for the latter form, using fiction and other forms of literature as sociological data is well established among scholars of teaching and learning in sociology (see Castellano, DeAngelis, and Clark-Ibáñez 2008, for a recent overview). Our focus in this chapter, how-

212

ever, is on sociology *through* fiction. That is, we make the case that writing stories can be an invaluable way of doing sociological research.

Although not widely recognized as a method of social inquiry, fictional methods have recently gained some acceptance in the social science literature. Most notably, Banks and Banks (1998) edited *Fiction and Social Research*. This collection of fifteen chapters details numerous examples of researchers using fictional narrative as an emerging form of social research. Focusing on the themes of representation, understanding, suspicion, and vulnerability, the contributors to this volume give us hope that we can change our direction. As Bochner and Ellis note in the introduction to *Fiction and Social Research*, using fiction as a form of social investigation "encourages the kind of self-examination, risk-taking, and creativity that can clear the way for reforming our research practices and curriculum and making the products of our research more interesting, more accessible, more evocative, and more inspirational" (1998, 8).

Most of the contributors to *Fiction and Social Research* come from departments of communication. Within sociology and anthropology, a few scholars have used fiction in the context of ethnography. For example, Rinehart (1998) advocates using fictional techniques in ethnography. He discusses how fiction and fictional devices are effective in "conveying certain aspects of lived experience" especially because fiction is often based on the writer's interpretation of actual events. Fiction is just another way to communicate our observations and "we must constantly work to enhance our toolbox of writing implements, to write scenes, to show rather than tell" (1998, 207).

A central point for Rinehart (1998) is that there is no need to apologize for the use of fictional methods. We can see why there might be an inclination to justify the use of fictional methods. As Richardson (1994, 517) says, "We have been encouraged to take on the omniscient voice of science, the view from everywhere." The use of fictional methods may leave us feeling insecure because it is a departure from conventional social science methods that many of us have been trained to employ. No apology is expected when one's work is viewed as scientific and objective and where the author is "absent"; however, some justification and rationale is often expected from scholars whose work is experimental, subjective, and evocative (Rinehart 1998, 213).

Frank (2000) is another proponent of mixing fiction and ethnography. She wrote a fictional short story about an encounter between an exotic dancer and a customer at a strip club. The short story gives insight into the complicated nature of relationships between dancers and their regular customers and explores several facets of the strip club setting: empowerment, intimacy, gratification, degradation, alienation, disenchantment. While none of the characters in the story have an "objective existence," the story is based on her experiences working in strip clubs when she did participant observation for her dissertation research. As such, the short story can be categorized as "ethnographically grounded fiction" (Frank 2000, 481). It can similarly be described as a fictional story that is "ethnographically informed" (482).

Brinkmann (2009) also makes a case for the use of literature in social scientific inquiry. He conceives of literature as a form of "qualitative social and human inquiry" (2009, 1378). Working more from a perspective of sociology of literature than sociology through literature, he analyzes the work of French novelist Michel Houellebecq and concludes that the writer is actually a sociologist who expresses himself in literary tropes. He argues that we "can learn as much from Houellebecq about contemporary human lives, experiences, and sufferings as we can from more traditional forms of empirical qualitative research" (1379). Brinkmann concludes by drawing an important parallel between literature and more mainstream methodologies: "Like traditional forms of research, literature can be done well or poorly, but when done well, it enables readers to understand the world and themselves better than they did before and may even animate them to act differently, both of which are legitimate aims of research" (1392).

As one final example, we consider the stories of criminologist Lonnie Athens (2004; 2010). Athens explains that his stories are drawn from an unpublished novel. He notes that the novel is closely based on the café he frequently visited in his childhood. A glimpse into Athens' background shows the connection between his life and his fiction (James 1999). One of the main characters in his stories is Pop, a Greek immigrant who operates a segregated café in Virginia. On one side of the café are whites, on the other side blacks, and Pop often finds himself in a no-win situation. If he favors the white customers, he may lose his black customers. If he is fair to his black customers, he alienates his white customers. And some of his customers (both black and white) don't see Pop as a *real* American. He is forever a foreigner. In their eyes he is not really white, and definitely not black.

Although these examples, and this chapter, focus on fiction, we acknowledge that others forms of literature, such as poetry, may be employed as tools of social research. For example, Harnett and Engels (2005) make a case for investigative poetry which combines the art of poetic representation with the evidence-based details gleaned from scholarly research. Chan (2003) uses poetry as a way to write about anorexia. Informed by a background in nursing, women's studies, and social work, she brings perspective to a complicated and common condition through a literary lens. And, in *Poetry as Method: Reporting Research through Verse*, Faulkner (2010) argues that poetry should be taught and employed as a method of gathering and conveying social research. In short, whether one uses fiction, poetry, or some other genre of literature, these scholar-authors are breaking from conventional norms and changing the direction of social research.

Our work in this chapter builds on these efforts by making a case for using fiction as a legitimate method in sociological research. The obvious questions here are: Why use fiction? With so many established forms of sociological methodology, why introduce a new interdisciplinary approach, much less one that is based on imagination instead of concrete truths? We believe there are four central reasons for using fiction as a method to capture, analyze, and convey sociological insights.

First, fiction is well-suited to capturing the intersectionality that characterizes social life-in-motion. Many traditional forms of sociological inquiry rely on methods that disaggregate the complexity of social life in order to study the constitutive elements. Typical sociological research focuses on a select few variables and then attempts to control for the influence or effect of other variables. The problem with this approach is that by separating the parts from the whole we are often ill-equipped to see the forest for the trees. Using fiction negates any need for such an artificial interpretation of the social world. Fiction does not occur in a vacuum. Instead, fiction, like other forms of literature, employs a "multiperspectival approach ... by building a constellation of multiple voices in conversation" (Harnett and Engels 2005, 1044). Most fictional stories are based on a number of plots and sub-plots interacting concurrently. Writers of fiction have no need to control for one or more variables because they are depicting the fluid process of reality rather than the static laboratory of the social scientist. Ironically then, fictional stories may actually feel more true to life than objective social science.

Second, the language used by fiction writers is often more accessible and more understandable. Sociology, like most academic disciplines, is often criticized for being difficult to comprehend. Mills (1959) was one of the first to level this critique in his skewering of grand theorists and abstract empiricists, and yet as a discipline we remain saddled with these problems. Many of us still rely, indeed many of us are still taught to rely, on obfuscating jargon to depict social life. Moreover, many of our top journals are still bastions of abstractly empirical, and often-times indecipherable, work. Fiction, more so than sociology, uses common, everyday linguistic practices. The goals of using fiction sociologically are not to impress the reader with intellectually pompous academic language nor are they to present relevant insights in such a way that they are comprehensible to only those select few with specialized statistical training. Instead, the point of most fiction is to convey the wonders of social life in a way that is creative, engaging, and available to all readers.

Third, and on a related note, we agree with Frank (2000) that fiction is more adaptable than traditional sociological language. There are times when the existing theoretical language and frameworks do not work. Sometimes ideas cannot be conveyed satisfactorily using tightly prescribed and antiseptic scholarly vernacular. Real-life experiences are not always easily captured with academic language. Maybe obscene, vulgar, or even offensive language is necessary to accurately depict a moment or an interaction. Maybe a stream of consciousness narrative is needed instead of a logical, point-by-point rendering. Or maybe the sociologist needs the space, not to mention the creative license, to describe something fully in depth. In all these instances, fiction may be a more flexible tool for the researcher than traditional sociological language and the accompanying methodologies. As Richardson (1990, 120) suggests: "*How* we are expected to write affects *what* we can write about." Sociologists who use fiction are not limited by what can be said, how it can be said, or when it can be said.

Fourth, most fiction, if not all fiction, implicitly speaks to the intersection of agency and structure. Whereas some sociological studies look at individuals apart from the social world they inhabit, and other studies look at reified social institutions seemingly devoid of individual actors, it is rare to find a work of fiction that detaches the individual from the larger social structure. Most fiction tells a story about actors in a social world or a social world filled with actors. It is hard to imagine, much less write about, one without the other (unless, of course, one is a detached social scientist). In this sense, fiction has the potential to achieve greater levels of analytical insight than many traditional forms of sociology because it embraces what Alexander (1988) termed the "new theoretical movement"— the fusion of agency and structure. Conversely, too much sociological work is still characterized as an either-or, micro-macro proposition. But for those who do sociology through fiction there is, in essence, a built-in methodological safeguard to ensure that both individuals and social structures will be critically relevant.

So how does one do sociology though fiction? There are a number of different ways that fiction may be employed as a methodological tool of the sociologist. We discuss two examples below but these are by no means the only ways that sociologists may use fiction or other forms of literature. Part of making an argument for fiction, or any of the other new methodological forms detailed in this volume, is to encourage others to be methodological innovators and cultivate further changes in direction. By offering our own novel (pun intended) approach to doing sociological research, we hope that we foster some creative momentum for others to step outside the strict confines of traditional sociological research.

* * *

A few years ago Todd traveled to London for the first time. Having been stimulated by a new environment he sought a way to capture, sociologically, his experiences. He was intrigued by the social interactions he observed and was equally fascinated by the myriad ways in which globalization, cultural imperialism, and materialism were present. He was not interested in walking around with a recorder and IRB consent forms to systematically capture these social interactions; nor was he interested in producing a formal treatise on the globalization of American culture. Instead, he wanted to write creatively about his observations of macro-level forces *and* depict the various micro interactions he observed. So he chose fiction. As we have suggested above, fiction allowed Todd to not only capture the interplay between agency and structure, but to depict the intersections of individuals' biographies and histories. Moreover, by using fiction as a method to analyze and convey, Todd was able to more freely communicate his sociological insights in an accessible manner without incomprehensible jargon.

*   *   *

Famous Like Rothko

I should have known I was in trouble when, in a dream, I was at the foot of the Bridge to Nowhere. Most bridges attract lovers of architecture. This bridge draws losers and never-beens. I asked the bridge tender "Which one am I?" He laughed before answering: "Both." He laughed some more.

What a dream. Or was it?

It's a sunny day in London. I've been looking forward to this day for a long time. I'm at Tate Modern waiting for the museum to open. My purpose is clear. It's the Mark Rothko collection that interests me. When the doors open a pleasant young man greets me and asks if I am here to see the Kandinsky exhibition. "No I am not," I say with an edge, "I'm here to see Rothko." He is puzzled by my response but points me in the right direction. When I enter the Rothko room I am captivated by the paintings that were commissioned by the Four Seasons restaurant in New York. When Rothko finished the paintings he decided they were better suited for a museum, so he gave them to Tate. Brilliant.

Two hours pass. I can't pull myself away from Rothko. People come and go but I stand here, mesmerized, imagining what it is like to be a famous artist. I fantasize about people staring at my work the way that I am staring at Rothko's. I picture historians arguing about the meaning of my paintings. I think about art students being influenced by my style. But I am probably kidding myself. In my realistic moments I fear my work will never be known.

Another hour passes. I could stay here all day if it weren't for the people around me. A man wanders in with an attractive woman and scoffs at what he sees: "I don't get it." She smirks with approval. That's my cue to leave.

I flip through my travel guide and read about the Portobello Road market. It says Saturday is the best day to go. I find the subway and ask for directions. The train I need arrives in a few minutes. When I sit down I smell fried chicken. The man sitting across from me is eating food from KFC. Should I be impressed or terrified of globalization? It's an easy decision: terrified. Thankfully it's a short ride. I exit at Notting Hill Gate and follow the herd of tourists to Portobello Road. At first I am happy. The houses are smart and colorful and one has a sign that says "George Orwell lived here." I make a mental note to read 1984 when I get back to New York.

As soon as I reach the market I realize I've made a mistake in coming here. It's hot and steamy and there are too many people. I am annoyed at the sight of people from all over the world throwing empty Coke cans to the curb. To escape the crowd I move to an alleyway and sit on a crate. A nice policeman stops and chats with me briefly. Afterwards I close my eyes, trying to achieve a quiet moment, but a couple interrupts to ask if I will take their picture. The couple appears to like each other, something I don't normally see. In life I prefer to be by myself but the sight of them makes me feel lonely. After I take their picture they engage me in small talk. But I just want to go to my hotel and sleep. I excuse myself and venture into the street. I have to fight through the crowd to get back to the subway. I bump into a man wearing a team Brazil soccer jersey. I bump into a woman who carries a dog in a purse. I bump into another man wearing a team Brazil soccer jersey. Where am I?

It's too damn hot, I am broke, and people keep running into me. I'm starving. I walk by a fish stall and the smell disgusts me. I have to go to the bathroom but can't find one. I'm jealous of children drinking lemonade. A man steps on my foot and doesn't care. I yell at him but he ignores me. I shout "DO YOU KNOW WHO I AM? I SAID DO YOU KNOW WHO I AM?" He looks confused. Of course he doesn't know who I am. I am nobody. I curse at him. He doesn't respond. I curse at him again and raise my fists. He looks down on me and shoves me to the ground. He kicks me a few times for good measure. He laughs and walks away. No one offers to help me off the ground.

I get up to the sight of people giving me dirty looks. I hear someone mutter "homo." I stumble my way through the crowd back to the subway. The entire time I have been in London I haven't waited more than five minutes for a train. This time I wait thirty. Finally the train arrives. On the train I endure a silly conversation between two people who are on their way to a costume party. I am relieved when the train reaches Earl's Court. After a miserable ten-minute walk I'm at the hotel. The concierge, a kind Nigerian man, wonders aloud if I have been robbed. I tell him I slipped and fell to the pavement. I go to my room and apply ice to my head — unfortunately, it doesn't help. I have two channels from which to choose: the BBC and a station that shows reruns of *The Simpsons*. I watch an episode of *The Simpsons* and drift to sleep.

I wake up twelve hours later, the longest I have ever slept in my life. I feel refreshed and am glad to be going home. I pack my suitcase and catch a shuttle driven by a hotel employee named Sal. He drives fast enough that I am scared for my life but slow enough for me to realize I didn't do very much while I was in London. I arrive at Heathrow and check in with time to spare. I watch people at the Starbucks kiosk and try to figure out the relationship between two people chatting at the end of the line. I read newspapers that other people left behind until it's time to board the plane.

On the plane I am seated next to a man who seems desperate to make conversation with his teenage daughter. It's no use — she just wants to watch a movie. Their awkward interaction makes me cherish my freedom. I become hopeful as I think about home and getting back to normal. I think about all my unfinished paintings and promise myself that I will finish them this year. The plane takes off smoothly. I ask the flight attendant for water, even though I want beer. I write one sentence in my journal: "I am happy as long as I get to define what happy is."

It's a seven hour flight back to New York. I spend all seven hours wondering if I'll ever be famous.

* * *

"Famous Like Rothko" is a rendering of a social world through fiction. This format served as a vehicle for expressing what Todd observed and experienced during his trip and allowed him to depict social life-in-motion. In the words of Lewis Coser, fiction, like all literature, "is social evidence and testimony" (1963, 2). In this relatively short work of fiction, Todd was able to capture, analyze, and convey a number of sociological concepts. Using traditional methods of social research, it would be difficult to encapsulate all of the sociological themes that are present in this 1,200 word story. Feelings of anomie, the extent of globalization and cultural imperialism, the sociology of high culture, and the multifariousness of social interactions are common themes of interest to sociological researchers. But using standard sociological practice, one would not be able to comment on *all* of these themes simultaneously. Instead, each theme would likely be studied separately given the imposing, (sub)discipline-specific walls that narrow our analytical focus.

Fiction also allowed Todd to convey real-life experiences using real-life language. For example, in his story the protagonist is kicked on a busy street and called a "homo." Although that didn't actually happen to Todd in London, something like that did happen to him elsewhere as he details in an autoethnography (Schoepflin 2009). And during the time this chapter was written, a car pulled in front of the house next door to Todd's. Two young men yelled something obscene. When the same men returned a few minutes later one shouted, *"Come outside, faggot!"* In effect, these social processes are creatively reflected in his story of the man being knocked around and called a "homo."

With fiction, one does not have to represent interactions and events exactly as they occur. Rather, the writer can use imagination as well as creative and adaptable language to extend the reality of experiences and observations. Some may be uncomfortable with this approach because it is not real, true, or objective. But there is no denying that this brief scene in "Famous like Rothko" captures a fundamental perspective of hegemonic masculinity and depicts how men relate to other men: as adversaries who resort to violence and employ homophobic language to "resolve" a situation.

Another main theme of the story is the pursuit of celebrity. Throughout much of the Western world, people have a desire for fame and notoriety. See YouTube. Watch *American Idol*. Peruse the magazines at the checkout aisle. Consider the Balloon Boy hoax in 2009. As sociologists, we understand this fame-seeking behavior as an outgrowth of larger social-cultural forces. Technological innovations allow us to easily broadcast ourselves to millions of others around the world; however, these same technologies may curtail our face-to-face interactions resulting in a greater sense of disconnect. To thoroughly understand this pursuit of attention requires that we approach this cultural phenomenon through the intersection of agency and structure. Only by identifying the social structural rules and resources will we be able to understand how our agentic capabilities — i.e., our behaviors — are impacted. And similarly, we must be cognizant of how our behaviors contribute to the perpetuation of those structural rules and resources that are deemed to be most desirable.

In "Famous Like Rothko," the intersection of agency and structure is a prevailing theme that becomes readily apparent when one begins analyzing the story. Whether one explores the story through the micro-interactions of the narrator or through any of the marco-forces such as consumer culture, art, or globalization, it is nearly impossible to understand the plot without accounting for both levels of analysis. For example, the narrator's agency, specifically his angst, could be read as a consequence of our collective infatuation with fame. Given the cultural messages we receive from the media there is a normative impulse that affects our behavior and compels many of us to crave notoriety, recognition, and even celebrity. On the structural level, the narrator's agency is bolstered by his access to multiple structural resources such as money for airfare, the technology of air travel, and the geo-political arrangements that let him visit foreign lands and experience (or lament) the cross-cultural effects of globalization. Whereas most social research would be narrowly focused on either the narrator's agentic angst or one of these structural variables, fiction, almost by its essence, directs our attention to the lives of individuals *and* the larger world in which they inhabit. There is no disaggregation of the two, nor should there be, if we want to accurately capture, depict, and analyze social life.

*   *   *

Next, we offer another illustration of a sociological story. Todd wrote this story at a difficult time in the lives of his friends. For example, one friend's baby died in infancy, a tragedy that profoundly affected his peer group. Though the story was written with his peer group in mind, he tried to write it in ways that extended beyond his circle of friends and their feelings. One the one hand, fiction offered a way for Todd to incorporate things that happened in the lives of people around him. He used fiction as a means to communicate their feelings, their limitations, their challenges, and he tried to do so in a way that didn't insult them, or judge them, or demean them. On the other hand, this story allowed Todd to use this difficult experience as sociological data.

It is ironic that sociology is happening all around us all of the time but most of us only attempt to capture it during prescribed moments of social research. Although our personal experiences sometimes give rise to our research questions, standard methodological protocol does not allow us to tap into our daily experiences, observations, interactions, and emotions. By doing sociology through fiction, we avoid this severe methodological constraint. As a tool of social research, fiction gives us the intellectual autonomy to exercise our sociological imaginations whenever and wherever we choose.

*   *   *

Spare Some Change?

Thanks for asking how I'm doing. You're the first person to ask in a very long time. I guess I would sum up my state of mind in the following way: lately I feel like punching myself in the face. I try not to think too long about what it means. Maybe it means that I want to feel something. I've had a feeling of numbness for so long. It's been forever since I've had an edge. Man I would give anything to get my edge back. I used to feel like no one could outwork me or outthink me. But now I just feel tired.

I feel like I want a lot but I don't have the desire to do what I need to do to get what I want. I also feel shallow for wanting. I've always been the type to be happy with what I have. But now what I have just doesn't seem to be enough. What I have doesn't seem like anything. I think about people living in their big houses and all I feel is envy.

I find myself driving up and down streets with homes I can't afford. Last week I drove down a street I'd never seen before — Tudor Place — and stupid questions kept running through my head: What the hell do these people do for a living? What do they know that I don't know? What are they doing that I'm not doing? I had this urge to run up to the biggest house on the block and leave my resume in the mailbox. I figured maybe somebody important would give me a chance.

Life has become a series of wakes and funerals. There are no signs of happiness anywhere. I'm obsessed with choices. I keep reading "The Road Not Taken" by Robert Frost. Everybody close to me says I should take the safe route. Just about everyone I know takes the well-traveled road. The few who don't are regarded as deviant and treated with no respect. I'm pulling myself in opposite directions: on the one hand I have a hunger to be different, on the other hand I feel the need to be accepted. Like Frost, I look at the road ahead as far as I can. But all I can see is sameness. The sun has not shined in days. Where have all the good times gone?

This year was supposed to be different. Late last year I had an interview with a company that I've been interested in for a long time. On the day of the interview I had this amazing feeling that it was the first day of my new life. I felt like a new chapter was about to be written. I woke up at 5:00 and had this weird urge to work out. I found some old dumbbells and worked out like a madman. I kept thinking *This isn't so hard. No more being lazy. No way. I'm gonna start working out everyday.* Then I ate some oatmeal for breakfast. Remember that professor from our Media Studies course in our freshmen year? The guy who was like 70 years old but looked like he was 50? Remember he said he ate oatmeal everyday and did a bunch of pushups? I thought of him and I felt inspired. I felt so confident getting ready for my interview. I felt like a new man. I couldn't wait to answer the typical questions: What are your strengths? What are your weaknesses? I was cracking myself up thinking of things I would never actually say: *My weaknesses? Oh, you mean "areas of opportunity." Well, there's always room for improvement. Tell you what ... to be honest, I'd like to develop a killer instinct. I'd like to have it in my repertoire. Not as my main play, but just as an option. Every once in a while you need to stare somebody down, beat them at their own game, put a foot on their throat. Leave them no chance to come back. Finish them. Metaphorically speaking, of course.*

I really was excited. I left my apartment in plenty of time before my interview. But it was the strangest thing. As soon as I left my apartment a bunch of obstacles appeared. I hate to use the word "surreal" but God it was surreal. First I drove to the ATM but I couldn't get anywhere near it because a bakery truck was blocking the entrance to the drive thru. No problem. I parked across the street and ran up to the machine. I got my money and ran back to my car. Then I needed gas. When I left the gas station I ran over some broken glass. It was everywhere in my path, I couldn't avoid it. Now all these negative thoughts were running through my head: *What if my tire goes flat on the way to the interview? Why didn't I get gas last night? I felt so great ten minutes ago, why do I have a headache all of a sudden?* I stopped at the deli to get some coffee because I don't feel right if I haven't had my morning coffee. I was still on time but now there was no room for error. I got stuck behind a bus that made it impossible to take a short cut to the interview. So I took the longer route. I was barely on time but I still had a chance to make it. Now that I was drinking my coffee I was starting to feel better. That Traffic song "Feeling Alright" came on the radio. I took it as a sign. I was feeling alright, in fact I was feeling much better. So there I was singing along, feeling confident again, feeling hopeful. I was almost there and still on time. And then, and I can't explain why, but when I got to the street where I was supposed to turn I kept driving straight. I couldn't get myself to go to the interview. I'm telling you I wanted to work for this company so desperately for so long but now I was terrified at the thought of going to the interview. I was sweating profusely. I was cursing myself. Next thing I know I'm twenty miles from the interview. What happened to me? I'll never know. I'll never know what stopped me from going to that interview. I was like a deer in headlights thinking *what the hell am I supposed to do?* I was too embarrassed to call. What was I supposed to say? Finally I called the woman who set up my interview. I lied. I said I was in an accident and expressed how sorry I was that I missed my interview. She said her boss would understand and that she would call me to reschedule the interview. I felt a little bit better. I told myself that if I got another chance I'd make good on it.

I got home about an hour later and there were two messages on my answering machine. The first was my mother wanting to know how I did on my interview. The second message was from the secretary. *Hello Mister Green, we spoke a little while ago about rescheduling your interview. I'm sorry to inform you that we won't be able to do so. It turns out that the position has been filled. Thank you for your interest in our company. We will keep your resume on file for six months. We will be in touch if something opens up.* I was crushed. I felt so sorry for myself. I got sick to my stomach. I spent the rest of the day curled up on my couch, like I did when I was seven years old and was too sick to go to school.

I didn't know what to do next. Send out more resumes? Christ I'm so sick of writing those stupid cover letters. *I think, if given an opportunity, I can make a positive contribution to your company. I think a position with your organization will help me meet my professional goals and allow me to help you continue to deliver first-rate services.* What a bunch of crap. So now I'm collecting unemployment and bartending at Dominic's once in a while for some quick cash. For a while I was thinking about going back to school but I've given up on that idea. I'm reading some pretty depressing shit these days: *Black Coffee Blues* by Henry Rollins and anything resembling existential literature.

I spend my days bumming around Delaware Park. What else can I do with so much time on my hands? What can I say, I enjoy walking around the park in the middle of the day. It's interesting to be surrounded by a bunch of retirees who actually worked for a living. I try to figure out where to go from here but I have no answers. Remember in college when I thought I had all the answers? What a difference ten years makes. How can you explain the fact that I was so confident back then but have no confidence now?

I need change and I need change now. I don't know what kind of change I need, I just know it has to be radical. When I'm at the Laundromat I sit and stare at the change machine and fantasize: if only I could put dollars into the machine and have change come into my life.

Maybe I'm sad because I haven't written in so long. You're the only person I know who doesn't judge me, who doesn't look sideways at me when I say I'm feeling down. I don't think there's anything wrong about not feeling whole. I'm unhappy and I don't feel bad about that. Why should I pretend that I'm content? Why should I put on a happy face? I've been faking it for too long. That only time I feel better is when I listen to "One of These Things First" by Nick Drake. It's a beautiful song. Every time I hear it I thank God it was written. It sort of makes me happy, at least for a few minutes. Other than that my thoughts of being happy are thoughts of being someone, something, or somewhere else. Most days I feel regret. Mostly I ask *what if?*

Yesterday was the worst day of all. I had to meet with someone at the unemployment office in order to be eligible for more checks. I had to provide proof that I've been looking for a job. This guy was the most miserable man I've ever encountered in my life. All I could think is *how does this guy make it through the day? He might actually be worse off than me.* Sitting there I made a promise to myself to get my life back on track. I told myself "tomorrow is a new day" and that I'd start my new life first thing in the morning.

After the interview I went to the store to get some cigarettes. There was a man in front of the store. The man was haggard. He caught my eye and asked "Spare some change?" Change. The magic word. It overwhelmed me. My legs felt weak. The words "I wish" spilled from my mouth. I sat down next to him. Sitting there in my suit, clean-shaven, we appeared like a portrait of contrast, but I felt there was no difference between us. A young woman headed towards the entrance of the store. The kind of woman that has it all together. Simultaneously the man and I shouted "SPARE SOME CHANGE?" She just kept walking, pretending we didn't exist.

Do you think it's random, what we all become? Do we have any choice in the matter? I cry when I think about what I've become. I'm crying right now. I woke up this morning and my first thought was "I don't have anything and even if I did, I have no one to share it with." And I broke my promise. I didn't do anything today to improve my lot. All I've done today is write to you.

So that's how I'm doing. I gotta tell ya, I wish you would have asked sooner.

* * *

"Spare Some Change?" is a story about a miserable man who is down on his luck, envious of those who have gained material success, and frustrated with his inability to succeed. In two notable ways, this story is like a good classroom lesson in sociology. First, the story invites us to walk in Mr. Green's shoes and experience his world of misfortune and despair. Even if our personal lives are largely devoid of such unforeseen and unfortunate circumstances, we can relate to the narrator's predicament to the extent that we have all been "down in the dumps" at one time or another. But beyond this basic level of empathy, the way the story is told allows us to embrace it, and its sociological relevance, at an even deeper level.

"Spare Some Change?" was written in response to an inquiry from an old friend. This is significant because even if we cannot relate personally to Mr.

Green, many of us may feel connected to the role of the supportive and questioning friend. And the fact that the story is told as a stream-of-consciousness letter is also significant. This format provides another entry point for readers to connect with the story. Most of us have had moments where we have ranted about all that is wrong in our life, in the world, at our job, in school, etc. And many of us have probably done so in a letter, an e-mail, a text message, a Tweet, a Facebook posting, or a face-to-face interaction.

Once we become hooked into this story on a personal level the second component of a good sociology lesson becomes manifest: The story compels us to raise more questions about the social world than it, or we, can readily answer. When we feel a connection to characters in a story we become invested in their existence and we yearn to know more about their lives, their predicaments, and their possibilities for transformation. So we ask ourselves questions. The questions underlying "Spare Some Change?" reflect the central themes of sociological analysis: Who succeeds and who fails in society? Who gets to define success and failure? Why do some people seem to have all the luck and live a life of privilege whereas others always experience hard times? How easy is it to change one's situation and become upwardly mobile? Is it just a matter of hard work, dedication, and attitude? Or are there larger forces that push some ahead and pull others down? Why do people respond differently to the challenges and obstacles in their path?

Because they speak to central sociological themes, these questions suggest the interplay between agency and structure, and the age-old question of free will and structural determinism. In the last thirty years or so there have been rigorous theoretical efforts to synthesize agency and structure (Archer 1988; Bourdieu 1977; Giddens 1984; Sewell 1992; Sztompka 1991). Although these efforts have advanced our sociological understanding considerably, one sometimes feels a sense of detachment from these analytical elucidations. Maybe it is because of the reliance on jargon — some of which is either foreign (i.e., *habitus*) or fabricated (i.e., structuration); or maybe it is because these conventional accounts of social action often fail to consider the feelings and emotions that shape our choices (Maynes, Pierce, and Laslett 2008).

Writing fiction such as "Spare Some Change?" helps us avoid these shortcomings because we do not get bogged down with obfuscating language, and we are better able to tap into the affective underpinnings that motivate behavior. And the benefits to writing fiction are enjoyed not only by the reader but by the researcher. What a relief it is to be able to write about agency and structure without feeling compelled to engage in the requisite name- or term-dropping. Equally gratifying is being able to channel one's creative energies and craft a story that can be appreciated by many readers on both affective and analytical levels.

There is another theme in "Spare Some Change?" that bears mentioning because it further expounds on the benefits of using fiction as a sociological method. This theme is conventional behavior. The narrator of this story feels constrained by convention, he is tired of doing the same thing over and over again, and he feels like he needs a change. At times, many of us have probably felt a similar type of treadmill existence. But unless we break out of this convention, act against the norm, and essentially become deviants, it is unlikely that we will garner much attention from sociological researchers. The reason for this is that sociologists are not very interested in the mundane behaviors of what Brekhus (1998) termed the "unmarked." Sociological researchers are much more interested in the "ontologically unusual." If Mr. Green was a real person, it is unlikely he would be the focus of sociological scrutiny unless his alienation became manifested into some creatively atypical (or better yet, criminal) activity. Sitting around lamenting does not make him a prime candidate for a research subject. This is unfortunate because as we see from this story, Mr. Green's plight is full of sociological insight if only we take the time listen to him. Doing sociology through fiction gives us the flexibility to consider both the outliers (the sexy, the unusual, and the utterly destitute) as well as the majority of us who fall within a standard deviation or two of the norm.

Concluding Thoughts

Picture yourself in any environment with interesting activity occurring. Even the mundane unfolding of social life stimulates the sociologist's mind. For example, think of a food court filled with consumers eating bland fast-food before they head back into the stores that can be found in Anywhere, U.S.A. Maybe it is consumer activity or eating habits that interests you. Or perhaps it is screaming kids and frustrated parents that catch your attention. Whatever happens to be fascinating, as a sociologist you seek to capture, analyze and depict these social processes. But what sociological methodology should you use? (Non)-participant observation? In-depth interviews or focus groups? Quantitative analysis of a national dataset of opinions and attitudes? Historical analysis of trends and patterns? All of these are legitimate sociological methods, of course. We believe that writing fiction should be added to the list. By promoting fiction as a conduit for the sociological imagination we seek to change our methodological direction and avoid currently fashionable theoretical views (Krieger 1984) so that we can investigate the social world in more provocative and creative ways.

It is important to note that we do not view sociology through fiction as a superior methodology compared with standard and long-practiced sociological methods. Nor do we believe it should supplant traditional methods. Rather, our perspective is that sociology through fiction is a valuable alternative. Fiction allows us to fully embrace the world sociologically in ways that may not be viable through standard methodological procedures. Whether it is through the use of flexible, adaptable, and jargon-free language, or from the inherent multiperspectival approach, fiction provides a unique medium through which we may capture, depict, and analyze social life. By writing fictional stories about real-life social processes, the sociologist will escape the imposing and constraining walls that often dictate how we see, how we say, and how we understand. In short, sociology through fiction can help us broaden our horizons as writers and researchers. And as Lackey (1994) demonstrates, a sociology through literature approach can be used in the classroom. He teaches his students to use sociological theories and research to craft short stories. The assignment is structured in a way that guarantees students will immerse themselves in their characters' worlds and relive their characters' lives in sociologically relevant ways.

A little over ten years ago, Herbert Gans (1997) published a study of the best-selling books in sociology. In 2010, this study was revisited in an essay in *Contexts* (Longhofer, Wesley, Baiocchi 2010). In both instances, the authors found that the books mostly likely to make it on this select list reflect the qualities of good literature: engaging, interesting, and accessible. More specifically, the authors noted that the best-selling books in sociology are free of jargon, are driven by stories, and cross disciplinary boundaries. In other words, sociology that uses the methodological writing style of fiction is the type of sociology that is most likely to be read. The obvious disconnect here is that most sociologists are trained methodologically with an eye toward writing for the *American Sociological Review*, the *American Journal of Sociology*, and other such academic journals. But as we all know, the writing in these journals is not free of jargon, is rarely driven by stories, and even in those instances when it is interdisciplinary, is still highly specialized and often esoteric. Consequently, very few non-sociologists have the ability, much less the interest, to read sociological journal articles.

This point becomes even more pronounced when we realize that many bestselling authors that write sociological books are not trained as formal sociologists: Malcolm Gladwell (*Blink, Outliers, The Tipping Point*), Barbara Ehrenreich (*Nickel and Dimed*), and Eric Schlosser (*Fast Food Nation*) spring immediately to mind. Given the sales of these books, it is clear that the public has a hunger to read analyses that offer sociological insights. Unfortunately, most sociologists cannot satiate the public's appetite because our writing style, which partially develops from our methods, does not fit the characteristics of good literature. We would do well to heed the advice of Berger and Quinney (2005, 10): "We need to cultivate a writing that reaches a broader audience, not just a writing that impresses our colleagues with our ability to master theoretical abstraction or mathematical technique." We need writing that appeals to both the intellect and emotions. As we have argued in this chapter, we believe that sociology through fiction is one major way to achieve this goal.

References

Alexander, Jeffrey C. 1988. The New Theoretical Movement. In *Handbook of Sociology*, ed. Neil J. Smelser, 71–101. Newbury Park, CA: Sage Publications.

Archer, Margaret. 1988. *Culture and Agency: The Place of Culture in Social Theory*. Cambridge: Cambridge University Press.

Athens, Lonnie. 2004. Three Tales from *Melting Pot Boils Over*. *Qualitative Inquiry* 10(3): 443–62.

_____. 2010. Trouble Comes in Threes. *Qualitative Inquiry* 16(2): 155–60.

Banks, Anna, and Stephen P. Banks, eds. 1998. *Fiction and Social Research: By Ice or Fire*. Walnut Creek, CA: Altamira Press.

Berger, Ronald J., and Richard Quinney. 2005. The Narrative Turn in Social Inquiry. In *Storytelling Sociology: Narrative as Social Inquiry*, ed. Ronald J. Berger and Richard Quinney, 1–11. Boulder: Lynne Rienner.

Bourdieu, Pierre. 1977. *Outline of a Theory of Practice*. Cambridge: Cambridge University Press.

Brekhus, Wayne. 1998. A Sociology of the Unmarked: Redirecting our Focus. *Sociological Theory* 16(1): 34–51.

Brinkmann, Svend. 2009. Literature as Qualitative Inquiry. *Qualitative Inquiry* 15(8): 1376–94.

Castellano, Ursula, Joseph DeAngelis, and Marisol Clark-Ibáñez. 2008. Cultivating a Sociological Perspective using Nontraditional Texts. *Teaching Sociology* 36(3): 240–53.

Chan, Zenobia C.Y. 2003. A Poem: Anorexia. *Qualitative Inquiry* 9(6): 956–57.

Coser, Lewis. 1963. *Sociology through Literature*. Englewood Cliffs, NJ: Prentice Hall.

Faulkner, Sandra L. 2010. *Poetry as Method: Reporting Research through Verse*. Walnut Creek, CA: Left Coast Press.

Frank, Katherine. 2000. "The Management of Hunger": Using Fiction in Writing Anthropology. *Qualitative Inquiry* 6(4): 474–88.

Gans, Herbert J. 1997. Best-sellers by Sociologists: An Exploratory Study. *Contemporary Sociology* 26(2): 131–35.

Giddens, Anthony. 1984. *The Constitution of Society: Outline of the Theory of Structuration*. Berkeley: University of California Press.

Harnett, Stephen J., and Jeremy D. Engels. 2005. "Aria in Time of War": Investigative Poetry and the Politics of Witnessing. In *The Sage Handbook of Qualitative Research*, ed. Norman K. Denzin and Yvonna S. Lincoln, 1043–67. Thousand Oaks, CA: Sage Publications.

James, George. 1999. Why They Kill? He Thinks He Knows. *New York Times*, October 10.

Krieger, Susan. 1984. Fiction and Social Science. *Studies in Symbolic Interaction* 5:269–86.

Lackey, Chad. 1994. Social Science Fiction: Writing Sociological Short Stories to Learn about Social Issues. *Teaching Sociology* 22(2): 166–73.

Longhofer, Wesley, Shannon Golden, and Arturo Baiocchi. 2010. A Fresh Look at Sociology Bestsellers. *Contexts* 9(2): 18–25

Maynes, Mary Jo, Jennifer L. Pierce, and Barbara Laslett. 2008. *Telling Stories: The Use of Personal Narratives in the Social Sciences and History*. Ithaca: Cornell University Press.

Mills, C. Wright. 1959. *The Sociological Imagination*. New York: Oxford University Press.

Richardson, Laurel. 1990. Narrative and Sociology. *Journal of Contemporary Ethnography* 19(1): 116–35.

_____. 1994. Writing: A Method of Inquiry. In *Handbook of Qualitative Research*, ed. Norman K. Denzin and Yvonna S. Lincoln, 516–29. Thousand Oaks, CA: Sage Publications.

Rinehart, Robert. 1998. Fictional Methods in Ethnography: Believability, Specks of Glass, and Chekhov. *Qualitative Inquiry* 4(2): 200–24.

Schoepflin, Todd. 2009. On Being Degraded in Public Space: An Autoethnography. *The Qualitative Report* 14(2): 361–73.

Sewell Jr., William. 1992. A Theory of Structure: Duality, Agency, and Transformation. *American Journal of Sociology* 98(1): 1–29.

Sztompka, Piotr. 1991. *Society in Action: The Theory of Social Becoming*. Chicago: University of Chicago Press.

CONCLUSION

Ieva Zake *and* Michael DeCesare

As stated in the Introduction of this volume, our goal was to give voice to the ideas of the new generation of sociologists. We asked them to think broadly and ambitiously about what they would like sociological theory and methodology to look like in the future. To conclude, we would like to analyze the common themes that emerged from their chapters. First, we look at the theoretical directions in which the new generation is taking us. Then we review the methodological innovations and emphases that young methodologists suggest. Finally, to live up to the promise of this volume, we discuss the ways in which theory and methodology are related in order to bridge the persistent gap between the two sides of the discipline today.

New Directions in Theory

Sociological theory has continuously debated issues of whether social structure determines individuals or people have independent agency and free will. Theorists have also disagreed on whether sociological research has to make normative statements about what ought to happen in the society or it has to present and help us explain the facts of social reality without necessarily giving recommendations for change. These classical debates are, naturally, discussed in the theories of the new generation as well. Today's sociological theory forms in relation to the dominant approaches of the late 20th century. There, for example, critical theory dedicated itself to analyzing how social structure penetrated and shaped the deepest levels of individual psyche. Conflict theory and its offshoots argued that social structure was shaped by inherent power imbalances and individuals played the roles assigned to them by power arrangements. Ironically, even though Mills tended to lament the loss of individual's independence in contemporary society, his theoretical perspective fundamentally failed to see people as capable actors designing their own lives. Similarly, feminist, postmodernist and post-structuralist theories in the late 20th century talked about not only individuals but entire reality as constructs of particular societies in specific historical moments. In their mind, there was nothing cross-cultural or cross-historical about the humans and their behavior in the society. Although symbolic interactionists were somewhat different in the sense that they focused more on individuals as opposed to macro-level social forces, they still maintained that one's identity was essentially a performance of and for the social. Rational choice theorists argued on behalf of the will of a reasonable individual, but — they were in minority among sociologists. In addition, almost all of the dominant theories of the late 20th century stood on the side of values as opposed to facts in sociological research demanding that sociology pursues normative research agendas oriented toward building the "good" or at least "equal" society. In other words, they all evaluated social facts according to a specific value system and believed that the purpose of this was to make sure that sociology participated in the liberation of humankind. But as it turns out, not all of the young sociologists are willing to walk in the shoes of the previous generation as far as the debates about facts vs. values and individual agency vs. social forces are concerned.

From the start it is hard to miss the new generation's opposition to the way in which late 20th century theory (in particular, postmodernism) attacked theories of human agency and universal and fundamental principles. The new generation of sociologists wants a general sociological theory akin to what postmodernists called the Grand Theory (foundational/final explanation). They are no longer interested in pursuits of immediate, contingent and context-based knowledge and solutions, and they are not afraid to demand research on human essence as well as universal social foundations.

For example, Debbie Kasper powerfully argues that sociology is ready to develop a unifying theory that analyzes everything social from the point of view of relations and is closely connected to contemporary research in cognitive and neural sciences. Joshua McCabe and Brian Pitt propose that the Austrian School of economics could be the theory to save sociology from postmodernist relativism and nihilism. It could lead sociologists toward studying the universal ways in which individuals perceive the world, make rational decisions and constitute society through their actions. Isaac Reed and Benjamin Lamb-Books suggest that we need a reliable interpretive sociological theory, which could help us differentiate between better and worse explanations in sociological research. In other words, according to the new generation, sociology needs a fundamental theory (either hermeneutic, relational, critical realist or Austrian school-based) as a point of reference and criteria for sociological knowledge. To them, sociological theory is not dead at all, in fact, it is desperately needed to lead sociology out of value confusion and potential irrelevance vis-à-vis other types of knowledge.

What exactly do they want the general sociological theory to do for them? Some want the new general theory to help sociologists revisit and "liberate" certain concepts and areas of study from the dominance of postmodernism. For example, Boyns demonstrates that postmodernist interpretations of contemporary culture have made wild overstatements akin to science fiction. Consequently, the sociology of tomorrow would have to rescue sociological analysis of postmodern culture by constructing a new model where culture is actually studied sociologically, that is, by looking at how and by whom it is created. Patricia Snell invites us to return to the concept of space as Simmel developed it and use it to overcome increasingly inconsistent approaches to spatial analysis in contemporary sociological research. Isaac Reed and Benjamin Lamb-Books propose that concepts such as interpretation and meaning should be rethought through the larger framework of classical (historical) hermeneutics as opposed to leaving them in the hands of recent theories, which have claimed that no final explanations were possible.

Another expectation that the younger sociologists have from sociological theory is to be able to bring back conceptions that have been either marginalized or completely excluded (usually for political reasons) from the theoretical canon of the late 20th century. In fact, the new generation of sociologists has a sense that the sociological theory since the post–1960s era pursued distinct agendas and was not quite as open to considering diverse approaches as it claimed to be. To remedy this tendentiousness, McCabe and Pitt argue on behalf of introducing sociological ideas of von Mises and Hayek — two prominent thinkers who have been persistently erased from sociological theory as too conservative, too pro-capitalism and too critical of socialist ideologies. McCabe and Pitt convincingly demonstrate that actually there is nothing ideological about the Austrian school's theory and methodology. Similarly, Ieva Zake brings up Karl Popper who has been excluded from the contemporary sociological theory. Zake shows that Popper revealed the ideological presuppositions of sociological understanding of the society and therefore his writings could be a valuable instrument for helping sociology be more reflexive about its own assumptions and their political consequences.

Other authors suggest that we do not need to go back as far into sociological thought to find inspiration for a new theory. They find valuable ideas in the sociological writings of the 1970s and 80s and combine these perspectives into the so-called critical realist approach, which they recommend as a viable direction for future sociological research. For example, Boyns suggests that we use critical realism to analyze the production of contemporary culture, while Snell argues that critical realism enables sociology to analyze both material and ideational aspects of space.

What do young sociologists want to accomplish with their search for a new general theory? One of the clearest goals that emerge from their writing is a renewal of sociological interest in social and historical agency of individuals. Sociology of the late 20th century was persistently moving toward the idea that individual actors were mere constructs of the social structures. In addition, Hegelian approach of studying History as independent of people and declaring everything to be historical dominated macro-sociological analyses. The new ideas suggested in this volume lead us instead toward analyzing history as a manifestation of meanings and intentions generated by individuals as they create, are affected by and respond to the social structure. Concretely, the new generation of sociologists sees social system as being internalized and then again externalized by individuals (see Boyns), social institutions as (often spontaneous) products of individuals' actions and relations (see McCabe and Pitt, and Kasper) and social structures as having an impact on individuals and individuals in response acting upon the social structures (see Snell). Moreover, the new generation points out that studying individuals as fully enveloped by their social context has caused ideological problems for sociology as a whole (see Zake). Overall, many, if not all, sociologists of the new generation are looking for a new theory of individual agency. This applies also to how we should understand the development of sociological theory itself as proposed in Keith Kerr's chapter on theory formation from the point of view of personal biography of a theorist.

The new generation also wants sociology to return back to its scientific aspirations. This does not mean that they want to reintroduce positivism. Instead, they want to see sociology paying closer attention to how it performs research and what presuppositions guide it. Most, if not all, young theorists disapprove of the past tendencies of sociology to assume that people are simple units who are or could be manipulated from above. They are critical of the assumption that sociology itself can become a "science" of social planning and thus essentially act as a political ideology. For example McCabe and Pitt, Kasper and Zake propose that sociology is not to participate in social engineering and instead pursue value-free and scientific research. Other young sociologists such as Reed and Lamb-Books disagree (but not completely) and suggest that future sociology would still have to deal with issues of power and social criticism, while Snell argues that future theory of space would have to incorporate accounts of spatial inequality and class-based social contexts. But none of them explicitly argue on behalf of normative or prescriptive sociology. This is a notable difference from the theoretical perspectives of the late 20th century. It is clear from their work that purely ideological agendas (such as introduced by critical theorists, conflict theorists, feminists or postmodernists) are no longer sufficient for sociology of the future. Instead the new sociological theory cares deeply and seriously about questions of loyalty to objective empirical research, scientific standards, criteria and validity of sociological explanations.

New Directions in Methodology

Perhaps even more than sociological theory, sociological methodology is in need of fresh ideas and innovative approaches.

The popularity of sociological methodology has waxed and waned among

American sociologists over the past 75 years or so. Even when sociologists have given serious and conscious attention to matters of method, it has usually been to one particular aspect — operationalization during the 1930s, or measurement during the late 1940s and early 1950s, for example. Today, as it has been for several decades now, the concern is with refining our statistical techniques. Rarely, if ever, has a critical mass of American sociologists reflected on methodology in a holistic manner.

About as far as sociologists have been willing to go is to consistently differentiate between so-called "qualitative" and "quantitative" methods, and then to set up camp on one side of the river and proceed to loft insults toward the tents on the opposite bank. And although the distinction can be found in nearly every research methods textbook, it has not been a fruitful approach in terms of advancing methodology. One can reasonably wonder, in fact, whether the distinction is more illusion than reality.

Tellingly, only two contributors to the Methodology section of this volume allude at all to the seemingly endless skirmish between the so-called "quantoids" and everyone else. One is Mikaila Mariel Lemonik Arthur, who points out that the variety of comparative-historical methods "transcends the qualitative-quantitative division" by relying on five fundamental and unique characteristics: searching for consistent connections, accumulating knowledge of specific cases, selecting the dependent variable, looking for configurations of factors that interact and lead to outcomes, and considering counterfactuals. For Arthur, comparative-historical methods cannot and should not be classified as quantitative or qualitative; these methods are, to a greater or lesser extent, both.

Like Arthur, Peter Moskos has no interest in continuing the fruitless debate. He simply says, in his chapter on the utility of introversion: "Qualitative and quantitative research complement each other very well (an idea too often lost on both sides of the great methodological divide)." He is undoubtedly correct, on both scores. The lack of discussion about, and other references to, the long-standing debate between quantitative and qualitative methods is an important feature of the chapters on methodology. It would appear that, at least among the younger generation of sociologists, it is a debate that is and should be relegated to the past.

Aside from minimizing, or ignoring altogether, the traditional split between "quantitative" and "qualitative" approaches to social research, the methodology contributions to this volume appear to be united by three primary themes. *The first is the importance of recognizing and understanding the history of sociological methodology.* So Arthur reminds us that sociology, in its American and European varieties, has always been both comparative and historical at heart. If there remains anything "classical" about the "classical" sociologists — Karl Marx, Max Weber, Emile Durkheim, and the like — it was their ability to bring an intellectual understanding of history to bear on the comparison of cultures or societies. Arthur also invokes Weber, John Stuart Mill, and George Boole in her effort to guide us through the most recent trends in comparative-historical analysis, all of which build on the method's long-standing foundation.

In a similar vein, Michael DeCesare argues for the historical and contemporary importance of measurement. If we cannot measure accurately, he asserts, we cannot hope to build theories of human behavior. He points out that his is not a novel argument; in fact, the lineage of methodologists concerned with measurement extends back to the physicist Percy Bridgman and, in sociology, to George Lundberg. The heirs of their wisdom were Otis Dudley Duncan and Hubert Blalock. But, DeCesare suggests, since Blalock's repeated calls during the 1970s and 1980s for a systematic and collective conversation about measurement, sociologists have ignored the subject altogether.

Although they do not reach back as far as Arthur and DeCesare, the other contributors to the Methodology section of the volume also appreciate the historical roots of the methods they discuss. And so Todd Schoepflin and Peter Kaufman point out the theoretical, methodological, and disciplinary influences on sociologists who use fictional stories as a method; these include ethnography, symbolic interactionism, communication studies, anthropology, and criminology. Natalia Ruiz-Junco and Salvador Vidal-Ortiz discuss the "Origins and Influences of Autoethnography" in a separate section of their chapter, and trace their analysis back to the 1970s. And Peter Moskos relies on the work of Carl Jung to frame his initial consideration of introversion as a methodological tool. Clearly, then, this group of younger sociologists recognizes and understands the importance of the history of methodology — both within and outside of sociology.

The second theme of the methodology chapters is the importance of looking forward. This is not surprising, given the objectives of the volume. But the unique way in which the contributors suggest moving forward is indeed surprising: by turning *inward*. For they wish to emphasize the personally involved first-person scholar, rather than the dispassionate, objective third-person researcher that professional sociologists have traditionally been trained to write to, for, and about.

Schoepflin and Kaufman, for instance, point out that using fiction as a method of doing sociology "is a departure from conventional social science methods that many of us have been trained to employ." They continue: "No apology is expected when one's work is viewed as scientific and objective and where the author is 'absent'; however, some justification and rationale is often expected from scholars whose work is experimental, subjective, and evocative" — like those who rely on fiction as a research method.

Ruiz-Junco and Vidal-Ortiz, to take another example, explain the importance of autoethnography as a method, but also explore its consequences. The subtitle of their chapter is telling: "The Sociological Through the Personal." For these authors, utilizing autoethnography both necessitates reflexivity on the part of the researcher and uncovers the multidimensionality of any particular researcher's positions vis-à-vis his/her subject and subjects.

While Schoepflin and Kaufman, as well as Ruiz-Junco and Vidal-Ortiz, focus their attention on different methodological strategies, Peter Moskos zeroes in on tactics. Given the obvious importance of ethnography in sociology, one cannot help but wonder how best to go about carrying out the kind of ethnographic research that has made minor celebrities of Michael Burawoy and others. Burawoy and almost every other sociological ethnographer over the past 30 years have played the extrovert at their research sites—actively reaching out to informants and ingratiating themselves with them. But Moskos convincingly argues that ethnography need not be limited to the extroverts among us. In fact, introversion and even shyness can be, and often are, useful qualities. And what can be more personal, what can be a better illustration of looking inward, than the provocative assertion that introversion is a useful methodological tool?

So, while some younger sociologists urge us to revisit established, but neglected, methodological techniques and concerns—comparative historical methods, for instance, and the importance of measurement — others enthusiastically push us down new paths, such as relying on fictional stories, practicing autoethnography, and embracing one's natural introversion. While some methodologists rightly ask us to heed the lessons of the past, others look forward. While some encourage us to think more scientifically about our methods of data collection and analysis, others suggest moving away from the traditional limitations of a scientific approach to studying the social world. These tensions have marked American sociology for several decades now, and they certainly mark the Methodology section of this volume.

The third and final noteworthy aspect of the chapters on methodology is that they are not dogmatic; that is, the contributors do not insist that their methods are the only methods— or even the best ones. All of the authors of the methodology chapters share this belief, but it is Schoepflin and Kaufman who state it most explicitly:

> It is important to note that we do not view sociology through fiction as a superior methodology compared with standard and long-practiced research methods. Nor do we believe it should supplant traditional methods. Rather, our perspective is that sociology through fiction is a valuable alternative.

What the contributors to this volume have done, instead of shouting down the competition in a desperate attempt to push their own methodological agendas, is simply to suggest paths forward. They do not arrogantly wipe away what came before. They do not discount out-of-hand other current methods. And they do not pretend that the paths they suggest are clear of obstacles or free from danger. Rather, the tone of the chapters seems to be, "These methods have worked for us, in terms of arriving at a fuller understanding of the social world, and it behooves all of us to pay some attention to them." That seems to us to be a reasonable position to assume.

Connecting Theory and Methodology
for the Sociology of Tomorrow

We suggest that it is of paramount importance that theorists and method-ologists see themselves as more aligned and connected than in the past. A good sociological theory must be translatable into research methods that will generate high-quality data, while employing methods without a theory produces results that are lacking on context and, therefore, sociologically meaningless. Without claiming that in this volume we have presented perfect theories or the best methods, we still find a number of important parallels between the theory and methodology of the new generation. These parallels, we believe, are a good way to begin building bridges between theory and methodology for the sociology of the next generation.

First, it is very noticeable that both theorists and methodologists are searching back into the history of sociology. They argue that sociological research as a whole needs to be more aware of its historical roots. This involves revisiting already established approaches and connecting them explicitly to what we do today as well as reviving methods and theories that have been forgotten, pushed to the side or intentionally erased from sociology's history. The new generation of sociologists wants to make it clear that the sociological perspective does not need to be reinvented by every new generation. There are valuable lessons to be learned from the past. Methodologists in this volume recommend that we do our homework about the methods that we use and make sure that we know when and with what success these instruments have worked in the past. The-orists propose to make sure that our contemporary conceptualizations include references to classical or other old outside-the-canon sociological writings not only as a formality but using them as true sources of intellectual inspiration. Overall, it appears that the period when the dominant push in sociology was to reject or re-do the work and ideas of previous generations (as, for example, was the case with the sociology of the 1960s) might be over. The new generation of sociologists is concerned about and interested in the historical trajectory of sociology's development and they want to position their work as a contribution to a continuous tradition of sociological thought

Second, both theorists and sociologists are interested in researching the nature and role of individual in the society. This does not mean that they are abandoning macro-level research or exchanging questions about large social forces for inquiries into microscopic social situations. In other words, the turn toward the individual as a social actor does not mean that we are witnessing the psy-chologizing of sociology. Instead, the new generation is interested in analyzing individuals as creators and receivers of social impact. Methodologists explore this using more individualistic or introverted methods of research, while the-orists are asking questions about what it means to analyze society, its nature and changes from the point of view of individual's agency. The new generation has serious doubts about suggestions that history, society, culture and other large social forces can exist and exert power without the direct involvement of particular individuals. In other words, the new generation is concerned with the search for the constructive agents in social processes and for the best methods to find these social actors. Although attempts to analyze individuals as creators of the social reality have been made before, this generation is unique in its efforts to avoid sliding into the subjectivism that occasionally plagued similar sociological studies of the last couple of decades.

Third, the theory and methodology of the new generation strive to be more self-reflexive, self-aware and self-critical than before. The position of the new generation seems to be that sociologists ought to think more clearly and honestly about the limitations of their own research. To our mind, this indicates an interesting trend aimed of making sociology more into a scientific (or at least more rationally rigorous) discipline as opposed to an ideology or public policy agenda. Politicized thinking is incapable of self-criticism, and this has been a major problem for a lot of recent research in sociology. As a result, it often has failed to generate meaningful knowledge because it was more concerned with following a political "party line" (as, for example, was often the case with feminist sociological writing about gender). Based on the writings presented in this volume, the new generation seems to be interested in leading sociology away from this danger. As noted, this does not mean that the new generation advocates a return to pure positivism. It rather suggests that sociological research should be concerned with generating knowledge through rigorous theory and methods as opposed to necessarily helping to "change" or "improve" the world around us.

Fourth, the chapters presented in this book testify that the new generation is actively trying to overcome conflicts and distinctions that have been created within the discipline. There seems to be a noticeable desire among the new generation of sociologists to unify sociology. Therefore they do not want to see sociological theories act as opposed ideologies, or methodologies battle each other as disparate camps. Whether they are offering suggestions about how to reconcile theoretical strands in sociology (see, for example, the chapters by Kasper, McCabe and Pitt, and Reed and Lamb-Books), or actively resisting labels that differentiate between quantitative and qualitative methods (see Moskos' and Arthur's chapters), the contributors to this volume are unsupportive of the unnecessary and possibly imaginary distinctions that have characterized American sociology for so long.

These are the four primary characteristics that mark the "new voices" in sociological theory and methodology that contributed to this volume. We suggest in closing — hopefully without being too presumptuous or proscriptive — that they can be fruitfully used as a blueprint for tomorrow's sociology. If American sociology is to bear fruit in the coming decades, then it must be historically grounded; flexible enough to emphasize social actors but rigid enough to prevent relativism and subjectivism from pushing their way in; reflexive, self-aware, and self-critical; and aimed, if not toward a grand unification, then decidedly against the further fragmentation of the discipline. These are tall orders, and they force us to wonder: Can they be successfully executed? We join the contributors to this volume in the belief that they can.

About the Contributors

Mikaila Mariel Lemonik Arthur is an assistant professor of sociology at Rhode Island College.

David Boyns is an associate professor of sociology at California State University, Northridge.

Michael DeCesare is an associate professor of sociology at Merrimack College.

Debbie Kasper is an assistant professor of sociology at Sweet Briar College.

Peter Kaufman is an associate professor of sociology at the State University of New York, New Paltz.

Keith Kerr is an assistant professor of sociology at Quinnipiac University.

Benjamin Lamb-Books is a Ph.D. candidate in the Department of Sociology at the University of Colorado at Boulder.

Joshua McCabe is a Ph.D. candidate in the Department of Sociology at the State University of New York, Albany.

Peter Moskos is an assistant professor of sociology and criminal justice at John Jay College of Criminal Justice at the City University of New York.

Brian Pitt is a Ph.D. candidate in the Department of Sociology at the University of Delaware.

Isaac Reed is an assistant professor of sociology at the University of Colorado at Boulder.

Natalia Ruiz-Junco is an assistant professor of sociology at American University.

Todd Schoepflin is an assistant professor of sociology at Niagara University.

Patricia Snell is a Ph.D. candidate in the Department of Sociology at the University of Notre Dame.

Salvador Vidal-Ortiz is an associate professor of sociology at American University.

Ieva Zake is an associate professor of sociology at Rowan University.

INDEX

Abbot, Andrew 104, 109
Alpert, Harry 149
American Journal of Sociology 226
American Sociological Association (ASA) 3, 6, 7, 145, 208
American Sociological Review (*ASR*) 7, 151, 226
Amsterdam 42, 164, 167
Annenberg Foundation 154
Archer, Margaret 80–84, 115
Aristotle 67
Athens, Lonnie 214
Austrian School 30–47, 230, 231
autoethnography 193–208

Baltimore, Maryland 163; Police Academy 165; Police Department 166
Bank Street College of Education 154
Baudrillard, Jean 69–71, 73–76, 78, 86
Bauman, Zygmunt 31, 44–46, 50, 71
Beck, Ulrich 50
Becker, Howard 149
Berger, Peter 36, 80, 82–84, 169, 226
Blalock, Hubert 6, 145, 149, 150, 152, 157, 234
Boole, George 234
Boolean algebra 182
Boston College 154
Bourdieu, Pierre 1, 18, 50, 70, 90, 122, 126, 127, 129, 131, 133, 134, 138, 139
Bridgman, Percy W. 147, 148, 157, 158, 234
Burawoy, Michael 56, 194, 196, 206, 235

California State University-Northridge 154
Carnegie Corporation of New York 153
case methods 172, 178, 179
catallaxy 37
Census, U.S. 107, 152, 177, 186; Bureau 152, 158
Chicago school 105, 107–110, 112
Coleman, James S. 31, 43
Coleridge, Samuel Taylor 84

comparative-historical methods 172–189, 233–234
Comte, Auguste 33, 44
conceptualization 1, 7, 15, 35, 70, 79, 84, 108–110, 113–117, 145, 147, 149, 150, 195, 236
conflict theory 52, 59, 61, 62, 123, 125, 229, 232
Contexts 226
conventionalism 147
Cop in the Hood 163
counterfactuals 174, 233
crisis of representation 69, 73, 74, 75, 85, 86, 199, 208
critical theory 24–26, 31, 33, 43, 44, 50, 59–61, 229, 232; *see also* Frankfurt School
cultural studies 40, 42, 70, 197, 199

Dahrendorf, Ralf 59, 61, 63
Denzin, Norman 193, 197, 198–199, 204, 208
Derrida, Jacques 4, 50
dialectics 17, 23, 28, 80, 83, 96, 110, 114
Dilthey, Wilhelm 14–19, 22, 23, 26, 27
Duncan, Otis D. 6–7, 150–151, 156, 158, 234
Duneier, Mitchell 168
Durkheim, Emile 13, 27, 74, 91, 101, 110, 113, 127, 169, 172, 233

ecology 107–108, 109, 116, 135, 137
Ehrenreich, Barbara 226
Elias, Norbert 122, 126–131, 133, 139, 140
Ellis, Carolyn 193, 197–198, 199, 201, 202–203, 204, 207, 208
Enlightenment 19, 44, 45, 63, 93
epistemic privilege 17, 24, 27
ethnography 34, 160, 164, 165, 166, 168, 169, 183, 189, 193, 194, 196–197, 199, 204, 206, 208, 213, 234, 235; global 193; institutional 193
ethnomethodology 58, 160
existential spatiality 106